DATE DUE

DEC 1 5 1998			

JUSTINIAN
AND THE
LATER ROMAN
EMPIRE

JUSTINIAN AND THE LATER ROMAN EMPIRE

JOHN W. BARKER

THE UNIVERSITY OF WISCONSIN PRESS

Published 1966
The University of Wisconsin Press
Box 1379, Madison, Wisconsin 53701
The University of Wisconsin Press, Ltd.
70 Great Russell Street, London

Printings 1966, 1977

Printed in the United States of America
ISBN 0-299-03944-7; LC 66-11804

FOR JOAN,
CHRISTOPHER NEIL,
AND ELLEN CARLA

PREFACE

This book was written largely for the general public, and to some extent for the student, rather than for the scholar. It is designed to give a broad but concise picture of Justinian's life and reign. It cannot be expected to add new information, whatever its insights. Nor is it intended to compete with the more exhaustive coverage which may be found in other studies. Nevertheless, in one respect, at least, the author hopes it may contribute something of individual value.

This is an attempt to give the nonspecialist reader some substantial background to the specific period of Justinian, something which may not be found so readily in other books about him — save, of course, in general histories, in which this period is merely one episode along the way. A ruler's reign is, after all, rarely a self-contained entity. However unique he may have been as a personality, he was inevitably involved with events which both preceded and followed his time. In the case of Justinian, it is all very well to fill in a few comments on the Persian wars, or on the Monophysite question, or on the barbarian kingdoms, when they appear in the course of the narrative. But the age of Justinian was — as is true of any epoch — shaped by the periods which preceded it. Unless one has some awareness of how the world of Justinian's time came to be, one's appreciation of what his activities really involved is likely to be hindered. The same is quite true of the opposite: that is, that the meaning and significance of Justinian's reign cannot be recognized without some idea of how the problems and forces of his age were worked out after his lifetime.

This double need is particularly acute in the case of Justinian. As the book endeavors to demonstrate, his reign was a crucial phase in the transformation of the Later Roman Empire into what we call the Byzantine Empire. Here the reader should be warned against possible confusion in the words used. The expressions "Roman" or "Later Roman" are often applied to a state which might more regularly be referred to as "Byzantine." Of course, all are one and the same, which is perhaps the point itself. Such are the connotations of the word "Byzantine," however, that the author has preferred to stress the element of continuity by avoiding the word as much as possible. In most cases the dilemma has been side-stepped by use of the adjective "Imperial." This word may come closest to suggesting both the continuity and the essential nature of the state under consideration, a state whose proper history extends from at least 31 B.C., if not earlier, to A.D. 1453.

In an even broader sense, Justinian emerges as a pivotal figure in the development of the medieval European world out of the break-up of the ancient Mediterranean world. The traditional stereotypes of the "Middle Ages" — an utterly inept designation applied in scorn by later writers with highly biased outlooks — are still very much with us. Even now we tend to think of medieval Europe essentially in terms of its northwestern regions, rather than of the full European and Mediterranean world. The area of Eastern Orthodox Christendom (not to mention Islam) is somehow left hanging in limbo as a result of a Latin-rooted provincialism. Thus the period, say, from the fifth to the eleventh centuries, if not beyond, is somehow "the Dark Ages." This was perhaps true as regards northwestern Europe. As we broaden our perspectives to take in eastern Europe and the Mediterranean world, however, we come to understand the actual nature of those early centuries, with an awareness of the role played by the surviving Roman Empire in the East, the "Byzantine" Empire.

It is within this context that Justinian must be viewed, and not merely within the narrow confines of his own lifetime.

Hence the opening and closing chapters of this book. If the sketches they attempt to give of the centuries before and after Justinian seem overly detailed for a book of this size and title, they should be seen as a proper part of its rightful scope. For this is a book not so much about a man as about a reign: what the reign was, what it meant, and where it belongs in the scope of Western history. It is therefore to be hoped that the reader will find this book of use in providing, within one compact format, both a substantial account of Justinian and his reign, and at the same time some idea of the context within which it belongs. In this sense, then, the book has two themes.

As for the sections on Justinian himself, even they cannot be offered as a biography in the usual sense of the word. It is one thing to trace the life of a figure in more recent history. We would then be more likely to have extensive contemporary information on him, and would be able to trace his personality and thoughts more fully. In the most ideal cases, we would be able to utilize his own papers and writings as well as the accounts of others, and we might also, perhaps, be able to consult people still alive who had known him. The further one goes back in history, however, the more difficult the task becomes as these sources of information drop away. In some more distant periods we find information of this kind to be so fragmentary that the personalities involved may be difficult to know at all. It is true that in the case of Justinian we do have extensive sources of information, which enable us to form a fairly well-defined picture of the man. Yet, caution is always necessary, for the line between knowledge and speculation is all too easy to cross. Essential as speculation is for the historian, if pursued too far it produces mere fiction.

Certainly historical fiction has its place for the general reader. The bookshelf on Justinian includes a substantial section of it. Some efforts in this line have won some popularity, such as the two by Harold Lamb: *Constantinople: Birth of an Empire* (New York, 1957), and its predecessor, *Theodora and the Emperor: The Drama of Justinian* (New York, 1952). More distinguished as literature are those by John Masefield (*Basilissa, A Tale of the Empress Theodora*, New York, 1940), and Robert Graves (*Count Belisarius*, New York, 1939). Historical novels such as these are, of course, pleasantly readable, occasionally offering fine flashes of insight into their subjects. These books can thus give the reader an imaginative re-creation of the period. Nevertheless, it is a re-creation as seen entirely through the author's eyes. As such, it is not necessarily reliable, and at worst it can be irrelevant, if not grossly mistaken, distorted, and misleading.

Fortunately, Justinian, his era, and his Empress Theodora have also attracted the attention of the responsible historian as well as the creative writer. Given the fascination of these subjects, such attention is fully understandable, even though it may needlessly cast into the shade proximate or related subject matter, overemphasizing Justinian out of fair proportion. Those who wish to avoid or supplement fantasy through more carefully grounded, if less colored, narrative have at their disposal many admirable historical accounts which can be trusted. They range from the popular to the scholarly. For those who wish to read further on this subject, a selection of them is discussed in the listing appended at the end of the book, pages 298–304: included in it are works in languages other than English, since the reader is entitled to a full indication of those which are important. Besides this Selected Bibliography, there is also, on pages 269–275, a Chronology (which is limited for the sake of convenience to Justinian's lifetime only), and, on pages 276–285, a set of Historical Lists of rulers and officials, secular and ecclesiastical (in this case covering the time span embraced by the entire book). Elaborate documentation has been avoided in the footnotes; but it was considered worthwhile to cite extensively one original source, the writings of Procopius, since they are readily available in English translation should anyone wish to pursue such references.

Finally, attention is called to a complementary publication, now in the process of preparation, designed as a companion to the present book. This is a large compilation of bibliographical references, which endeavor to give a thorough exposition of the vast scholarly literature on the Empire's history during the period of the book's coverage, that is, from the third to the eighth centuries A.D. By these means, the author hopes that he has rendered some service to both the general public and the specialized scholar, whose respective needs and outlooks have become so increasingly different in recent years.

JOHN W. BARKER

Madison, Wisconsin
December, 1965

AUTHOR'S NOTE

For this reprinting, I have drawn upon the constructive suggestions of many reviewers, as well as on ideas of my own, to make some small changes or corrections. These must be made within the existing format because of reproduction restrictions. Among desirable alterations not possible at this time are some revisions and additions to the Bibliography that are called for. Regretting what cannot yet be done, I thank my helpful critics for their advice, and the University of Wisconsin Press for providing this much of an opportunity.

JOHN W. BARKER

Madison, Wisconsin
July, 1977

ADDENDA

(To note 1 on page 4)

A particularly penetrating discussion of reasons and explanations for the "fall" of the Empire may be found in the final chapter (25) of A. H. M. Jones's *The Later Roman Empire,* pp. 1025–1068.

(To note 9 on page 76)

Note also two other operas, by Handel: his *Ezio* (London, 1732) and his *Giustino* (London, 1736), fancifully treating the stories of Aëtius and Justin I, respectively.

(To middle paragraph on page 262)

Mention should also be made of one more testimonial of Justinian's enduring memory, in connection with religious matters. To him is attributed the authorship of a hymn which is, to this day, a fixed part of the Divine Liturgy (equivalent to the Latin Mass) of the Eastern Orthodox Churches. This is the *Troparion* that begins with the words "Ho monogenés Hyiòs kaì Lógos toû Theoû" ("O Only-begotten Son and Word of God"). It is a poetic synopsis and paraphrase of the Creed, and some of its wording is paralleled in parts of the Emperor's ecclesiastical decrees. A case can be made for ascribing it to Severus of Antioch, the Monophysite prelate, or at least to his influence. But the ascription to Justinian himself is very strongly affirmed by weighty testimony and tradition, and his authorship is conventionally accepted, with 535 or 536 suggested as its date of composition.

ACKNOWLEDGMENTS

There are, first of all, a number of individuals to whom I owe expressions of thanks for their various involvements with the publication of this book. I wish to thank Dr. Hans Trefousse of Brooklyn College, a respected former teacher, and Mr. Jacob Steinberg, for the original suggestion and encouragement to write this book. Acknowledgment is due my successive graduate assistants, Miss Sally Ann Proctor (Mrs. T. Rackley) and Miss Robin D. Gibbs, for their help in preparing the manuscripts of this work. My thanks go also to my wife, who patiently read the drafts of the book and gave me the benefit of her constructive badgering. An important background to my remarks on Haghía Sophía are my valued contacts with Mr. Robert Van Nice of Dumbarton Oaks, whose research on the great building is soon to be published. I have profited from the suggestions of Professor Irfan Kawar (Shahid) of the Institute of Languages and Linguistics at Georgetown University in Washington, D.C., on material dealing with the Arabs. My distinguished colleague at the University of Wisconsin, Professor Charles Edson, was also kind enough to peruse my manuscript and give his ideas on it. Above all, I am deeply indebted to Professor Glanville Downey, then of Dumbarton Oaks in Washington, who read through this book as it was being written, and who gave freely of his time, experience, learning, and humor to offer invaluable advice on it. Many of its merits and none of its faults are to be credited to him.

In addition, I am greatly indebted to several individuals for help in illustrating this book, beyond the institutions and agencies cited as their sources. Professor Gyula Moravcsik of Budapest secured a photograph of the statue sketch with gracious efficiency and kindness. Of the faculty at Dumbarton Oaks, Ernst Kitzinger provided some useful information, while Paul Underwood was extremely generous with both advice and material; and I owe Professor Alfred R. Bellinger, and his assistant, Miss Julia A. Cardozo, my gratitude for their selection of the Justinianic coins reproduced here. Finally, I acknowledge thanks to the personnel of the Cartographic Laboratory of the University of Wisconsin, who produced the maps for this book.

Secondly, I wish to express formal thanks to the respective publishers who have granted permission to use the various passages by other authors which I have quoted in the course of the book. They are as follows:

To the Macmillan & Company, Ltd., for the quotations from J. B. Bury's *A History of the Later Roman Empire from the Death of Theodosius I to the Death of Justinian.*

To the Public Trustee and The Society of Authors, London, for the quotation from George Bernard Shaw's *Caesar and Cleopatra.*

To the Harvard University Press for the quotation from the H. J. Thomson translation of Prudentius in the Loeb Classical Library edition.

To the Dumbarton Oaks Library for the quotation from A. A. Vasiliev's *Justin the First.*

To the University of Oklahoma Press for the quotations from *Constantinople in the Age of Justinian* by Glanville Downey.

To Harper & Row, Inc., for the quotation from J. M. Hussey's *The Byzantine World.*

To Penguin Books, Ltd., for the quotation from P. N. Ure's *Justinian and his Age.*

To the Cambridge University Press, for the quotation from Charles Diehl's Chapter (I) "Justinian's Reconquest in the West" in Vol. II of *The Cambridge Medieval History.*

To John Murray Ltd. for the rights to reproduce the diagram of the Land Walls from John E. M. Hearsey's *City of Constantine, 324–1453.*

CONTENTS

ILLUSTRATIONS

Following page 158

Maps and Plans

JUSTINIAN
AND THE
LATER ROMAN
EMPIRE

I THE BACKGROUND: THE ROMAN WORLD BEFORE JUSTINIAN

"476 and All That"

Few events have been so misunderstood as the supposed "Fall of the Roman Empire," and few dates so abused as A.D. 476.

Historians and laymen alike have a fondness for tidy generalizations and for specific dates on which to hang them. Certainly there do exist decisive dates in history: 31 B.C., A.D. 800, 1066, 1492, 1789, 1848, 1917, and 1945 are some which immediately bring to mind pivotal events that changed the course of history. To such a list it has been easy to add the year A.D. 476. For many, this date has conjured up a dramatic picture of the collapse of one of the greatest powers the human race has ever known. The might of Rome, sovereign of the Mediterranean and much of Europe, once irresistible in arms, omniscient and omnipotent in its great system of law, benevolent in its unifying rule of all civilized men, proud author of the unique Pax Romana, patron of the arts and letters, culmination of all past glories — Rome, the incomparable civilizer and pacifier of the nations, is broken, ruined, and trampled in the dust. Hordes of barbarians swarm over the Roman world, spreading violence, destruction, chaos. The ancient world is at an end, and "The Dark Ages" have begun.

Themselves captivated by this picture, successive generations of historians have hovered figuratively over the corpse of the Roman Empire, performing their own autopsies to establish the cause

3

4 · JUSTINIAN AND THE LATER ROMAN EMPIRE

of death. The verdicts have been numerous and varied. Some have gone to dangerous if briefly fashionable extremes by basing their explanations on single or oversimplified causes: the debilitating effects of Christianity; the exhaustion of the soil; a change in climate; a conflict of social classes; the role of the army; a breakdown of the labor supply; the corrupting effects of excessive luxury, self-indulgence, and immorality; the results of unconscious food-poisoning; and even the absurdities of racial "mongrelization" or dilution. Other reasons advanced have been more moderate and have in fact contributed valuable points of view.[1] Yet, despite the undoubted learning, earnestness, and perception of these examinations, all too many of them have been conducted very much under the spell of the symbolic date of 476 and the dramatic picture it suggests.

A dramatic picture it is, undeniably; but also an inaccurate one. It involves a double fallacy. In the first place, it seriously distorts

1. Besides the vast scholarly literature and discussion on the cause of the decline and fall of the Roman Empire, there are a few guides the general reader may find helpful. A very good, if brief, survey has been contributed by G. Downey in his Introduction (pp. xi–xxiii) and annotations to the paperback edition of the English translation of F. Lot's *The End of the Ancient World and the Beginnings of the Middle Ages*, published in America by Harper in the Torchbook series (TB–1044, New York, 1961); this book is itself, of course, one of the most valuable works on the subject. There is also a useful selection and review of various interpretations of the question in two new paperback volumes: *Decline and Fall of the Roman Empire: Why Did It Collapse?*, prepared and edited by D. Kagan in the series "Problems in European Civilization" published by D. C. Heath and Co. (Boston, 1962); and *The Fall of Rome: Can It Be Explained?*, edited by M. Chambers in the series "European Problem Studies" published by Holt, Rinehart and Winston (New York, 1963). Of some use also is *The Myth of Rome's Fall*, by R. M. Haywood (New York, 1958; Apollo Edition, Paperback A–34, 1962). Note, however, the comments by the eminent J. B. Bury, *History of the Later Roman Empire from the Death of Theodosius I to the Death of Justinian* (A.D. 395–565) (2 vols.; London, 1923; also reprinted as a paperback by Dover Publications, T–398/399, New York, 1958), I, 308–313, in which he suggests that the collapse of Roman authority in the West was not at all an inevitable result of internal decay: "The gradual collapse of the Roman power in this section of the Empire was the consequence of *a series of contingent events*. No general causes can be assigned that made it inevitable" (p. 311, my italics).

the actual nature of what happened. And, secondly, it is rooted in the tendency to think in terms of only a portion of the Roman world, not the whole of it. Moreover, attempts to interpret the course of events in terms of a single cause or type of causes only oversimplify deceptively what is surely one of the most complex processes in the annals of western civilization.

But the ultimate delusion of the date 476 and its connotations is the suggestion of something that did not actually happen. No empire fell in 476. It is true that a specific line of Roman sovereigns ended in that year. They were not the sole representatives of Roman authority, however, and their extinction in fact only set the seal on a process which had already been in operation for several decades.

We are thus confronted with a dual enigma. We must not only interest ourselves in why the Roman Empire "declined and fell," but also we should try to appreciate the real nature of that "decline and fall." Debate on the first point has at times discouraged, or distracted from, consideration of the second. Certainly the question of cause alone is an irresistibly fascinating one, and one that will long continue to attract speculation. By this time, however, the scope of that debate is shrinking. On the whole, we believe we know fairly well *what* the causes were. The remaining and enduring uncertainty concerns rather the relative importance, the interplay, and the relationships of these various causes in their intricate context, something which no glib or monothematic diagnosis can solve. Once one can rise above the complexities of this debate, the importance of examining the nature of the "decline and fall" becomes apparent. Even if we cannot always explain this problem in definite detail, we can understand its broad lines and implications. In so doing, we can grasp readily the general outlines of what happened in the Roman world from the third century to the eighth or even the ninth century, the period which witnessed the transition from the ancient to the medieval world. In that transformation the span of the Emperor Justinian's activities, from 518 to 565, stands out more than ever as a pivotal epoch, of far more significance than the single year 476.

That date has its place, but on a much lower scale of importance. The demonstration of this point is the real theme of any proper background to Justinian's age itself.

The Reorganization of the Roman World-State

Few phases of civilization have left so deep an imprint as the Roman. The development of modern Europe, or of "Western Civilization," is inconceivable without its universal foundations in Rome. Survivals and derivations from Rome surround us on all sides. Our literature, our law, our statecraft, our political, religious, and social institutions were all to some degree shaped by Roman origins. The example of such a unified, pacified order as the Pax Romana has haunted men's imagination and tempted their ambitions ever since the days of the Empire's decline. In the Middle Ages in particular, the image and glory of Rome, at least as it was then understood, exercised an influence on the minds of active men and theoreticians alike in ways which would have amazed the Romans themselves.

The point of departure for that which came later was also the point of focus for that which had come before. The Roman Empire was in some ways the culmination and final flowering of Antiquity. Its literature, art, architecture, and science represented the distillation — if not always the purification — of all that had been achieved up to that time in the Mediterranean world and its surrounding areas. All these separate developments were gathered up by Rome, synthesized, and diffused to the confines of the civilized Western world. Indeed, Rome had *become* the civilized world. For the first and perhaps the only time in history, all the civilized portions of the West (as distinguished from what we would now call the Far East) were gathered together in a single, universal political entity, at peace with themselves, free within limits to prosper in their own way, a diversity within unity.

Contemporaries who enjoyed the benefits of this Pax Romana recognized what it meant. The Romans themselves felt they were fulfilling a mission. Vergil, the official poet of the Augustan Age, which saw the perfection of the Roman Imperial system, sang memorably of this mission. For him the genius of his people was clear:

> Others will fashion the breathing bronze to softer shapes,
> And, I do concede, will draw living portraits from marble;
> More eloquent will their oratory be, and their instruments
> Describe the movements of heavenly bodies and predict
>   the star's rising;
> But it is for thee, O Roman, to rule the nations in thine
>   empire;
> These shall be thine arts: to impose the law of peace,
> To be merciful to the conquered, and to beat down the
>   proud.[2]

The more practical Pliny the Elder, the great Roman encyclopedist, boasted in the first century A.D. of his people's accomplishment as the world's unifiers and civilizers. For him Italy was:

. . . at once the nursling and parent of all the world; chosen by the will of the gods in order to augment the glories of the very heavens, and to bring together the scattered powers, and to mellow customs, and to assemble the rough and crude tongues of so many peoples in the intercourse of one common dialect; to give to men the benefits of cultivated discourse and civilization; and, in brief, to serve as a single fatherland for all races in the whole wide world.[3]

The real meaning of the Pax Romana was thus much more than the glory of universal conquest and rule. For all those who were brought under the sway of Rome there were, beyond mere sub-

---

2. Vergil, *Aeneid*, Book VI, ll. 847–853; my own translation. Compare these sentiments with those suggested, curiously enough, by George Bernard Shaw in his delightful play *Caesar and Cleopatra*, in an exchange which Caesar has (in Act V) with the Greek-Sicilian merchant Apollodorus:

CAESAR. . . . Remember: Rome loves art and will encourage it ungrudgingly.

APOLLODORUS. I understand, Caesar. Rome will produce no art itself; but it will buy up and take away whatever the other nations produce.

CAESAR. What! Rome produce no art! Is peace not an art? is war not an art? is government not an art? is civilization not an art? All these we give you in exchange for a few ornaments. You will have the best of the bargain. . . .

3. Pliny the Elder, *Natural History*, Book III, chap. 6, my own translation.

jection, innumerable blessings. Even the Christians, who abhorred the pagan element of the Roman tradition, were well aware of these blessings, and in particular of what Roman rule had meant for the Christian Faith. Here is the late fourth-century Christian poet Prudentius:

. . . Shall I tell you, Roman, what cause it was that so exalted your labors, what it was that nursed your glory to such a height of fame that it has put rein and bridle on the world? God, wishing to bring into partnership peoples of different speech and realms of discordant manners, determined that all the civilized world should be harnessed to one ruling power and bear gentle bonds in harmony under the yoke, so that love of their religion should hold men's hearts in union; for no bond is made that is worthy of Christ unless unity of spirit leagues together the nations it associates. Only concord knows God; it alone worships the beneficent Father aright in peace. The untroubled harmony of human union wins His favor for the world; by division it drives Him away, with cruel warfare it makes Him wroth; it satisfies Him with the offering of peace and holds Him fast with quietness and brotherly love. In all lands bounded by the western ocean and lightened by Aurora at her rosy dawning, the raging war-goddess was throwing all humanity into confusion and arming savage hands to wound each other. To curb this frenzy God taught the nations everywhere to bow their heads under the same laws and become Romans — all whom Rhine and Danube flood, or Tagus with its golden stream, or great Ebro, those through whose land glides the horned river of the western world, those who are nurtured by Ganges or washed by the warm Nile's seven mouths. A common law made them equals and bound them by a single name, bringing the conquered into bonds of brotherhood. We live in countries the most diverse like fellow-citizens of the same blood dwelling within the single ramparts of their native city, and all united in an ancestral home. Regions far apart, shores separated by sea, now meet together in appearing before one common court of law, in the way of trade in the products of their crafts they gather to one thronged market, in the way of wedlock they unite in legal marriage with a spouse of another country; for a single progeny is produced from the mixed blood of two different races. Such is the result of the great successes and triumphs of the Roman power. For the time of Christ's coming, be assured, was the way prepared which the general good will of peace among us had just built under the rule of Rome. For what room could there have been for God in a savage world and in human hearts at variance, each according to its different interest maintaining its own claims, as once things were? Where sentiments are thus disordered in man's breast, agreement upset, and faction in the soul, neither pure wisdom visits nor God enters. But if a supremacy in the soul, having gained authority to rule, checks the impulses of refractory appetite and rebellious flesh and controls all its passions under a single order, the constitution of life becomes stable and a settled way of thought draws in God in the heart and subjects itself to one Lord.

Come, then, Almighty; here is a world in harmony; do Thou enter it. An earth receives Thee now, O Christ, which peace and Rome hold in a bond of union. These Thou dost command to be the heads and highest powers of the world. Rome without peace finds no favour with Thee; and it is the supremacy of Rome, keeping down disorders here or there by the awe of her sovereignty, that secures the peace, so that Thou hast pleasure in it.[4]

Thus could even the Christians, though the persecuted victims of Imperial policy, recognize how inconceivable would have been the spread of their faith without the peace and unity, not to mention the unhindered freedom of communications and travel, provided by the blessings of Roman rule. To them, Roman universal sway was part of the Divine Plan, though its blessings could also be enjoyed as fully by all the peoples of the Empire, whatever their spiritual outlook.

Yet, it was in vain that the panegyrists extolled the glories of Rome and the benefits of its governance, and in vain that poets and seers prophesied eternal sway for Roman rule. The Empire aged and changed. It was not an imperishable monolith. It was in some ways even a house built upon sand. Embodied in its structure were many elements of potential collapse: some were merely inherent aspects of the ancient world, but others were distinctly Roman qualities.

To begin with, the Roman world was not a technological one in the modern sense. Ancient scientific knowledge and awareness, for all its brilliance, was essentially philosophic speculation with

4. Prudentius, *A Reply to the Address of Symmachus* (*Contra Orationem Symmachi*), Book II, ll. 583–640, reprinted by permission of the publishers and the Loeb Classical Library from *Prudentius*, translated by H. J. Thomson (Cambridge, Massachusetts: Harvard University Press, 1953), II, 53–57.

little or no relation to actual life. Ancient society neither was able to develop a mechanized economy, nor was interested in trying to do so. Our knowledge of the considerable inventiveness and gadgetry of Antiquity makes it clear that such a development would not have been impossible. Nevertheless, it never came about, partly because of conventional philosophic scorn among great thinkers for the idea of any practical application of abstract scientific and engineering theory to everyday life; but, more basically, simply because ancient economy was already firmly based upon slavery. Quite apart from purely moral considerations, slavery was an unrealistic economic pillar. On the one hand it tended to encourage an inferior quality of labor, and on the other hand it was weakened by the fact that the number of slaves could only decline — the end of major conquest had dried up the principal source of them, and the increasing frequency with which slaves were freed reduced the number in existence even further. Thus, the deceptive straitjacket of a slave system hindered the development in Antiquity of any extensive industrial economy. Ancient economy remained largely agricultural, and was not very sophisticated even in that sphere. What little industrial activity did exist was relatively primitive, while commercial activity concentrated on the importation and diffusion of luxury goods from the Far East. Production of purely practical commodities developed increasingly into small-scale on-the-spot manufacturing, which discouraged long-range commerce, lowered standards of quality, and fostered a trend toward local self-sufficiency in at least the western provinces.

Economic activity was also hampered by social taboos that cut off vital capital. It was unfashionable, if not improper, for the wellborn and wealthy to put their money into trade. Land was the only acceptable area for investment. Far back into Roman history can be traced the growth of large landholding at the expense of an increasingly pauperized, dispossessed, and diminished free peasantry, though the process was not consistently uninterrupted. The area of land under cultivation also seems to have declined, as did the manpower force, if not the total population as well. The taboos against investment likewise worked against commerce, so that Rome never had a stable or a fully developed middle class in modern terms. Within the Empire, Rome and Italy in particular produced less and consumed more in an essentially parasitical relationship. Moreover, the Empire as a whole was caught in an unfavorable balance of trade since its craving for eastern luxury items, such as silks and spices, forced it to suffer a steady drain of its money to oriental lands beyond its borders. With its financial resources continually diminishing, debasement of the coinage and inflation followed in due time.

The roots of decay went even deeper, beyond exclusively material considerations. Most of the achievements of ancient civilization, particularly Hellenic, came from an age characterized by a different political order, the age of the city-state. Within its limited confines the individual found his fulfillment and his place as a part of a community. But fertile as the city-state had been as a matrix for creativity, it was also the breeder of the hatreds, rivalries, and constant civil struggles which helped weaken and destroy Classical Greek civilization. The city-state had been superseded in the Hellenistic Age (i.e., after the death of Alexander the Great in 323 B.C.) by the great kingdom as the basic political entity, and then in turn these had been absorbed and replaced by the Roman Empire. The city continued to be both the focus of cultural life in the Roman world and its unit of administration; indeed, the Empire has even been called little more than a network of city-states. Nevertheless, this continued use of the shell could not disguise its emptiness. The municipality was ceasing to be a stage for the social and political aspirations of local ability, or the focus of a real sense of identification. Rome itself could not be a substitute for what the city-state had been. However much its power was respected, and however much the blessings of its peace were enjoyed, Rome was after all but a distant, parasitical, and increasingly, an oppressive ruler. Though it survived in Roman times, municipal office was gradually transformed from an honor to a burden, and the average individual citizen probably regarded the Empire to which he belonged, at best, with apathy, and almost certainly with little personal sense of overriding loyalty.

While public spirit declined, the spiritual outlook also changed. Christianity has often been accused of weakening or destroying older civic virtues. Actually, Christianity was in this respect but a part of the much broader religious scheme in late Antiquity. The individual, lost in the great mass of large states, and often ground down by the trials and burdens of daily life, needed a new perspective which would give his life some meaning. In response to this need, a host of new religious cults flourished. Most of them came to stress personal salvation and the preferability of the next world to life on earth. The general spirit of other-worldliness could only encourage individual apathy toward the community and the state. Service on behalf of the state, in office as much as arms, seemed that much more contemptible. The growing popularity of celibacy added further encouragement to withdrawal from normal life, be it the withdrawal of pious believers to the growing way of monastic life, or simply the withdrawal of many of the most upright and able men from the contamination of earthly activities. The Christians were all the more inclined to look upon the state's decline and calamities merely as divine retribution for the sins of mortal men.

Finally, there was a peculiar weakness in the basic political machinery of the Roman state. The foundation of Imperial sovereignty was, in the last analysis, the army. The stability of one-man rule and the defense of the frontiers required the maintenance of a force which was a heavy drain on the resources of the state, a force which also became increasingly irresponsible in behavior and alien in composition. In addition, the role of the army in the government complicated the matter of form and appearances. The delicate façade of republican formalities, which had rendered the Augustan principate more palatable to lingering traditional sentiments, was gradually worn thin as the open tyranny of the Emperors increased. Moreover, the Augustan system had never established any orderly process of succession. Hereditary transmission was not always possible, and civil wars over the throne broke out from time to time, becoming more the rule than the exception during much of the third century. By then, crises of succession had been joined by external pressures and by a degree of internal disintegration which required drastic action.

That action came under the Emperor Diocletian (A.D. 284–305). Unfortunately, his attempt to cope with the succession problem was a failure. The idea of co-Emperors was not new, nor was it a novel conclusion that the responsibilities of the Roman state were becoming too broad for one pair of shoulders to bear. But Diocletian's new plan of collegiate rule went far beyond anything yet attempted in these respects. It was to be a tetrarchy of co-Emperors, two senior (each with the title of Augustus) and two junior (each with the title of Caesar), with ultimately a regular procedure for abdication, replacement, and promotions through the scale. Its weakness was that it ignored all logic of heredity and ambitions. It only initiated in short order a new phase of the very kind of civil war it had been designed to prevent. Out of the collapse of this abortive system came the triumph of Constantine the Great as sole Emperor by 324. In other respects, however, Diocletian's reforms were to have more lasting impact, and were in fact completed by Constantine himself.

These reforms can easily provoke revulsion. They amounted to nothing less than a despotic regimentation of all aspects of life, reaching into all branches of society — the political, the social, the economic — in a desperate effort to shore up the sagging ancient world. The economy was manipulated and regulated by fiat, not always with complete success. The taxation system was reorganized, imposing new burdens on most levels of society, including the municipal officials. The latter were charged with responsibility for assessments, out of their own pockets if need be, thereby confronting the lesser moneyed classes with ruin or extinction. All people were fixed in their rank or calling, tradesmen to assure vital goods and services, and cultivators to assure food supplies. As for the latter, not only were the remaining free cultivators fixed in their occupation, but they were also bound legally to their land, and began to assume a status foreshadowing that of medieval serfs. The entire administrative system of the Empire was reorganized, so that the central government was in a more advantageous position to control and check its powerful officials. Civil and military authority was carefully separated to prevent the concentration of excessive power in the hands of ambitious or potentially rebellious commanders. At the same time, in order to run the expanded machinery of the state, a complex bureaucracy was established to replace or supplement the local municipal authorities, and to give the Emperor checks and balances and informers at all levels of the Empire's administration. The ruler was thus provided with new means of control, while new stability and continuity were added to the Imperial governmental structure. Such changes also introduced a new element of expense, stubborn reaction, abuse, corruption, and oppression. Finally, the very nature of the Imperial office itself was transformed: the Emperor became an oriental despot, surrounded by pomp and ceremonial, bedecked in dazzling splendor that was set off by an ostentatious court, and isolated from his subjects. Thereby was he made more lofty and awesome in their eyes, as well as removed to some extent from the more immediate dangers of assassination. At the same time, he became more dependent upon advisers, and more submerged in the debilitations of boundless luxury and self-indulgence. The Augustan principate had been replaced by what has been called the *dominate*, the rule of an absolute master along Near Eastern lines.

Totalitarian and repugnant though these reforms seem to us, and oppressive and burdensome as they made life for the peoples of the Empire, they cannot be idly dismissed as only negative steps. These reforms became the basis for the development of the subsequent Byzantine state and system. More immediately, they helped save the Roman Empire for a while, if only after a fashion. It is true that some of the reforms were ill-advised and unsuccessful. But the bulk of them served their purpose in that they arrested the decline of the state and its economy and enabled Rome to face its challenges with bolstered strength: the Roman Empire was a considerably more viable state in the early fourth century than it had been in much of the third. Moreover, the reforms of Diocletian were also, it should be remembered, the work of men who were earnestly trying to save the ancient world from the collapse it seemed to be facing. For Diocletian at least, personal ambition, lust for power, and selfish interest had nothing to do with his activities. His idealism encouraged by failing health, he abdicated after some twenty years of rule, and he steadfastly resisted all temptations to return to the throne during the rest of his life, which ended in 313.

Out of the crises of the third century A.D. had come a complete reorganization of the government and society of the Roman Empire. Nevertheless, these changes alone do not explain the events to come. There are two basic facts which must be grasped before those events can be understood.

The first is what we might call the "de-Romanization" of the Roman Empire. This was not a sudden process. Even in the late periods of the Roman Republic it had become plain that the entire Mediterranean world could not be successfully ruled simply as the subject territory of a single city. The strains and the corruptions of empire were among the factors which wore down and helped to destroy the Republic as a system. The new order established by Augustus (31 B.C.–A.D. 14) might maintain the trappings of traditional Roman institutions, but it transformed the Roman state into a monarchy, ruled on the basis of military command and administered from Rome as a capital. By the second century men of provincial background emerged to prominence, even rising to the throne, though at first they originated from the families of Roman aristocrats and colonists settled in the provinces. This trend, however, is meaningful only as a symptom. The Roman world was no longer the province of a Roman master race. Even the very privilege of citizenship, once so exclusively guarded and so jealously treasured, was given out with increasing frequency. Rome had always been willing to adopt and assimilate alien nationalities and races, with little sense of prejudice. This policy of amalgamating stock of diverse origins can be traced back even to the traditional legends of the city's supposed founder, Romulus. It was thus as a kind of final touch that in 212 the Emperor Caracalla issued his edict making virtually all freeborn men full Roman citizens. By this time the leveling of social status within the Empire was completed. Intermarriage and broadened enfranchisement had long been placing native-born Romans and free provincials on a more nearly identical level.

Thus, the Roman state had become a world-state. It was no longer an empire owned by Rome: it was in fact the civilized world of the Mediterranean and European lands of which Rome was the administrative capital, but it was also a political entity which had ceased to have a narrowly Roman spirit in the sense of its origins from the city on the Tiber. This process was to be symbolized by the very position of Rome itself hereafter. From the beginning Italy had held a privileged status in the Empire, as an area apart from the rest of its territories. Under Diocletian's reorganization it became merely another province, shorn of its old privileges and status. Meanwhile, Rome itself had ceased to be the actual capital of the Empire, at least as the residence of the Emperor. From Diocletian's time it was abandoned by virtually all of the Emperors. Scornful of its old republican and religious associations, and in need of more practical or strategic locations, they avoided it except for very rare visits. Later, when a capital was needed in Italy, Milan was chosen as closer to the threatened frontier, and then Ravenna as an all but impregnable fortress.

The second fact to be borne in mind is that the Roman Empire was always composed of two distinct spheres. On the one hand there was the Eastern Mediterranean world. This was the true center of ancient civilization. Most of ancient culture had developed here. Its language was generally Greek, and its intellectual outlook was likewise Hellenic. Here lay the chief cities of Antiquity, the largest population, the greatest wealth, the most extensively developed trade and commerce, and the most stable prosperity. The Eastern half of the Empire had, in short, both the deeper background of civilization and the more firmly rooted resources of recovery and continuity.

On the other hand there was the West, by contrast the inferior half of the Empire. Its economy was less extensive, less diversified, and less secure, its commerce was more limited, its cities were fewer and more sparsely populated, its manpower was smaller, and its prosperity was more fragile. Both politically and culturally it was a parvenu. Though Greek colonization had graced parts of Italy and Sicily, the bulk of the Western Mediterranean had but lately become part of the civilized world and had produced little by comparison with the East. Carthage had been a center of power and commerce, but hardly of civilization. The Etruscans have their interest for us, but were as nothing in this context. Rome itself was a cultural pygmy until it waxed great on what it absorbed from the East; only by conquest and its genius for government had it acquired a claim to status in the ancient world. To be sure, it was through Rome that the rest of the Western

Mediterranean and much of Europe had been brought into the pale of civilization. But in the Western sphere that civilization was largely Latin in language and outlook, lacking either the tradition or the flexibility of what the Greek East could boast.

The Roman Empire was therefore really a union of two components, the Greek Eastern Mediterranean and the Latin Western Mediterranean, not entirely compatible, and eminently separable — a marriage of convenience resulting from the all-embracing sway of Roman power. There was no doubt at the time which of the two components was the more cultivated or durable. Indeed, even in the West, Greek was freely recognized and read as the true language of culture among the educated. It must be stressed that these facts — on which so much of what followed was based — were as evident to contemporaries as they should be to us. Even the brilliant Julius Caesar recognized it, and toyed with the idea of moving his capital from Rome to an Eastern city, probably the great Hellenistic center of Alexandria — though the attractions of Cleopatra may have played a role in this scheme. This very idea was one of the outrages which shocked Caesar's conservative countrymen, and it helped to hone the daggers awaiting him when he last entered the Senate House on the fateful Ides of March in 44 B.C. Caesar's kinsman and eventual heir, Octavian-Augustus, realized the indiscretion of so drastic a step as moving the capital eastward. He and his successors retained Rome as the capital of an Empire which was, however, no longer the private preserve of an exalted and self-governing city. It was also an Empire whose center of gravity was moving increasingly eastward. So it was, three centuries later, that Diocletian, never one to fear breaking with the past, indicated his own recognition of which part of the Empire counted most: not only did he abandon Rome as his residence, but he himself took the Eastern provinces as his personal portion of the Empire in its collegiate administration. Nevertheless, it fell to his chief successor to make the final and formal step, confirming the relatively greater significance of the East in the Roman world.

Constantine the Great (306–337) is most readily associated with his momentous conversion to Christianity. Rightly so, for this step became a vital landmark not only in the history of the religion's spread, but also in the course of history in general. This small and obscure yet vital sect had driven the Roman state, otherwise one of the most religiously tolerant in history, into occasional spasms of persecution — though by no means consistent or continuous ones. Christianity emerged from the last and most determined persecution (in the first decade of the fourth century) in an ambiguous position, suddenly to find itself with the stunning success of having captured the allegiance of the triumphant new Emperor himself.

It was a capture, but in a sense captivity as well. Challenging as is the story of the rise of Christendom, the problem of the conversion of Constantine is an even more challenging one, absorbing as it has the attention of many analysts. We can hardly go deeply into this question here. To a degree it is perhaps an academic one, since we will probably never know fully this controversial ruler's mind. Nor will we ever know precisely why he cast his lot with a sect which represented only a small percentage of the Empire's population, and adopted its beliefs as his personal faith. He did *not*, it should be noted, make it the sole and official state religion. It was not until later in the fourth century that paganism was overtly persecuted, and not until the end of that century, under Theodosius I, that it became the sole acceptable state faith. What Constantine did do was to make Christianity an acceptable religion; by his personal conversion he gave it new attractiveness and promoted its surging growth; by his Imperial favor he gave it privileges and preferments, though he also intervened in its affairs. What remains mysterious is his original motivation. Was it sincere piety and personal faith that prompted Constantine's actions? Was it, as some interpreters suggest, an act of calculated political foresight? Or was it an inscrutable move, not to be understood in rational terms? Or was it a complex interaction of such motives? Many ingenious hypotheses have been advanced, but they can amount to no more than that. Whatever the reason or reasons may have been, the fact remains that Constantine took the step, one which affected the entire course of history.

Yet, Constantine's conversion has overshadowed another act, or rather another aspect of the same act, which had consequences at least equally significant. Here we return to our point concerning the imbalance between the Eastern and Western spheres of the Roman Empire. For it was Constantine also who took the ultimate step of moving the capital of the Empire officially to a more natural center, away from its artificial and outmoded location in Rome, to the more viable East. Again, this is a step which has provoked endless debate. Plainly, many factors must have been involved in Constantine's decision. At least one of them may have been simply his desire for a new Christian capital, divorced from the pagan and republican associations of Rome. Other considerations there must certainly have been also, not the least of which could have been the matchless qualities of the site he chose, in terms of defensibility, and of commercial and strategic location. No matter what his final choice proved to be, however, it had to be an Eastern city; we actually know that he considered more than one such city before making his final decision. Whatever the factors involved in the choice, it was on the site of the ancient city of Byzantium that the new capital finally rose. To it were brought the old forms and trappings of Roman government. Large elements of the Roman aristocracy were encouraged to move there. Even the Senate, a body whose power was by now mainly formal if still occasionally to be reckoned with, was re-created in the new seat of Empire. New Rome it was to be called officially; but it was as the City of Constantine, *Konstantinoúpolis*, that it would come to be known. Whatever his various reasons for selecting it, and however much he appreciated what he was doing, he was in actuality establishing one of the principal factors through which the Roman Empire would survive in at least some form — an impregnable bastion which would hold off almost all threats, however formidable, and a nucleus from which the surviving Empire could repeatedly regenerate itself.[5] This was Constantine's most tangi-

5. See the highly stimulating interpretation by Lot, *The End of the Ancient World*, pp. 38–39, in which he portrays Constantine's act as having a long-range significance utterly different from what this Emperor himself had intended. Lot also maintains (pp. 36–37) that the transference of the capital to the East was "not the culmination of a process of evolution," insisting with some technical plausibility that "Never had the idea of doing away with Rome as a capital occurred to an Emperor." But his argument is based on an absence of acts only, while the ideas in question are somewhat less easy to perceive

ble accomplishment, his definitive if perhaps unconscious designation of the East as the key to the survival of the ancient world and of the Roman world-state.

Under Constantine's successors in the fourth century the reorganization of the Roman world was pursued along the lines he had laid down. Christianity was well on its way to its absolute triumph, to come at the end of the century, as the state religion. The attempt at a pagan revival under the last member of Constantine's house, the brilliant but futilely visionary Julian "the Apostate" (361–363), bore no fruit. Christianity's progress was irresistible, while paganism was doomed, and within a generation the old cults were discriminated against, persecuted by Gratian, and finally proscribed by Theodosius I. Yet, in the wake of the new Faith's triumph came also conflict. If Constantine had any illusions about using Christianity as no more than a unifying force in the reconstituted Roman world, he was soon to be disabused of them when the Arian controversy, the first of the early Church's great Christological disputes, broke out. It was under Constantine that the first attempt, though not the last, was made to settle it, by means of assembling the first "ecumenical" or universal council in 325 in Nicaea. Symptomatically, the First Council was held in an Asiatic city, and was dominated largely by the clergy of the East. Even in ecclesiastical and theological matters the East would continue to be ahead of the West in this formative epoch of the Church. Another great conclave was required, the Second Ecumenical Council, held in Constantinople itself in 381, to discredit Arianism fully within the Empire. By that time the Christian Church was not only triumphant over all rivals, but was also embarked on the long and variable path of its relationship with the State, each party ready and willing to use the other for its own purposes whenever possible. With Constantine himself began the development of the Emperor's role in Church affairs, a development which was to reach an important stage in the reign of Justinian.

---

or trace. In point of fact, the idea was not an entirely new one, as we have seen. Constantine's transference was a symbolic act in itself and was indeed a culmination of a broad process of evolution in which the predominance of the Eastern half of the Empire had become undeniable.

Constantine's return to the sovereignty of a single ruler was not to be maintained consistently, for there were renewed divisions of the Imperial authority after his death. Family interest was the cause. Constantine left behind three sons, each of whom was given a share of joint power until civil wars reduced them to only one survivor, Constantius II (337–361, alone from 353). These civil wars were ruinous for the military strength of the Empire, especially with the carnage of the Battle of Mursa (351), which attended Constantius' repression of the usurper Magnentius (350–353).

Another reason for renewed collegiate rule was practical necessity. The tasks of governing the entire Roman world and of facing mounting external pressures were becoming more than ever too much for a single ruler. Nor was it enough to delegate responsibility to subordinates, if the Emperor was to avoid the danger of usurpations by the all-powerful supreme commanders of the type required by the military situation. And so a renewed division of authority came with the accession of Valentinian I (364–375). As a soldier he was guided by the fact that the frontier threats in the West were more acute than those in the East. Accordingly he reversed the usual procedure: he took the West for himself and assigned the Eastern sphere to his brother Valens (364–378). Valentinian's sons, Gratian (375–383) and Valentinian II (378/83–392), were maintained in power in the West after his death; while in the East, Valens was succeeded by Theodosius I (379–395). Theodosius I, often called "the Great," was destined to be the last man to rule the entire Mediterranean world. After the successive overthrows of Valentinian I's sons by usurpers, Theodosius punished their murderers and then, for the final year of his life, assumed the rule of both the East and the West. Nevertheless, when Theodosius died in 395 the pressures and burdens which had encouraged collegiate rule in the latter half of the fourth century still made unthinkable any continuation of united authority.

The chief of these pressures was by no means a new one. It may be easy to think of the barbarians as constituting a threat which menaced Rome only by the third or fourth century A.D. In reality the barbarian cloud had long hung over Roman history. Even in the early days of the Republic the Romans knew the danger of barbarian attack; as when the Gauls, the masters of much of northern Italy, actually attacked, captured, and sacked Rome, about the year 390 B.C. according to the traditional account. It was with long memories of such disasters in mind that Julius Caesar had mounted his campaigns in Gaul in 58–51 B.C. By then the Romans had already confronted specifically German threats: in 102–101 B.C. a menacing invasion of several Germanic tribes was crushed just in time to prevent their descent into Italy. Much of Caesar's own campaigning was concerned with erecting barriers across German routes of penetration southward. This policy was extended by Augustus, who dreamed of pushing beyond Caesar's boundary of the Rhine and of making the Elbe River the northern frontier of the Empire. A disastrous defeat in A.D. 9 and unsuccessful operations thereafter early in the first century shattered that dream. Had it been realized, the Roman frontier position and much of the later development of the Germanic people themselves might have been considerably different.

For the next century or so the Germanic frontiers were relatively quiet, but ripples of unrest appeared occasionally, while the restlessness of the Germanic tribes beyond the Rhine was a never-ending danger. Such restlessness increased late in the second century, and the great Marcus Aurelius (A.D. 161–180), one of the most pacific of all rulers, was to pass his final years in the weary toil of campaigning against Germanic uprisings. With the growing internal disorder and crises of the third century the Roman Empire was more open to attacks by the barbarians, who proceeded to violate the frontiers and to menace exposed Roman territories. One Emperor, Decius (249–251), actually lost his life in battle against the Goths when he went forth to resist their depredations.

Fortunately, these dangers were met by the heroic efforts of a series of energetic military Emperors in the latter part of the century. Almost to a man these Emperors were provincials, originating from the area of Illyricum in the northern Balkans. Hence the frequent designation of them as the "Illyrian Emperors": most notable were Claudius II "Gothicus" (268–270), the great *Resti-*

tutor orbis ("Restorer of the World") Aurelian (270–275), and Probus (276–281). Under them, Roman forces hurled back the invaders and restored the integrity of the frontiers, although even Aurelian was forced to abandon some territory in eastern Europe. As a none-too-subtle symptom of changing times, however, it was the victorious Aurelian who built a great new wall around the city of Rome to protect the sprawling and long unfortified capital against any possible attacks. Nevertheless, by the beginning of the fourth century the barbarian menace was to some degree under control again.

Still, the pressure did not abate. On the contrary, the fourth century was to witness its further concentration. By this time the age of the barbarian migrations had begun. The Germans and other peoples were on the move and were developing a formidable momentum. The reasons for the migrations of these semi-civilized tribes were varied. Some of these peoples, like the Asiatic Huns, were by nature nomads and raiders. Frequently there was a chain reaction of pressures, of one people on another, when they migrated or were attacked. Many of these tribes, however, were in search of land. With their primitive farming methods they were particularly attracted by the fertile soil of the Mediterranean world. In most cases they were not interested simply in plundering and destroying, at least not as a prime objective. On the whole, though they may have hated Rome as one will often hate a superior, they also admired it and wanted to become part of the more advanced and wealthy Roman world, to enjoy its benefits themselves, preferably on their own terms. Finally, it is worth emphasizing that these barbarian peoples did not constitute immense, numberless hordes; they rarely amounted to more than tens of thousands and their occupation of Roman territory usually involved little beyond the spreading of a thin veneer over the provincial populations in a given area.

More formidable than ever by the fourth century, the barbarians confronted the Roman Empire all along its European frontiers: Franks, Alemanians, Vandals, Suevians, Alans, Burgundians, Goths, and many other lesser peoples. The reorganized Roman state had to live with this mounting menace — and cope with it. The story of how it did cope with it, to one degree of success or another, especially in the focal period of the fifth century, is the story of the establishment of the world which confronted Justinian in the sixth century.

The Survival of the East

When the new barbarian storm broke late in the fourth century, it did so over a Roman Empire which was not a seamless monolith, as has been seen, but which was more than ever separating into its two spheres, East and West. Inevitably, each sphere reacted differently, in accordance with its respective position, capacities, and general circumstances.

The first and most dramatic of the barbarian breaches came in the East. While Valentinian I and his successor Gratian were struggling with the Germans on the Western frontier, his brother Valens found himself faced with a dangerous opportunity. One branch of the Gothic peoples, the Visigoths (the "West Goths"), had been moving in a southwesterly direction towards Roman lands. In the middle of the fourth century the process of converting them to Christianity had been begun by their great apostle Ulfilas, or Wulfila; but their conversion was to *Arian* Christianity, a fact which was to be another source of friction when they and other barbarians who had followed their religious example came into contact with the largely anti-Arian Roman Christian world. Then, in the 370's, the Visigoths came under violent attack from the Huns, who were themselves moving westward. In 376 the Visigoths appealed to Valens to be allowed to cross the Danube and settle in Roman frontier territories, which they would engage to occupy and defend. Valens accepted, and what seemed a mutually satisfactory arrangement began. However, the needless and excessive misconduct of corrupt Roman officials antagonized the new Visigothic settlers, driving them into rebellion. In short order they began to ravage their way southward, deep into Roman territory. Valens marched out to meet the Gothic army at the city of Adrianople, where battle was joined on August 9, 378. Thanks to the Emperor's mismanagement, the Roman army was utterly defeated; in the course of the battle Valens himself perished.

The defeat was a shocking disaster. A Roman Emperor had been killed in battle defending his own territories against the first major German tribe to push far into Imperial territories. The disaster was the worse in that it was a needless one, and was largely the result of Valens' own blunders. Still, if the defeat was shocking, it was far from decisive. The Goths did not attempt to press their advantage; though they remained menacingly in revolt, their victory did not mean the collapse of Roman defenses before them. Several years of determined campaigning ensued before Valens' successor in the East, Theodosius I, could bring about, by the year 382, their pacification.

The Goths remained on Imperial territory and had to be dealt with somehow. Theodosius, a man of energy, earnestness, and great competence, an administrator and reformer of undoubted capacity, chose a solution which seemed workable at the time but which was fraught with the most dangerous implications for the future. He incorporated the Visigoths into the Roman army. The principle of assimilating new blood into the population was, of course, old and well-established in Roman history. But even though there were precedents for such assimilation, the scope of this attempt was something of a strain on the Empire's digestion. Imperial armies had long been heavily dependent upon alien soldiers. They now became largely dominated by Gothic and other barbarian elements, often incorporated en bloc into the Imperial ranks. Obviously, it was a dangerous thing for a state to be dependent for its defense on people who were related to or identical with its enemies. Moreover, not only did Theodosius Germanize the army to a considerable degree, but he also accepted many Germans, including Goths, as his generals and counselors and friends. This served for the moment to disunite the Germans, dividing them into those who wished to continue hostility to the Empire and destroy it, and those who were now eager to serve it. But it had a more serious impact on the outlook of the leading Romans, who saw the barbarians — both aliens and Arian Christians — winning preferments and dominating court and military life. Soon a substantial nativist, anti-German, party came into being. The German problem had assumed internal as well as external implications, and there is no doubt that Theodosius I, for all his merits, must bear the responsibility for complicating and compromising the position of the Empire in relation to the barbarians for decades to come.

Upon the death of Theodosius in 395 another division of Imperial authority was effected; or, rather, a familiar one was renewed. As it happened, it was to be the final division. We should understand that the Empire itself was not officially divided. There was still theoretically only one Roman world-state, even though the obvious economic and cultural cleavage between East and West was recognized by the establishment of two separate courts, with their respective spheres of authority corresponding to the two naturally distinct halves of the Roman world. It is true that there were periods of rivalry and real cleavages of policies and attitudes between the two courts. Nevertheless, they also often cooperated wholeheartedly, and the two Emperors were in theory still colleagues, co-rulers over the same Empire, even if quasi-independent in their own spheres.

Both the heirs of Theodosius were feeble and inconsequential ciphers as individuals. To the elder son, Arcadius (395–408), about eighteen years of age, naturally fell the better of the spheres, the East, with its court at Constantinople. The younger son, Honorius (395–423), not yet eleven years old, received the Western sphere, with its court not at Rome, or even Milan, but at Ravenna, on the Adriatic coast of Italy. In accordance with Theodosius' wishes, Honorius was placed under the care of the late Emperor's close adviser and friend, Stilicho, a Vandal in origin. Stilicho has been indicted by some historians for dereliction of duty, for selfish ambition, and for his excessive intrigue and intervention in the affairs of the East.[6] A case can be made to explain some of his policies, and there is no denying that he was a man of considerable ability. From many points of view, however questionable some of his activities, Stilicho can be taken as a perfect example of how a barbarian German could be caught up in the Roman idea and become its relatively loyal and effective instrument.

At the Eastern court, also, German influence bulked large, if less impressively than in the case of Stilicho. Among the many

6. E.g., Bury, *History of the Later Roman Empire* . . . (A.D. 395–565), I, 172–173, and 312.

important members, barbarians or otherwise, of the intrigue-
ridden entourage of Arcadius was the Gothic commander Gaïnas, who had dreamed of becoming in the East what Stilicho
already was in the West. To oust native opponents he joined in
the conspiracies of rival courtiers against each other. In the course
of these manipulations the docile Arcadius was himself married
to the daughter of a Frankish commander, thereby bringing German blood into the Imperial family itself. But Gaïnas' ambitions
carried him too far. A flourishing nativist faction in the capital
joined with his enemies to bring about his fall. With the aid of
the loyal Gothic commander Fravitta, Gaïnas was destroyed by
the year 400; and then, with appropriate treachery, Fravitta himself was eliminated when he had served his purpose, lest one alien
threat be replaced by another. For all its shadiness, however, the
anti-German victory was a substantial one. It was then possible to
reorganize the army, which, while still retaining barbarian elements, managed to integrate them more successfully thereafter
into what native forces were available.

While the German problem in the East was being checked internally, an external German problem remained. The Visigothic
people as a body were still on Roman territory. They could be
pacified with status in the armies and with preferments, but they
continued to be a dangerous cancer in the East's military and
political system, especially with the rise of their energetic and
ambitious chieftain, Alaric. As his demands increased, the Eastern
court attempted to buy him off with high commands and titles.
In 397 he was even given virtual license to plunder Greece unopposed, under the pretense of "guarding" it. Thus the ancient
lands of Hellas were opened to barbarian ravages for the first
time, and in particularly shameful fashion. Thereafter, Alaric was
shunted into Illyricum as the official commander there for the
Eastern court. While the East could offer plunder and preferment,
it was the West, however, which held the best prospects of land.
With the further encouragement of intrigues involving Stilicho,
Alaric found himself drawn out of the Eastern sphere and into
the Western. By 402 it was the turn of Italy to face the menace of
the Visigoths.

As in the East, nativist (anti-German) factionalism was flourishing, with the all-powerful Stilicho as its natural object of hatred. In the West, however, the implications of factional agitation were to be quite different from those in the East. Stilicho, whatever his merits or defects, was faced with an overwhelming and complex challenge. He was obliged to stave off Alaric — though by avoiding any decisive encounter he raised suspicions as to his motives — while at the same time coping with other distractions. Gaul was being ravaged by various Germanic tribes, including his own people, the Vandals. In or about 405 a mixed force of barbarians under the command of one Radagaisus plundered its way through northern Italy until Stilicho annihilated it. In the following year a revolt broke out in Britain and Gaul. Amid all this, Stilicho's enemies and detractors would not rest until he had been eliminated. At length, in 408, the anti-German faction triumphed over Stilicho and secured his disgrace; he dutifully submitted to arrest and execution. But Stilicho was not Gaïnas. Whereas the nativist reaction in the East had paved the way for a healthy purge of the internal German threat, its victory over Stilicho in the West was a hollow one. With his removal the principal obstacle to Alaric was gone. Freed at last, the Visigoths ravaged unchecked through Italy, past the apathetic Honorius in his stronghold of Ravenna, and in August of 410 they entered the defenseless city of Rome. For the first time since 390 B.C. a barbarian foe violated the city which had been the conqueror and queen of the ancient world. The damage and the long-range effects of the Visigothic sack of Rome in 410 were trifling, but the psychological effects of the blow were immense. The end of the world seemed at hand.

Alaric was neither to consolidate nor long to enjoy his stunning success. After a frustrated attempt to cross the sea to Africa by way of Sicily, he turned back and, at the end of the year 410, he died. His successor, Aistulf, or Ataulf, led the Visigoths out of Italy and into southern Gaul. Here, after various hostilities and negotiations, the Visigoths began to build their position, established a kingdom at Toulouse, and eventually extended their power into Spain, where their kingdom would ultimately be centered. In theory their kings absorbed and ruled Roman territory as Roman commanders and viceroys, but in actuality they had begun the dismemberment of the Empire in the West.

Nor was the remainder of the West invulnerable. After the revolt of 406, Britain seems to have been abandoned by the Romans. Thereafter, the unhappy island was left exposed to raids, and then conquest, by the Saxons, to be lost to Christian Europe for nearly two centuries. Gaul continued to be devastated alike by German attacks and by local rebellions and usurpations. The feeble government of Honorius struggled on ingloriously. After a new period of civil war upon his death (423), he was followed by his nephew, Valentinian III (425-455). A child at the time of his accession, Valentinian was dominated for years by his mother, Galla Placidia, and then grew up to be a vicious and worthless wretch. His reign witnessed only further dismemberment of the Western provinces. The Vandals and other tribes plundered their way through Spain, and as a result of intrigues in 429 won entry into North Africa, long the goal of land-hungry barbarians. Under their able King Gaiseric, they made rapid progress. By 430 they had taken the city of Hippo Regius — during the siege of which its Bishop, the great St. Augustine, died — and in 439 they finally won Carthage. Thus was established in North Africa a new and powerful German state. It was the only one of the emerging barbarian kingdoms to become a great naval power; a power whose ravages the Empire's shores were soon to feel, even in the East. In the face of such disasters the feeble Western court was helpless. The emergence of the general Aëtius, the last major Roman commander of any genuine talent, was of some help in Italy and Gaul, but by the middle of the fifth century Germanic encroachments in the West had become irresistible.

While the Western sphere of the Empire was being parceled out among the barbarians, the East was by contrast able to hold itself together with remarkable success. It had a number of distinct strategic advantages over the West, as we shall see. For one thing, it had a less extended and perhaps a more defended European frontier; and it was of course from Europe that the Germanic pressure was coming. The profusion of powerful senatorial landowners with vast estates, though extensive also in the East, was less so than in the West, where these semi-independent magnates served to weaken the power of the central government in the provinces and were not unwilling to betray their Emperor to preserve their wealth under new barbarian regimes. The East also had, in its Asiatic provinces, resources of revenue, wealth, and man-power as yet untouched by barbarian ravages. To be sure, its leadership was not much less degenerate than that in the Western court. The feeble Arcadius (395–408) died young, and gave way to his infant son, Theodosius II (408–450). The latter grew up to be a retiring and relatively inconsequential figure in almost everything but ecclesiastical affairs. He was dominated alternately by his elder and more forceful sister Pulcheria, and by his cul-tured but overtly ambitious wife Eudocia, as well as by various advisers and ministers. Some of them, however, were exceedingly capable men. In point of fact, for all the disasters which the early fourth century brought to the Roman world, the reign of Theo-dosius II in the East was generally a time of peace and even prosperity.

There were indeed important constructive accomplishments during this reign. In 425 the Emperor chartered the Higher School in the capital, what we have come to call the University of Constantinople. It was designed to be a new intellectual center, emphasizing Greek culture, and of cardinal importance for the cultural life of the East Roman world. In 438 Theodosius II issued the law code which bears his name, the *Codex Theodosianus*, a milestone in the systematization of Roman Law, and an important precedent for Justinian's own work in this sphere a century later. Finally, the reign of Theodosius II also witnessed the construc-tion (in 413; repaired and extended 447) of the great Land Walls of Constantinople. Combined with the city's natural position, these fortifications helped make the capital the virtually impreg-nable bastion it was to be for centuries to come — a factor of de-cisive consequence for subsequent history.

Such fortifications were not works of idle ostentation; they were vital necessities for the East as the middle of the fifth cen-tury drew on. While the German threat had temporarily waned there, a new one had come to replace and overshadow it. This was the rise of the Huns. These hordes of nomadic Mongoloid peoples had been moving westward for some time. In the 430's, concur-rently with the rise of their greatest leader, the fearsome Attila, they were accumulating a vast empire of conquered lands and

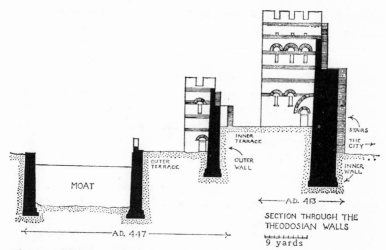

The Land Walls of Constantinople, cross-sectional plan. (Reproduced from John E. M. Hearsey, *City of Constantine, 324–1453*, by permission.)

subject peoples, including many of the Germanic tribes in eastern Europe, while operating from their center of power in the plains of modern Hungary. The Empire in the East was again placed in great peril, especially with very limited defensive military forces free or at its disposal. Somehow the Eastern court succeeded in spinning out negotiations and intrigue, and was able to buy peace with Attila through tribute and subsidies.

However heavy and humiliating these payments were, they demonstrate another important advantage which the East enjoyed over the West: more ample resources of wealth. Though it is true that tribute was paid by the Western court as well as the Eastern, and also that Attila's exactions nearly ruined the East financially, its capacity to pay seems to have contented him, so that he left it an independent, if degraded, victim. Having bled the East, Attila now found his ambitions attracted to the West. When Theodosius II died in 450 his successor, Marcian (450–457), the husband of his sister Pulcheria, ended the ruinous tribute payments. By then Attila was already committed to an invasion of the West, though popular stories of his being invited by the unhappy princess Honoria, sister of Valentinian III, to claim her as his bride are exaggerated if not apocryphal.

Attila's hopes of devouring large chunks of the Western part of the Empire were not, however, to be realized. The courageous Aëtius, though lacking sufficient forces of his own, was nonetheless able to win the cooperation of the Visigoths. German and Roman momentarily united against the common Asiatic foe. In the summer of 451, at the Battle of the Mauriac Plain (or Campi Catalauni, near Troyes), the Huns were defeated. Gaul was spared from the Huns thereafter, though the Visigoths themselves remained to menace it.

Attila was far from curbed. Aëtius was powerless to organize sufficient resistance when the Hun turned in the following year, 452, to ravage Italy. Into the peninsula he swept, and it seemed as if Rome would be subjected to a second and even more devastating sack. Then Attila suddenly turned back, leaving Rome untouched. The precise reasons for this are unknown: the practical difficulties of thinning forces, overextended lines, and particularly disease may have played some part in his decision. There is also the tradition of an embassy by the influential, persuasive Bishop of Rome, Leo I "the Great," a story which may very well have some basis in fact. Whatever dissuaded him, however, Attila's retreat from Italy marked the ebb of the Huns' threat. Within a year, Attila was dead. His successes had been those of conquest and plunder. He left behind him no true governmental machinery or institutions; unlike so many of the Germans, he had built a power that was purely negative, without constructive accomplishments. Deprived of his forceful personality, the Hun Empire fell apart. The German and other subject peoples threw off their yoke, and thereafter the various tribes of Huns remained lesser powers in eastern Europe. The Eastern and Western courts alike were freed from the frightful menace which Attila had represented in his lifetime.

This was to be little comfort to the Western court. In the face of hostile fortune it did not enjoy capable or stable leadership. Its one hope, Aëtius, received his reward in falling victim to petty intrigues. In 454, with the connivance of the contemptible Valentinian III, he was murdered. With this one last prop removed, the Emperor himself was to reap the fruits of his own folly: he was assassinated in his own turn early in 455. With him died the Theodosian house in the West. His throne was usurped by the chief conspirator, the Roman Senator Petronius Maximus. The latter's futile government was powerless against a new menace. The crafty and able Vandal King Gaiseric, exercising his maritime muscle with increasing success, had been watching the chaos in Italy with a sharp eye. In the spring of 455 his Vandal forces swooped down upon Italy and entered Rome. Once again the former seat of empire was subjected to barbarian pillage — though the ravages of the Vandals were not so excessive by comparison with those of others as to justify the modern connotations of their name.

Chaos now descended upon the West. With the support of the Visigothic King, the commander Avitus was installed as Emperor. After a reign of barely one year (455–456), he was deposed. Antagonized by this failure, the Visigothic kingdom ended all semblance of allegiance to the Western Emperor; it ruled in Spain and southern Gaul as a fully independent power. North Africa was, of course, in the hands of the powerful and hostile Vandals. Only portions of Gaul and the whole of Italy remained under the control of the Empire in the West. Even here the real power was held by local commanders, especially Germans, while genuine central authority was almost nonexistent.

Worse still, Italy itself was by this time under the domination of a series of powerful German commanders. Since they respected the unwritten law that a barbarian German (and an Arian Christian) could not himself sit on the Imperial throne, they chose instead to be kingmakers. The chief of these was the barbarian Master of Soldiers, Ricimer. After an interval in which the Emperor in the East was theoretically recognized as the sole sovereign of the Roman world, Ricimer was able to elevate his own candidate in the West and was himself given the title of Patrician. His first creation was the Emperor Majorian (457–461), of good Roman antecedents. Surprisingly enough, Majorian proved to be a man of considerable energy and ability. He achieved some success in cleansing parts of Gaul of barbarian raiders. His success made Ricimer uneasy, and then, when Majorian's bold attempt

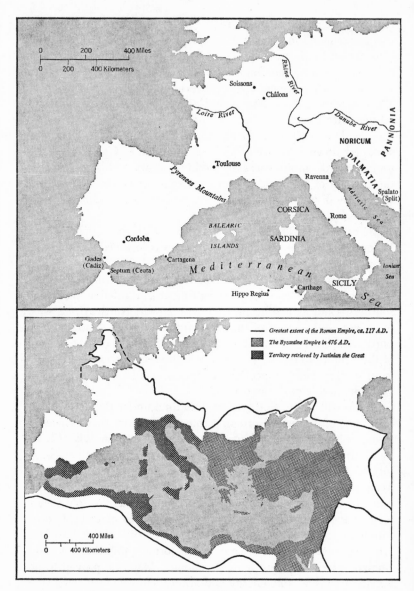

Europe and the Mediterranean world in the Age of Justinian. (Map courtesy of University of Wisconsin Cartographic Laboratory.)

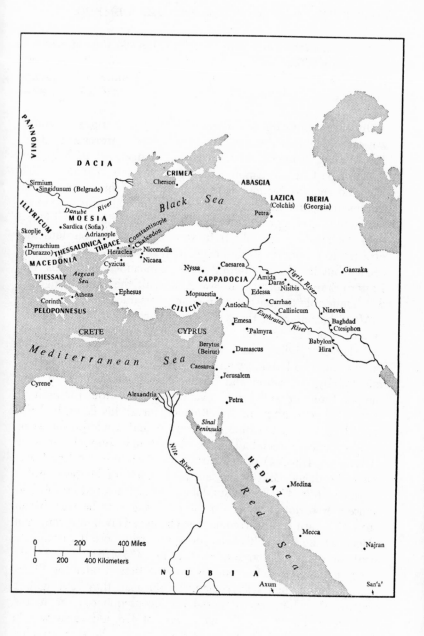

at an assault on the Vandals in Africa failed in 460, the unfortunate Emperor's position was undermined. Ricimer had him deposed and executed by the following summer. After another interregnum Ricimer chose a more docile figurehead named Severus (461–465).

Under the pressure of Gaiseric's threat and intrigues Ricimer was eventually forced to appeal to the Eastern court for assistance. The Eastern Emperor Leo I was not undisposed to help the Western part of the Empire; during a new interregnum in the West he sent to Ricimer a new candidate of his own for the throne there, the Eastern noble Anthemius. Leo also agreed to the mounting of a great new expedition against the Vandal kingdom. Originating entirely from the East, and at burdensome expense to its treasury, this expedition of 468 might have succeeded but for the blundering of its commander, Basiliscus, the Eastern Emperor's brother-in-law. As a result, the Vandal kingdom was again able to resist Roman counter-assaults.

After the failure of the great expedition of 468, the latest co-operation of the two courts soon ended. Amid terrible pressures and dangers, Ricimer and Anthemius distracted themselves by falling out. The latter's reign (467–472) was presently to be terminated by deposition and death. The appointment of a new puppet Emperor (Olybrius) availed Ricimer little, for both of them died soon after, in 472. Ricimer, for all his flaws, had defended Italy to some extent. His nephew and would-be successor as kingmaker, Gundobad, established a new puppet Emperor (Glycerius, 473–474) in defiance of the Eastern court. Leo I was not to be defied, and again sent a candidate of his own, Julius Nepos, who in 474 drove Gundobad out of Italy and established himself precariously there. In the following year he was driven out in his turn by the commander Orestes. This new strongman placed on the throne his own young son, who bore the ironically symbolic name of Romulus Augustulus (475–476).

Again the Germanic elements grew restless. Under the direction of one of their leaders named Odovacar, they rose against Orestes, slew him, and deposed his inconsequential son in the summer of the supposedly magic year of 476. Odovacar was in complete control of the forces of Italy, but he chose to abandon the game of Imperial puppetry. He dispatched the Imperial insignia back to Constantinople, informing the new Eastern Emperor Zeno that one sovereign was sufficient for the Roman world, and that he, Odovacar, would administer Italy as the agent of the Emperor in Constantinople. Though the deposed Julius Nepos retained claim to the Western throne as an exile, and would continue to do so until his death in 480, Zeno was in no position to oppose Odovacar's *fait accompli*. Therefore Zeno reluctantly recognized Odovacar as Patrician in Italy, where he was to rule for the next seventeen years.

Once more there was only one Emperor in the Roman world. Rather than marking the "fall" of the Roman Empire, 476 marks its reunification under a single sovereign. But it was a sorry wreck of an empire as far as the Western provinces were concerned. North Africa was independent under the Vandals, while Spain and southern Gaul were virtually autonomous under the Visigoths. Italy was the preserve of the far-from-servile Odovacar. The remnants of Gaul muddled through on their own under quasi-independent Gallo-Roman regimes like that of Aegidius (d. 464) and his son Syagrius (d. 486), and those of other, less powerful, local magnates, continually menaced by Visigoths and Burgundians, though enjoying some support from the generally allied Franks. It was the Franks, however, rising to greater strength and unity under Clovis (481–511), who would eventually fill the vacuum by destroying Syagrius at the Battle of Soissons in 486, and begin their absorption of Gaul. Under the pressure of Clovis and his Merovingian successors, the Visigoths would fall back beyond the Pyrenees and be confined exclusively to Spain. Thus would Roman authority finally crumble in the West.

So then, it was only direct Roman authority in one sphere which disappeared by 476, not the Empire itself. It is all too easy to assume that once the Empire lost the West, and Italy, and the city of Rome itself, it was therefore no longer the Roman Empire and had become something else. Yet the state we are considering had long since ceased to depend on Rome or Italy for its identity. It was still *the* Empire, the *Christian* Empire of the civilized (i.e., Mediterranean) world, whatever territory it had lost.

What remained of the Empire in the East, of course, had still escaped such parceling out. It stood intact as the surviving sphere of the Roman world, with unquestioned legal claim to the full Imperial tradition, a claim which even many of the barbarian kingdoms recognized. Yet the East was not freed from all perils of its own. Indeed, for a while during Ricimer's regime in the West there was very great danger that the East would be dragged down a parallel course.

Upon the death of Theodosius II, his sister Pulcheria accepted as her nominal husband and as the new Emperor the aged commander and official, Marcian (450–457). Marcian was an earnest and capable ruler who, among other things, effected important financial and administrative reforms. His advancement to the throne was due in part to the sponsorship of a man who had been his previous superior, and who began to emerge as an ominous manipulator behind the scenes. This was Aspar, by birth of the Asiatic Alans. He had risen under Theodosius II to the highest military command and the rank of Patrician. But greater prospects lay ahead of him. In 453 Pulcheria died, ending the Theodosian house in the East; then in 457 Marcian himself died, leaving no specific heir or designated successor. As a barbarian and an Arian Christian, Aspar could not dream of the throne for himself, but he could seek to play the same role which Ricimer was playing in the West at exactly this time. Moreover, Aspar had behind him the support of a growing new barbarian element at the Eastern court. With the death of Attila and the ensuing collapse of the Huns' power, the Germans in the East became a powerful menace once again, both internally and externally. A new phase of danger from the Germans was beginning as Aspar sought to dominate the Eastern court, as Ricimer was doing in the West, through a puppet Emperor.

His choice was Leo I (457–474), a man of obscure background and unprepossessing qualities. Yet Leo I proved to be something different from what was expected, and was in fact determined not to be merely the docile tool which the Western shadow-rulers were. His relations with Aspar soon cooled, and even became hostile. Leo appreciated the fact that he needed some support to offset Aspar and the German element if he were to avoid becoming a creature of the Eastern kingmaker. He lacked any male heir of his own, but he did have two daughters. It was by marriage that Leo would secure the help he needed.

In this instance also the Eastern sphere of the Empire had an advantage which the West lacked: a native element which could be used as a counterweight to the Germans. This group was the Isaurians, a species of "home-grown" barbarians. These rough mountaineers had raided and demoralized the provinces in south-eastern Asia Minor since the beginning of the fifth century, and their depredations had distracted much of the Eastern court's attentions and limited military resources in the midst of its other dangers. Barbarians the Isaurians were in their outlook and way of life, but they were indigenous to the Empire, a part of it, and its subjects. Even under Theodosius II the central government had made attempts to use them in defending the Empire, especially the capital, against the Hun threat. Their chieftains proved unpredictable and were not readily pacified. Nevertheless, the Isaurians were hardy fighters, and in the eyes of the desperate Leo their potentialities outweighed their faults.

Within a precarious decade of his elevation by Aspar, Leo I had won over to his side the Isaurian chief Tarasicodissa, and had married him to his elder daughter, Ariadne. The groom changed his name, adopting that of an earlier Isaurian leader, Zeno — which also had the merit of sounding somewhat more Greek than his original name. By the years 466–467 he was firmly established in the capital as Leo's henchman and a definite counterweight to Aspar. Together Leo and Zeno organized a new force of palace guards called the Excubitors, which gave the Emperor a personal body of supporters on whom he could rely against the power of the German element.

The Eastern court was not yet the Western one. The East, far from presenting the picture of disintegration and chaos to be found in the West, was still a firm and well-ordered society, as yet untouched by the systematic ravages of barbarian invasions. The elaborate machinery of its civil government was fully intact. Its provinces had not slipped into the disorganized localism fostered by the great independent landowners in the West. Nor was Aspar actually anywhere near the dominant position which Ricimer enjoyed in Italy. As a result, the Alan commander could not openly block the hostile moves of his intended puppet and the new Isaurian rival. Nevertheless, Aspar was determined to assert himself and continue to build his power. When the scheme was formed for the great naval expedition against the Vandals in co-operation with Ricimer, it was warmly supported by the Empress Verina as a vehicle for her ambitious brother Basiliscus. Aspar had the good sense — and also the sobering experience of having commanded another such unsuccessful expedition earlier, in 431 — to oppose the plan. When his advice was ignored he remained aloof and dissociated himself from it. There is even the possibility that he encouraged the appointment of the incompetent Basiliscus with the deliberate idea of crippling the scheme. After Basiliscus' mismanagement had permitted the expedition to snatch defeat out of the jaws of victory in 468, Aspar's position at court was in consequence much stronger, and he proceeded to take advantage of it.

Intrigues were launched against Zeno to undermine his position. Further, new and humiliating obligations were imposed on the cowed Leo. The most drastic of these was the requirement that Aspar's eldest son be given the title of Caesar, with the status of heir to the throne. This concession was finally wrenched from Leo in 470, but the prospect of an heir apparent who was both barbarian in origin and an Arian Christian provoked violent popular opposition. Such indignation, coupled with innumerable further intrigues, prompted Leo and Zeno to strike back. In 471 they arranged the assassination of Aspar and most of his sons. Thus the would-be Ricimer of the East was cut down and the latest internal German menace eliminated. It was no small accomplishment on Leo's part, though hostile contemporary sources rewarded him with the appellation of "the Butcher."

This did not mean, however, that the German question was completely solved for the East. For by this time the other branch of the Gothic peoples, the Ostrogoths, had moved into Imperial territory and had settled for the time being. Once again there was a large and menacing body of Germans who might well do in the East what their predecessors had been doing in the West. A powerful element of these Ostrogoths was already in Thrace, close to the capital, and on Aspar's assassination their chief, Theodoric

Strabo, demanded the slain commander's title and prerogatives. Leo was forced to yield on this point, with the consequence that the German danger in the East continued after his death.

Leo I had eliminated the internal danger posed by Aspar, and as his own life drew to a close he became concerned about securing a stable and safe succession. Making Zeno his heir was a delicate matter, since the new Isaurian element was becoming as unpopular in the capital as the Germans had formerly been. Zeno and Ariadne had a little son, also named Leo, born about 467. It was therefore arranged that this child should follow his grandfather to the throne. When Leo I died in February of 474, the reign of the boy Leo II began. But the child was sickly as well as a minor. It was natural that his strong father, Zeno, should be immediately designated as his associate in actual rule. Then, the boy Emperor himself died in November of the same year. Zeno was left as the actual successor in title as well as fact.

The reign of Zeno (474–491) was in itself an answer to the German threat, but it also raised new problems. Upon the assumption of power by this former mountaineer chieftain, the influx into the capital of his people, the crude Isaurians, only increased popular resentment against them. Nor were these countrymen particularly reliable from his point of view. Zeno found himself faced not only with continued German dangers, but also with his own internal problems. He did his best, patching up a peace with the Vandals in the year of his accession, and trying to control the Thracian Ostrogoths of Theodoric Strabo, who was now friendly, now hostile. In short order, however, the reign of Zeno degenerated into a morass of conspiracies and revolts, with a cast of characters that grew bewilderingly. Included at the outset were the disgruntled dowager Empress Verina, her selfish and ambitious brother Basiliscus, and a pair of Isaurian brothers, the untrustworthy commanders Illus and Trocundes. Within a year of his elevation to the throne Zeno was driven out of Constantinople, and Basiliscus seized control of the government.

Basiliscus rode into power on a wave of anti-Isaurian sentiment, and his accession was attended by a massacre of Isaurians caught in the capital. Basiliscus, however, proved to be as spectacularly incompetent an Emperor as he had been (in 468) a general. By

476 Zeno's cause was prospering and the rightful Emperor was able to recover the capital. Even so, the atmosphere of rivalries, intrigue, assassination and Isaurian rebellion continued, while Theodoric Strabo hovered ominously in Thrace. In 479 a new actor joined the cast: Marcian, the husband of Leo I's younger daughter. When he attempted a usurpation of his own, he was put down, but in 483 he tried again, this time with the support of Illus. The two soon fell out, and the treacherous Illus abandoned him to go over to the side of a former enemy, the dowager Verina. Together they now advanced still another usurper, Leontius, in 484. The Eastern provinces were in an uproar, and it was becoming doubtful that the remaining Eastern portion of the Empire could survive such chaos.

To his credit, Zeno somehow managed to pull things back together. Bit by bit he pushed his various enemies to the wall and destroyed them. Hard pressed by him, Verina died in 485 and Trocundes was eliminated. The remaining rebels were systematically blockaded and reduced in their Isaurian strongholds and elsewhere. When Illus and Leontius were finally captured and executed in 488, Zeno had gone a long way towards putting down the restless threat of rebellion and disorganization which his own people represented. It was ironic that the reign of Zeno should both symbolize the contribution the Isaurians were making to the salvation of the Empire and at the same time begin their own destruction, itself necessary to secure that salvation.

Meanwhile, as Zeno was confronting the problem of his own people, he was also speeding the Eastern Empire on to its final escape from the Germanic menace. The Ostrogoths were not represented alone by Theodoric Strabo, in Thrace. Another group of these people was now located further north in Illyricum, under a second Theodoric, called the Amal. The two Theodorics were natural rivals, and their quarrels helped Zeno to neutralize the Gothic menace during his internal troubles. The death of Theodoric Strabo in 481 brought Zeno to a more direct confrontation with the Amal, who was conceded the rank of Patrician by 484. He was on good enough terms with Zeno to aid the Emperor in the final struggle against the rebellious Illus in 488.

Nevertheless, Theodoric the Amal was too much of a menace

to be left as he was. Fortunately, Zeno found himself in a position to achieve the perfect solution, in fact a solution to fit two simultaneous problems. The power of Odovacar in Italy had become a growing irritation to the Eastern court. Odovacar, for all his avowed dependence on the Emperor in Constantinople, reigned as an independent sovereign. Relations between him and Zeno had deteriorated badly. It was in the interest of the Empire to eliminate this separatist barbarian. Who was better qualified to do the job than Theodoric and his Ostrogoths? Few policies have ever killed two birds with one stone so neatly. Spurred on by Zeno and assured of Imperial support, the Ostrogothic attack on Odovacar soon began. Leading his forces into Italy in 489, Theodoric defeated his opponent, and then had Odovacar treacherously murdered in March of 493 as the culmination to Ostrogothic victory. Theodoric proceeded to establish in Italy his own Ostrogothic kingdom, the latest of the new barbarian states in the West, and in some ways the most remarkable. Though an untutored man himself, Theodoric (493–526) admired and respected Roman civilization. He did his best to preserve the society and governmental machinery which he found — it should always be remembered that the barbarian states usually represented the mere imposition of a very small Germanic ruling element over the existing Roman population and system still in a given province. He also surrounded himself with the most capable native leaders and the finest minds of Italy at the time.

With the transference of Theodoric and the Ostrogoths from Illyricum to Italy, the German threat came to an end in the East. That sphere of the Empire had managed, often by a hair's breadth, to escape the West's fate of dismemberment. For all the great personal unpopularity of Zeno and his reign at home, and for all the problems he left unsolved at his death, it is to him the credit belongs, as we shall see, for having ended at last the German peril, as well as for having laid the basis for the elimination of the counterthreat posed by the Isaurians. By such steps — the elimination of Gaïnas (and Alaric) in 400, of Aspar in 471, of Theodoric in the 490's — did the Eastern half of the Empire survive while the Western half disintegrated.

*The Religious Problem and the Reign
of Anastasius I*

Through all of the foregoing discussion of the deterioration of the West and the survival of the East we have ignored
a problem which was jeopardizing the internal unity: the chronic
religious strife in the Christian Church. This was, it might be
noted, a problem primarily for the East. For it was the Eastern
area of Christendom which was the more cultivated, the more
productive, and the more likely to provide leadership in the
fourth and fifth centuries, the so-called Patristic Age. Of the
Western or Latin Fathers of the Church in this period, St. Ambrose of Milan (340–397), St. Jerome (340–420), and the great
St. Augustine (354–430), only the last-named of them (admittedly
one of the greatest Christian thinkers of all time) could be mentioned in the same breath with the elder and more influential
Eastern or Greek Fathers: the "Cappadocians," the brothers St.
Basil the Great of Caesarea (330–379) and St. Gregory of Nyssa
(d. *ca.* 394), with their friend St. Gregory Nazianzus (329–389),
and of the same period, the eminent St. John Chrysostom, or "The
Golden-Mouthed" (d. 407). Even more, in the development of
the Church the accomplishments of Eastern Christendom were
the basis for most contemporary and subsequent religious thought,
in the West as in the East, while the center of religious activity
and controversy remained in the Eastern half of the Mediterranean world throughout this age. Although this religious ferment
was essentially an Eastern phenomenon at the time, it was, however, to be no less vital for the whole Roman world; and it was
certainly a grave concern of the rulers of the Empire as it struggled for survival.

The condemnation of Arianism had been first accomplished
under the leadership of Athanasius at the Council of Nicaea in
325, and then again more decisively at the Second Ecumenical
Council at Constantinople in 381. As a result, the Arian challenge
to the divinity of Christ had been repulsed, and the development
of the Trinitarian equation of the Son to the Father was assured.
It is true that Arian factions of dissent continued within the Empire after 381, such as that which flourished in Milan around the

Empress Justina, the mother of Valentinian II and the foe of that city's great Bishop, St. Ambrose. For the most part, however, Arianism was on its way to complete extinction among the peoples of the Roman Empire by the end of the fourth century. To be sure, thanks to the missionary work of Ulfilas in the mid-fourth century, the Goths and after them most of the other German tribes were converted to Arian Christianity. Thus, when the barbarians invaded the Empire and established their kingdoms in the West most of them were already Christians, though heretical Arians. Just as dissenting relatives will often hate and fight each other more bitterly than strangers, so between the two rival brands of Christian Faith there was inevitable friction which further complicated the relations of the new barbarian rulers with their orthodox subjects on the one hand and with the orthodox Emperor in Constantinople on the other. Nevertheless, by the end of the fourth century Arian doctrine itself had ceased to be a live theological force in the development of Christian thought.

This resolution by no means ended Christological controversy. Quite the contrary, the official confirmation of Christ's divinity obliged theologians to face more directly the central issue: If the Logos had become man as Christ, how were the Divine and Human elements within Christ compounded or related? By the early fifth century lively speculation had developed on this question. In the forefront was a school of thought emerging in the great Syrian metropolis of Antioch. Its answer to the problem was in essence to suggest that the two Natures of Christ, the Divine and the Human, were distinct and independent within His Person. This approach did not win consistent acceptance, but matters were brought to a head when a member of the Antiochene School, Nestorius, became Patriarch of Constantinople in 428 and attempted to impose the Antiochene outlook on the Eastern Church.

Violent opposition soon developed, on two levels. One level was purely theological. The Antiochene-Nestorian emphasis on the importance and the distinctiveness of Christ's Human Nature offended those convinced of His essential Divinity. It was also unacceptable to those dedicated to the growing veneration of the Virgin Mary as *Theotókos* or "Mother of God." The Nestorian position would make her only *Christotókos* or "Mother of Christ," that is, mother of a Being whose Humanity compromised His Divinity and made Him something less than God Incarnate. The principal theological reaction to the Antiochene-Nestorian offensive was formulated in Constantinople itself by an Archimandrite, or abbot, named Eutyches. His position stressed the absorption of the Human Nature of Christ in a single all-encompassing Divine Nature. This emphasis upon Christ as of a single *physis*, or Nature, is what came to be called Monophysitism.

But the theological reaction to Nestorius was not at all the sole or the decisive one. The truly crucial reaction was to be political. Much of the opposition to Nestorius was not to his theology, but to his pretensions as Patriarch of Constantinople. In the growth of the administrative system of the Church, power had naturally tended to be fixed in the large urban centers. Since the cities in the East were larger and more numerous, and had older histories and cultures than those in the West, this process was more striking there. It was also refined further by the growth in the early Church of the concept of the Apostolic See. Its essence is the idea that, above and beyond the normal administrative authority exercised in the various great cities by the Bishop (from the Greek word *epískopos*, or "overseer") and the Archbishop, or Metropolitan, there was also a further prestige attached to certain cities where the episcopal tradition had been established by or associated with one of Christ's own apostles. There came to be four such specific Sees: those of Antioch (St. Peter), Jerusalem (St. James) and Alexandria (St. Mark) in the Eastern Mediterranean world, and Rome (St. Peter) in the West — and the fact that Rome was the only Apostolic See in the Latin world was an important factor in the general acceptance in the West of the primacy of the Bishop, or Pope, of Rome.

It is apparent that the rank of these four Sees was established originally as a result of essentially practical, secular, and administrative considerations. Nevertheless, their apostolic associations, if to a degree rationalizations of their growing eminence, certainly helped to further the growth of their importance in the Church. Such was the respect for these Sees that their incumbents came to be called Patriarchs, and their prestige enabled them to exercise primacy over all other ecclesiastical authorities in their regions of the Roman world.

To these four Sees, however, a fifth was added. Prior to Constantine's transfer of the capital, the old city of Byzantium had not been sufficiently exalted to justify more than a dependent bishopric under the jurisdiction of the Metropolitan of Heraclea. With the refounding of the city as New Rome, or Constantinople, and its elevation as the new political center of the Empire, it was natural that some effort would be made to secure a corresponding elevation of its ecclesiastical status. In conformity with practical necessities and custom, Constantinople therefore came to be a far more important bishopric: no longer a dependent one, but a full patriarchate, claiming both a wide influence of its own and an artificial prestige to rationalize its inclusion in the same class with the already established Apostolic Sees. Whatever the justifications for this, the move was in fact simply a reflection of the city's new secular status. So it was that in the canons of the Second Ecumenical Council of 381 (conveniently held in Constantinople itself), the Patriarchate of New Rome was given wide new administrative jurisdiction and was officially graded as second only to the old Rome in rank among the Apostolic Sees, and ahead of the three others. It was not until perhaps the late sixth or early seventh century and thereafter that the artificial and administrative status came to be more firmly bolstered by the convenient development of a tradition of a legitimate apostolic background from St. Andrew.

The other Apostolic Sees, with older and more impeccable credentials, did not react cordially to the pretensions of the upstart capital. The See of Alexandria, established in the greatest metropolis of the old Hellenistic world, became a particular opponent of Constantinople's attempts to match its political position with an ersatz ecclesiastical status. Alexandria had pretensions of its own, for by the end of the third century it was not without dreams of primacy in the East itself. Not only were the Patriarchs of Alexandria far away from the overshadowing power of the Emperor, which the incumbent in Constantinople always had over him, but also the Alexandrian See was occupied by a succession of particularly able and aggressive men. Since the days of the Patriarch Athanasius (328–373), the great anti-Arian champion, the Alexandrian primate also had the blind devotion of the fanatic Egyptian monks and national sentiment to support him. Alexandria was the

most natural protagonist to oppose the rise of the Constantinopolitan See. The first round of their rivalry had already been
fought during the incumbency of the Alexandrian Theophilus
(385–412), who had played an important role in the fall of his
Constantinopolitan rival, St. John Chrysostom (398–404). For
Alexandrian purposes, the activities of Nestorius and the reaction
of Eutychianism provided a perfect opportunity for the newest
anti-Constantinople offensive. Moreover, Egypt was temperamen-
tally attuned to the Eutychian-Monophysite position: it had a
strong tradition of the worship of a strictly unified divinity, and
it boasted particular devotion to the veneration of the *Theotókos*,
especially in view of this region's own past association with the
worship of Isis, the pagan mother-divinity. The staunch persistence of pagan concepts or impulses in the shaping of Christian
tradition must always be remembered in understanding the religious developments of the era.

In retrospect it can be seen that Nestorius was largely the victim of a political conflict, the rivalry between Constantinople and
Alexandria for ecclesiastical primacy in the East. When examined
carefully, the Antiochene-Nestorian position is not entirely incompatible with the orthodox doctrine as ultimately established, while
the extremes of the Nestorian "heresy" are to some extent the
result of hostile portrayals and partisan propaganda. Obscure as
a theologian, Nestorius was, even worse, an inept politician. In
Cyril, Patriarch of Alexandria since 412, he found his nemesis: an
opponent who was able, forceful, cunning, resourceful, and unscrupulous. Amid the uproar of opposition raised against Nestorius and his activity, a new council was finally called to air the
matter. This Third Ecumenical Council met in 431, significantly
in the great city of Ephesus in Asia Minor, another center of pagan
mother-goddess worship, as the home of the orientalized "Diana
of the Ephesians." Outmaneuvered in advance, Nestorius found
himself arraigned before the Council, which was dominated by
the astute Cyril. In the inevitable outcome, Nestorius was condemned as a heretic. The Antiochene School was discredited, its
members dispersed and driven into flight or exile beyond the Empire's frontiers, especially to Persia. Nestorius himself was deposed
and ultimately exiled (appropriately) to Egypt. There he died

about 451, a symbolic martyr. His work was memorialized by the Nestorian Church which grew up in the East beyond the Empire's borders.

Cyril and the Alexandrian See were now in the ascendant. Eutyches himself became increasingly influential in Constantinople and at the court. Even the Emperor Theodosius II seems eventually to have been made sympathetic to the Monophysite position under the influence of an ally of Alexandria, the powerful eunuch minister Chrysaphius. Meanwhile, Cyril had died in 444, and had been succeeded by Dioscorus. As the one had been crafty and arrogant, the other was to become recklessly aggressive, determined to push Alexandrian advantages even further. One modern scholar, viewing Dioscorus' excesses in the light of contemporary perils, has dubbed him "the Attila of the Eastern Church," while another has waggishly suggested that such a comparison might be unfair to Attila! [7]

The triumphant progress of Alexandria began, however, to provoke a counterreaction. In its struggle with Alexandria, Constantinople was to find an ally in none other than Rome, its sister See in the West. The throne of Peter was at this time occupied by Leo I (440–461), the forceful Bishop famed as the dissuader of Attila. Leo's powerful personality put real flesh on the bones of Petrine pretensions to Papal primacy for the first time, and justly earned him the appellation of "the Great." Leo had no desire to see Alexandria ascendant in the Eastern Church. He proceeded to support action against the Monophysite faction by backing a synod which was held at Constantinople in 448 to depose and discredit the controversial Eutyches. Further, in 449 Leo took the initiative in the doctrinal struggle by issuing his *Tomus*, a compromise proposal on the issue. In essence his formula suggests that Christ be viewed as a single *persona* in which were united the two perfect and distinct Natures, the Divine and Human. The

7. The first scholar was A. Amelli, in his book *S. Leone magno e l'oriente* (Rome, 1882), as quoted and amplified upon by the second, N. H. Baynes, in his article, "Alexandria and Constantinople: A Study in Ecclesiastical Diplomacy," in the *Journal of Egyptian Archaeology*, 12 (1926), 155, or in its reprinting in Baynes' collection *Byzantine Studies and Other Essays* (London, 1955), p. 114.

Monophysite and Alexandrian faction would not be outdone. Dioscorus was determined to clear the field of all opposition to his dual causes of theology and primacy. Fortunately for him, he had the support of Theodosius II against both the Pope and his own Patriarch of Constantinople, Flavian. In 449 a new council was convened, in Ephesus once again, under the sponsorship of the Emperor and presided over by Dioscorus. This council was not to be regarded as an ecumenical one, but came, on the contrary, to be known as the *Latrocinium*, or "Robber Council." In the crudest possible display of raw ecclesiastical power-politics, Dioscorus had Flavian of Constantinople brutally deposed, and Eutyches restored; he then rammed through a program aimed at nothing less than a formal establishment of Monophysitism as Church doctrine. Alexandria seemed now to exercise undisputed primacy of the Church in the East.

At the apex of its victory, however, the Alexandrine-Monophysite position crumbled. Dioscorus' ally at court, Chrysaphius, fell from power early in 450. Then on July 28 of that year, Theodosius II died as a result of a riding accident. The religious affiliations of the Emperor's fatal horse have never been fully clarified, but one might well suspect that it was a dedicated equine anti-Monophysite, in view of the drastic change of events which followed the accident. The marriage of Theodosius' sister, Pulcheria, to Marcian brought to the throne an Emperor who was at once less sympathetic to the Monophysites than Theodosius II had been, and at the same time determined to put the strife-torn Church at peace. With ample precedents before him, and with the new alliance of the Churches of Constantinople and Rome behind him, Marcian exercised the old Imperial prerogatives of calling an ecumenical council, and of supervising its activities closely. Indeed, Marcian's action in this regard was to be remembered as his most important achievement.

Marcian resisted Pope Leo's demands that the new ecumenical council, the fourth, be held in the West. Instead, Chalcedon, the important suburb of Constantinople across the Propontis (Sea of Marmora), was chosen so that the Council would be under the Emperor's watchful eyes. There it met in 451. The ascendancy of Alexandria was ended, and its aggressive power was broken once and for all. The new council repudiated the Robber Council of 449 and all its works. The Monophysite theology was rejected, and a new formula of orthodoxy was affirmed which carefully charted a middle course between the extremes of Nestorianism and Eutychianism. Founded on Pope Leo's earlier *Tomus*, this formula laid down the belief in two distinct Natures united within a single *Prósōpon* or Person: "one and the same Christ in two natures without confusion or change, division or separation." Thus, in a direct line of development from the earlier councils, Chalcedon laid the basis for the Christological dogmas of universal Christian orthodoxy; but a long period of uncertainty and strife would elapse before that basis would be clearly acknowledged, by default if not otherwise.

Not the least interesting feature of this council was the fact that it was a relatively rare case of the Roman Bishop playing an important role in the great ecumenical councils of the Church's formative centuries. It was to be a rather unusual occasion, however, largely as a result of the vigorous personality of Pope Leo I himself rather than as a reflection of any actual recognition of the universal authority of the Roman See at this early stage. Certainly Rome was represented at all the councils by this time, but, whatever deference the Eastern prelates allowed the chair of St. Peter, its occupant was still regarded as but one of several exalted colleagues throughout Christendom; *primus inter pares*, but no more. The fresh example of Alexandria itself had taught the East the dangers of overweening aims at primacy.

As Chalcedon was a deathblow to the ambitions and pretensions of Alexandria, it was also, then, a triumph for the current alliance of Constantinople — endorsed by both Patriarch and Emperor — with Rome. Yet, at this moment of joint victory, the Church of Constantinople did not hesitate to look to its own interests. The controversial Twenty-Eighth Canon of the Council of Chalcedon's transactions contained nothing less than a bold new assertion of the pretensions of Constantinople. New Rome was declared equal in authority and prerogatives to Old Rome; where the latter held any primacy it was to be only in the barest formalities of honor. There was no wish to deprive Rome of any due rank. This arrangement was administrative and made it clear that the Eastern churches intended to be regionally autonomous. But it demonstrated Constantinople's determination to assure itself an ecclesiastical position commensurate with its political status in the East. When the Acts of the Council were received in Rome, Pope Leo angrily denounced the Twenty-Eighth Canon and refused formal ratification to it. In this fashion, and at this early date, were sown the first seeds of antagonism between Rome and Constantinople, and the ground was thus prepared for the further difficulties which were to follow. Consequently, Chalcedon furnished the ultimate cornerstone of the doctrines of the Church, but at the same time it set the stage for the later conflict between the Eastern and Western halves of Christendom.

Monophysitism had been condemned by the Council of Chalcedon, but hardly extirpated. There were also new political associations to further Monophysite dissent. By the second half of the fifth century the Patriarchal rivalry of Alexandria with Constantinople had ceased to be a vital issue. Instead, an equally disruptive factor was already available to take its place. Throughout history, doctrinal dissent has frequently been linked with local or national sentiment. There has been much debate on the point, but it is difficult to avoid the conclusion that Monophysitism became to a great degree linked with, if not the channel for and expression of, local disaffection in the Eastern provinces, especially of Syria and Egypt. Much of the population in these regions was resentful of the distant tyranny of Constantinople, a parvenu both politically and ecclesiastically. Ground down as they were by the ever-increasing oppression of the Imperial fiscal system, they would therefore snatch at any form of resistance to the central government and everything for which it stood. In a sense, it was as difficult to pacify the Monophysite religious dissent as it was to quell local disaffection and resistance. The fanatic devotion of Egypt and Syria to Monophysitism was something that the debates of theologians and the decisions of a council could not suffice to destroy.

The remainder of the fifth century was marked by the embarrassing continuity of the Monophysite problem. The decisions of the Council of Chalcedon, except the impolitic Twenty-Eighth Canon, were fully acceptable in the West among all Christians (save the Arians), and Monophysitism raised no problems there. The East, however, continued to be distracted, amid its other preoccupations, by this all but insoluble religious controversy, which was actually to last for almost two more centuries. Its political implications were extensive. Not only did the Eastern court have to cope with the Arianism of its German would-be masters, but it had to face the disaffection of the Monophysite provinces. Nor did Monophysitism have supporters only in its strongholds of Egypt and Syria. In the capital itself it had such factional support that it became a dangerous element in the various court intrigues and conspiracies, especially in the reign of the unpopular Zeno. The usurper Basiliscus, for example, built his position almost entirely upon a policy of courting Monophysite support. On his own authority he abrogated the decisions of Chalcedon; even worse, he went so far as to decree the abolition of the Patriarchate of Constantinople. The storm of outrage which greeted these high-handed and ill-advised acts forced him quickly to recall them. By then it was too late, and their impact only hastened the downfall of this inept opportunist.[8]

Recognizing that the unhealed wounds of religious controversy constituted such a dangerous political issue, Zeno himself made the first of a series of attempts by various East Roman rulers to settle the matter through Imperial intervention, compromise, and fiat. By 482 there were some indications of a growing conciliatory spirit. The Patriarchs of Constantinople and Alexandria, respectively Acacius (472–489) and Peter III Mongus (482–489, second reign), had been in contact with each other and seemed to feel that a resolution of differences might be possible. Heartened by this promising atmosphere, Zeno issued in 482 his *Henōtikón*, or Decree of Union. It was a frankly compromise measure. It attempted to ignore the controversial decrees of Chalcedon and simply to retreat to the previous positions established at the First and Third Councils. To satisfy each side, both Nestorius and Eutyches were again anathematized. Any commitment to or repudiation of the Chalcedonian formula concerning the two Natures,

---

8. Curiously, the opposite extreme of courting religious dissent was illustrated during this period by the rebellious Isaurian general Illus, who in 484 attempted to win support from remaining pagans.

as against a single Nature, was avoided. The decree merely suggested in vague terms that Christ was "of the same nature with the Father in the Godhead and also of the same nature with us in the manhood," a formula which politely led the argument nowhere.

At first it seemed that the *Henōtikón* might work. Conciliatory spirits in the leadership on both sides accepted it. Nevertheless, genuine compromise was impossible on any level. As so often happens, an effort to steer a middle course, however well-intentioned, only drew down the scorn of extremists on both sides. Zeno's endeavor quickly elicited rejection and fury from the more rabid partisans of the Monophysite and orthodox Chalcedonian persuasions alike. Worse yet, in turning its back on the accomplishments of Chalcedon, the Church of Constantinople forced a break with its erstwhile ally, the Church of Rome. Pope Felix III (483–492) condemned the *Henōtikón* and all that it stood for. An exchange of excommunications between Pope and Patriarch by 484 brought about the so-called Acacian Schism, the first rift between Rome and Constantinople and a symbolic prototype of worse schisms that were to come in later centuries, with increasingly tragic results. Thus, the *Henōtikón* accomplished nothing constructive, but instead only made matters worse than they had been before. When Zeno died suddenly in 491, for all the important accomplishments of his reign, he left behind the terrible legacy of the unresolved Monophysite problem, with which the next reign would deal in even more drastic fashion.

The process of choosing a new sovereign immediately gave evidence of the gravity of the religious question. The populace greeted the widowed Ariadne with cries of "Let the Empire have an orthodox Emperor!" and "Let the Empire have an Emperor from among the Romans!" The East Romans were as weary of the alien Isaurians as they had been of the Germans whom the Isaurians had checked. They were also weary of politically inspired compromise of the True Faith. For his part, the modern reader may himself be weary of the intricacies of subtle theology and blind sectarian devotion; but he should remember that in an age when this life was considered only a preparation for the next, the establishment of *orthodoxía* or "*correct*" belief" was a vital necessity in assuring the attainment of eagerly sought salvation. Given this attitude, the popular concern was understandable, and each aspect of the demand was important. The citizens of the capital demanded a native-born sovereign who would vindicate both their patriotism and their religious orthodoxy. Ariadne was to satisfy them on the first count, but not entirely on the second.

Her choice for her second husband and the new Emperor fell upon an aged and minor court functionary, who bore the lowly title of *Silentiarius*. If no longer a young man — he was apparently about sixty years of age — Anastasius had long experience in civil affairs to recommend him. He had the disadvantage of a personal background distinctly tinged by Monophysitism. This heterodox disposition was an open secret, and in order to calm apprehensions regarding it he was obliged by the Patriarch to sign a confession of faith and a profession of orthodoxy. With this precedent, the giving of these formal assurances ultimately became standard procedure upon the accession of Byzantine sovereigns in later times.[9]

In spite of his age, Anastasius I (491–518) proved to be an energetic and zealous Emperor. His reign was a busy and extremely important one in many respects. In the first place, it was under him that the Isaurian danger was finally ended. These rough

9. There is no survival of such a coronation oath or profession of faith in the major source for Byzantine court etiquette, the mid-tenth-century *Book of Ceremonies* by the scholar Emperor, Constantine VII Porphyrogenitus (A.D. 913/44–959). There is the text of such an Imperial profession of faith surviving in the very late *Book of Offices*, falsely attributed to the fourteenth-century official George Kodinos: chapter 17, in the edition of I. Bekker (Bonn, 1839), pp. 86 ff. Constantine VII's compilation does, however, give a transcription of the ceremonies attending the elevation of Anastasius (Book I, chap. 92, ed. J. Reiske, Bonn, 1829, pp. 417–425), including the exchanges between Ariadne and the populace and their acclamation of the new sovereign. (The cries quoted may be found in Reiske's text, on, respectively, p. 418, ll. 19–20; and p. 419, ll. 6–7. In both cases, the word translated as "Empire" is in the original Greek *oikouménē*, a word actually meaning the entire inhabited world, as in its use for "ecumenical" or "universal" councils; and this word was often used by the Byzantines as synonymous with their Empire, which was presumed to embrace theoretically all of civilized Christian humanity.)

mountaineers had served their purpose as the Eastern court's bulwark against the Germans, and such was the stability of the surviving Empire that it could now dispense with them. By 498 Anastasius' generals had firmly stamped out the last embers of Isaurian restlessness and rebellion; the surviving tribesmen were resettled elsewhere in the Empire. There were new external threats, although they were not nearly so frightening as those witnessed earlier in the fifth century. A new period of hostilities began with the Persians. In the Balkan vacuum created by the departure of the Ostrogoths, raids were launched by various Hunnic peoples, especially those called the Unogundur (or Onogur) Huns, ancestors of the modern Bulgarians. In view of their raids deep into Imperial territory, Anastasius built the so-called Long Wall across the Thracian peninsula some forty miles from Constantinople in order to protect the area of the capital. Anastasius did succeed in maintaining generally friendly relations with two of the western barbarian kingdoms, Ostrogothic Italy and Frankish Gaul, which both readily recognized the theoretical lordship of the Roman Emperor in Constantinople over their realms.

A particularly important sphere of Anastasius' activities was his administration. Just and benevolent in disposition, he undertook many pious and humanitarian works for his subjects. Above all, he was a fiscal reformer. Though he lacked expertise himself, his advisers helped him to resolve decisively the state's financial difficulties, particularly acute since the expenses of Leo I's abortive African expedition.

Anastasius was naturally concerned with the revenue system in particular. In 498 he abolished the so-called *chrysárgyron*, a highly unpopular and inequitable tax on urban business transactions. The move evoked great popular rejoicing and helped stimulate trade. By way of compensation, new sources of revenue were found and were more efficiently taxed. Greater emphasis was placed upon agricultural revenue. As an indication of how extensively the Eastern Mediterranean economy had improved since the days of Diocletian — and, we may suppose, not without the help of his own reforms — the latter's old tax paid in produce, the *annona*, could once more be paid in coin. The economy in general, even in rural areas, could be put on a much sounder monetary basis. While the government of Anastasius I devoted itself extensively to new methods of taxation and revenue assessment, it also imposed stringent economies to make the system more just and efficient. Such methods were at least earnest if not always fully successful or popular. There were in addition further clarifications and stabilization of the coinage system. The results of Anastasius' diligent administration were a restored and revitalized economy and greater fiscal stability. He even produced a treasury surplus which, according to reports, amounted to 320,000 pounds of gold.[10] This figure may be exaggerated, and the contemporary complaints that Anastasius was avaricious were perhaps unfair, but there is no doubt that the healthy and prosperous

10. In his *Anékdota*, or *Secret History*, the embittered Procopius makes the following statement, in the course of his denunciations of Justinian's supposed extravagance: "Now this Justinian, at the time his uncle Justin assumed the realm, found the government fully provided with public monies. For Anastasius, being at once the most far-sighted and the most able administrator of all Emperors, and fearing just what happened — that his successor to the realm, should he be in need of money, would probably plunder his subjects — filled his treasuries to overflowing with gold ere his life was ended. Yet, all this Justinian squandered with the utmost speed . . . even though it might have seemed that any ruler prodigal in the extreme might have taken one hundred years for this. In fact, those in charge of the treasuries and storehouses and all the other Imperial properties affirmed that Anastasius, after ruling the Romans for more than twenty-seven years, left behind in the public coffers three thousand and two hundred hundred-weights [*kentēnária*] of gold. At the same time, during the nine years of Justin's rule of the Empire, while this Justinian was bringing confusion and extravagance into the government, four thousand hundred-weights more were brought into the public coffers in illegal fashion, and of all these sums nothing whatsoever remained, [so they said,] but it had been consumed by this man while Justin was still alive, just as was related by me in the foregoing statement." (*Anékdota*, xix, 4–8. All quotations from Procopius are given in my own translation.) Though the context of this statement makes the compliment to Anastasius a somewhat back-handed one, intended to reflect the more discredit on Justinian, its veracity can be neither specifically refuted nor categorically denied. To give a meaningful evaluation of this sum in modern terms would be very difficult, but J. B. Bury, writing in 1923, estimated it at £14,590,000 (*History of the Later Roman Empire*, I, 446), while A. A. Vasiliev, in 1952, suggested a figure between $65,000,000 and $70,000,000 (*History of the Byzantine Empire*, p. 141). By any standards, it was a tremendous sum of money for the age. On the rapid dissipation of it by Justin and Justinian, see p. 73 below.

state in which Anastasius left the East Roman finances was no small factor in encouraging and supporting Justinian in his ambitious projects thereafter.

It was, however, the religious aspect of this Emperor's reign which proved to be the most crucial. Neither a dogmatist nor a fanatic, even though he was disposed generally towards Monophysitism, Anatasius was inclined to seek peace and compromise. From the beginning he chose to make his predecessor's *Henōtikón* the basis of his policies. Unfortunately, conciliation and the *Henōtikón* could not satisfy the inflamed passions of partisanship nor end the confusion raging in the Church. At the outset of his reign Anastasius attempted to end the embarrassment of the Acacian Schism with Rome. Pope Gelasius I (492–496), however, was ill-disposed towards compromise. His rejoinders to the Emperor constitute some of the first forceful statements of Papal doctrine of the duality of power, the spiritual and temporal, a guiding theme of later Papal history in the West. With the next Pope, Anastasius II (496–498), some genuine conciliation seemed possible, but in the years thereafter the Roman Pontificate was itself torn by schism and strife that made normalization of relations between Rome and Constantinople all the more impossible.

Meanwhile, the situation at home had been deteriorating. Resentful of Anastasius' persistent support of the *Henōtikón*, the Patriarch Euphemius (490–496) became openly hostile, even attempting to appeal to the Pope against the Emperor. Matters proceeded to such a point that Anastasius had Euphemius deposed by a synod in 496. A more tractable Patriarch, Macedonius II (496–511), was installed. Nevertheless, ecclesiastical affairs had become complicated further by political interests. For one thing, strong Monophysite elements continued to flourish in the capital. More particularly, there was a link with a crucial medium of popular discontent.

The old circus parties of the chariot races had been transplanted from old Rome to New Rome. Originally, the charioteers had been organized into four groups, each named after a color, but they had been reduced to two, the Blues and the Greens. The popular devotion to one or the other of these circus parties involved more than mere sports enthusiasm. The circus factions were organized bodies of the populace, identical with or related to the demes, which were the militia and public maintenance organizations in the city. Moreover, circus factionalism provided the sole outlet which the populace had for any expression of its opinions or will. The great Hippodrome was the only place where the Emperor and his subjects could confront each other directly and regularly. The factions therefore became important and volatile channels for mass opinion. Though it is dangerous to generalize, each of the factions tended to represent political and religious outlooks: the Blues were inclined to favor aristocratic interests and orthodoxy, while the Greens had something of a lower-class identification and were associated with Monophysitism. Both factions were represented by excitable street mobs always spoiling for a fight and prone to acts of hooliganism. In the unstable political and religious atmosphere, conflict between the two factions became more extensive. It was in the reign of Anastasius I that such conflict first became of grave concern and even a threat to the government and its policies.

Riots between the circus factions were nothing new, in the capital or even in the provincial cities where they also flourished. By this time they had become more frequent and more deeply involved with the government's religious policies. When Anastasius deposed the Patriarch Euphemius in 496, riots broke out to demand his reinstatement. The factions were ready, of course, to riot on smaller pretexts. In 498, after Anastasius had failed to release some imprisoned Greens, he was stoned by the mob in the Hippodrome. The Excubitors had to be mustered to protect him, but the Greens continued on their rampage, setting fire to buildings. Another serious riot broke out between the rival factions in 501 amid some traditional festivities. Obviously, the unruly factions comprised a dangerous and unpredictable element. They would become more so as Anastasius' religious involvements grew increasingly complex. Nor, as we shall see, were their disturbances to end with his reign.

Finding sectarian conciliation unsuccessful, Anastasius' government drifted increasingly into a pro-Monophysite position. This course was more than a reflection of Anastasius' own feelings. For one thing, the Emperor felt that the only way to maintain

Imperial control in the Monophysite-disposed provinces, especially in strife-torn Syria, was to favor the anti-Chalcedonian outlook. The Patriarch Macedonius was in his turn antagonized. After an attempt was made to win him over, Anastasius felt obliged to have him deposed also, and this was done in the summer of 511. The Emperor now adopted a more openly Monophysite posture. In 512 he sanctioned the introduction in the capital of a specifically Monophysite addition to the so-called *Triságion* formula, the threefold chanting of the Greek liturgical text beginning with and built around the word [h]*ághios*, or "holy." The orthodox faction was outraged. New riots broke out, this time too violent to be quelled even by force. Anastasius was compelled to appear before the mobs in the Hippodrome, standing in the *Káthisma*, or Imperial Box, without his crown or Imperial garb, in the fashion of a suppliant, offering to abdicate. Fortunately, this appearance calmed the populace, who urged the brave old Emperor to resume his throne. There the riot ended.

Nevertheless, the orthodox faction would not relax its opposition so easily. Though the mob had been placated, Anastasius' Monophysite drift continued. Combined with the unpopularity of his stringent fiscal economies, this process naturally increased opposition to him, and the ground was amply prepared for the rebellion which soon broke out. By 514, discontent among the European units of the army had joined with religious unrest to produce an open revolt. Its leader was an able commander named Vitalian, who was at least partly barbarian in origin. Leading a motley force and welcomed by dissidents along the way, Vitalian advanced upon the capital and threatened to overthrow the aged Emperor, whose own position within Constantinople was hardly very reliable. To the anti-Monophysite elements Vitalian appeared as a champion against the anti-Chalcedonian government. The religious controversy seemed to have reached its explosive point. Anastasius was not defeated yet, however, so long as he had his diplomatic cunning. He opened negotiations and won over Vitalian's emissaries with gifts, concessions, and promises to submit the religious difficulties to Papal mediation. Disgruntled and outflanked, Vitalian withdrew from the capital, but remained on alert nearby. Anastasius had no intention of keeping his promises and soon hostilities broke out again. When the Emperor sent a force against Vitalian under his nephew Hypatius, the latter was defeated and taken captive by the rebel.

Anastasius' difficulties were then further increased. Not only was he engaged in a climactic struggle-to-the-death over his religious policies, but he now had to face a renewed explosion of the quarrelsome popular factions. As a result of his cancellation of certain festivities in the capital, new riots broke out. The situation was again too tempting for Vitalian to resist: he advanced upon the disorganized Constantinople a second time. It seemed riper than ever for his plucking. Yet, again it eluded him. Once more Anastasius managed to save the day by negotiations. Hypatius was freed on ransom, and Vitalian was named the supreme commander of troops in Thrace. Anastasius committed himself to calling a council at Heraclea, complete with Papal representation, to settle the religious issues. Once again Vitalian withdrew.

This time Anastasius made a genuine effort to carry out his promises. After the elevation of the new Pope, Hormisdas (514–523), the Emperor began negotiations to arrange the projected council in Heraclea, planned for the new year, 515. Fruitless haggling between Anastasius and the Pope ended in complete deadlock, and a new breach was opened between the Emperor and Vitalian, who maintained that Anastasius had not kept his promise. In 516 the rebel commander moved against Constantinople in his third attempt to seize power. By this time the Emperor was prepared to meet force with force and not merely with negotiations. Loyal government forces were able to hurl back Vitalian's large barbarian army with decisive results. Vitalian's power was shattered, and he was compelled to withdraw in disorder. Although he was still at large, and still a factor to be reckoned with, his immediate threat was ended. Nevertheless, Vitalian had very nearly succeeded in converting the orthodox opposition to Anastasius' anti-Chalcedonian, pro-Monophysite policies into a lever for toppling the old Emperor's regime. In addition, the Huns and other barbarians from whom Vitalian drew his forces had been taught a few lessons about the vulnerability of the capital.

The remaining years of Anastasius' surprisingly long reign were occupied with a new sequence of futile negotiations with Pope

Hormisdas, marked by diplomatic sparring and intriguing on both sides. It was plain that as long as this Emperor occupied the throne nothing could be accomplished towards a resolution of the religious issues. The Empire was still in turmoil, and partisan feelings were, if anything, more intense. Clearly, the experiment which Anastasius' reign represented had failed: to placate the opposition of the unyielding Monophysites by favoring them had only led to greater complications. There would have to be a new government before any alteration was possible in the course of Constantinople's religious policies. Anastasius was an old man, and could not live much longer. The Empress Ariadne had died in 516. On July 8, 518, Anastasius himself died, by this time almost a nonogenarian.

The change of government was drastic and unexpected. Anastasius had made no arrangements for a successor. He left behind him three nephews, Hypatius, Pompeius, and Probus, but none of them seems to have been a serious or active candidate for the throne. One of the chief ministers attempted to install a dependent of his own. For this purpose he gave a sum of money to the commander of the Excubitors to serve as a donative for the troops to win their support. Instead, the commander chose to use the money for his own purposes. With careful manipulation of procedure and with apparent pressure on the Senate, he had himself proclaimed Emperor on July 9, 518.

His name was Justin. He was an Illyrian of humble peasant birth who had risen through the ranks in a relatively undistinguished career. He was totally inexperienced in rule and is believed to have been illiterate. His Empress had been a purchased slave and concubine before he had married her. He appeared to be rather unpromising material for the throne, and few people might have suspected that with him a new age was at hand.

The reign of Justin I (518–527) began with only a moderate initial reaction against the previous regime of Anastasius. It is true that by the following year the new government had formally abandoned the religious policies of its predecessor, and it was soon to attempt to chart a new course in ecclesiastical affairs. For the moment, however, Justin retained many of Anastasius' advisers. He was also at pains to pacify elements of possible danger and so initial caution was required. Efforts were made to secure the loyalty of the unambitious nephews of the late Emperor. Above all, the once-menacing Vitalian had to be conciliated. The latter obeyed a summons to the capital, where ecclesiastical policy more congenial to him was being formed, and he accepted the highest military and civil ranks as a symbol of his trust and devotion.

But the man who was really to put his stamp upon the new era was advancing onto the stage of events. Though childless, Justin I had a nephew and protégé who soon emerged as the real power behind the throne. His name was Flavius Petrus Sabbatius Justinianus.

II JUSTINIAN, THEODORA, AND THEIR COURT

The Origins of Justinian and the Reign of Justin I

Justin I and his successors were of Balkan provincial stock. Such origins were by no means unusual among Roman Emperors, especially among the East Roman rulers of the periods immediately preceding and following. There was a time when historians favored theories that the family of Justinian was of Slavonic blood. These theories have been disproved, so that we may now be certain that the new dynasty came from a background of the old Thracian peoples who had settled in Illyria and had become fully Latinized.

Justin was born about 450 and, like the rest of his family, grew up as a poor peasant — according to our information, as a swineherd. As a young man past twenty Justin journeyed to the capital with a few friends to seek his fortune. He arrived in time to join the important new body of Imperial guards, the Excubitors, then being formed by Leo I. A competent soldier, Justin rose to important commands under Anastasius during the suppression of the Isaurians, the wars against the Persians, and the civil war with Vitalian. By the time of Anastasius' death, Justin had progressed from the lowest rank in the Excubitors to become their Count, or commander. It was with this background as a field soldier, if not as much of a tactician, and certainly with no administrative experience, that he was thrust by fortune onto the throne.

Justin was in his late sixties in 518, even older than Anastasius had been at the time of his accession in 491. In view of his age and inexperience, Justin might well have been a weak figurehead Emperor. Intrigue might also have been multiplied by the fact that he and his wife Euphemia had no children, no son to succeed him. Fortunately, Justin did not lack for either support or a successor. Though indeed childless himself, he had several nephews. In the course of his rise in the Imperial forces Justin saw to it that these nephews enjoyed the fruits of their uncle's success by having them educated and trained under his sponsorship. One of them, for instance, was the future general Germanus. Chief among these nephews, however, was young Flavius Petrus (or Peter) Sabbatius, son of Justin's sister and her husband Sabbatius. The youth had been born about 482. When he was in his twenties, during Justin's service under Anastasius I, Justin had brought him to the capital as his ward, to be educated under his own direction. Eventually, Justin legally adopted his nephew, in token of which the young man added "Justinianus" to his name, and he ultimately chose to use this as his own official name.

It would be interesting to know the young Justinian's thoughts when he first came to the capital under his uncle's aegis. Justin's support could assure him of almost unlimited advancement in military service. How much more promising his prospects may have seemed we cannot tell; but, from what we know of the mature Justinian's self-confident personality, we may suspect that he was sufficiently aware of his abilities at this stage to look ahead boldly. Certainly the young man soon showed himself to be intellectually gifted. Whatever additional debts Justinian owed his uncle, and however limited old Justin's own intellectual attainments may have been, it is to Justin's credit that he gave his nephew a good education, and doubtless helped cultivate the youth's capacities in such fields as law and theology, which were to have such important impact on the decade to come in the Empire's history.

We do not know much of Justinian's actual military career after he was given a commission in the *Candidati*, the Emperor's personal bodyguard. He was in his middle thirties by 518, and at one point in the scramble for power following Anastasius' death he is reported to have been offered the throne himself; but he is said to have declined discreetly, in deference to his uncle. Upon Justin I's accession, Justinian was given a new command as the Count of the Domestics, an important contingent of the troops in the capital. He proved at the outset to be his uncle's strong right arm by clearing away the remnants of plots and conspiracies on behalf of a rival candidate to the throne.

Not that Justinian himself was without competitors for power. Among the exiles recalled by the new regime's amnesty was the former rebel, Vitalian. To secure the loyalty of this still dangerous man, oaths and promises were exchanged between him, Justin, and Justinian, and he was given the highest military command, together with the old distinction of the consulship — the traditional Roman republican office still maintained as something of an honorary award — for the year 520. Vitalian would naturally pose the greatest threat to Justinian himself. It is therefore no surprise to find that by July of 520 the murder of Vitalian was conveniently arranged, almost certainly by Justinian and with at least the connivance of Justin.

This move left Justinian without a serious rival as his uncle's successor. He promptly assumed Vitalian's high military command, and was given the rank of Patrician. Holding the consulship for 521, he used it to curry public favor through the displays and liberality that had come to be the chief responsibilities of this once exalted office. Such was his rise to favor and power that even old Justin became anxious. It seems to have been under pressure, and not by his own choice, that Justin set the final seals on his nephew's advancement. New titles were given him, and in 525 he was made Caesar, a rank which clearly designated him as heir to the throne. When Justin's final illness began, the old Emperor officially crowned Justinian co-Emperor with the full title of Augustus on Easter Sunday, April 4, 527.

Regardless of the formal processes by which Justinian emerged as his uncle's successor, there can be little doubt that his influence in the government was all but supreme virtually from the moment of Justin's accession. It seems likely that Justinian was, in effect, the true "brains" of the Roman government from 518 to 527, and that Justin himself had but little to do with, or only the slightest real understanding of, the policies conceived and executed in his name. For this reason the incumbency of Justin I as Emperor has often been regarded as little more than an interlude, an introduction to, or anticipation of Justinian's actual personal power.[1] There can be no doubt that Justin's reign had qualities of its own. Under the circumstances, however, discussion of the policies and events of that reign may reasonably be deferred so that they can be considered later as the proper beginnings of Justinian's own activities in various spheres.

Old Justin did not long survive the confirmation of his nephew's progress to the succession. His illness, resulting from the reopening of an old wound in his foot, had caused him to take Justinian as his full colleague in April of 527. The malady abated somewhat, but Justin was past his middle seventies, and his strength could not sustain him much longer. A few months later the end came, on August 1, 527. As Emperor in title as well as fact, Justinian was already sovereign, but it is this year that his sole rule began, and it is with this year that his official accession is usually dated. Nevertheless, the Age of Justinian did not suddenly begin in 527. It had been a reality since 518.

Theodora

By the time Justinian formally assumed the Roman diadem in his own name, he had enjoyed singular advantages. He had been raised, trained, and advanced under the aegis of his well-placed uncle, who had also given him a good education in addition to the benefits of influential sponsorship. Securing himself in power under his uncle when the latter rose to the throne,

1. In his fundamental monograph on this epoch, A. A. Vasiliev, *Justin the First; An Introduction to the Epoch of Justinian the Great* ("Dumbarton Oaks Studies" No. 1, Cambridge, Mass., 1950), gives the following comments on the question of the reign's significance: "Of course Justin's rule was unquestionably an introduction to that of Justinian; but it was an introduction of vital importance. It cleared the ground and laid a firm foundation for Justin's successor, and we should remember that Justinian's influence behind the throne was predominant from the opening years of Justin's reign, so that when Justinian wore the purple alone he was continuing policies already inaugurated" (pp. 3–4).

Justinian had an almost unmatched opportunity of apprenticeship in ruling the Roman world, which allowed him to obtain the very experience his uncle had lacked. His position also gave him the opportunity to experiment with policy, and to lay the basis for projects which would take shape fully during his personal reign. Finally, he possessed his own widely varied talents, the careful cultivation of which had prepared him admirably for the tasks ahead. Few rulers could hope to begin their reigns with so many advantages.

Justinian possessed a further advantage, one that cannot be overlooked. This was the woman who now stood beside him as his wife and Augusta, or Empress. Theodora brought to her husband and to her era talents and capacities that were no mean ones, talents which were fully complementary to his, and which played a vital role in the shaping of his reign. Thus, Theodora represents for the student of Justinian more than merely the spice which has helped attract so much interest in his age, scholarly or otherwise.

Theodora was without question one of the remarkable women of history. To call her a colorful figure is something of an understatement. Her reputation has largely been shaped by the writings of her contemporary, Procopius. Though he was a truly great historian, his *Anékdota* or *Secret History* is probably the most infamous and scurrilous piece of sustained character assassination in all of literature. The most sensational details of his portrayal of Theodora, primarily in the ninth chapter of this work, may be safely left to those who prefer their pornography gilded with the respectability of scholarship and history—whether in the book's many modern translations or, in Gibbon's phrase, "veiled in the obscurity of a learned language," in the original Greek. Yet, much of this gossip and defamation which Procopius has gleefully transmitted to us concerning Theodora must be taken into account in piecing together both a contemporary picture and a modern assessment of this woman.

We have a good idea of her appearance. Even the spitefulness of Procopius himself cannot disguise his admission of her beauty, for all the qualifications he adds: "And Theodora was of a handsome countenance and in all other ways attractive, but short, and while of not altogether pale complexion, at least somewhat sallow, and her glance was always keen and sharp." [2] In addition, we have several portraits of her, most notably in one of the two famous mosaic panels in the apse of the Church of San Vitale in Ravenna — perhaps the most celebrated individual works of Byzantine art — which shows her as a pale, perhaps ageing, but still strikingly handsome and commanding woman (see Plate V).

According to the most unfavorable accounts of her, Theodora was the child of a bear-keeper of the circus and grew into a life as a public performer. If she was not an outright prostitute, her career as an actress — at a time when the theatrical profession was supposedly of such a depth of moral and social standing as to make modern burlesque appear prudish — was certainly a low one.[3] Procopius describes with obvious malice the prodigious feats of wantonness and vice in which she allegedly excelled, and, however exaggerated, such stories may reflect some basis of truth. She does seem to have had at least one illegitimate child. The climax of her career is reported to have come after a period as mistress to the governor of a North African province, when she was cast onto the streets and was obliged to make her way back to the capital through the Eastern provinces by "practicing her profession in each city," in Procopius' phrase.[4]

It was, at any rate, only after a highly unsavory youth that her path finally crossed that of Justinian. This seems to have occurred after the accession of Justin, when the Emperor's nephew was already rising in power. Justinian fell passionately in love with her, and she became his mistress. Her bewitchment of him was more than the work of sensual wiles. In her Justinian recognized gifts far more striking, and he was determined to have her as a legal partner and wife. His aunt, the Empress Euphemia, would not hear of the idea. For all her own ignoble background, and in spite of Justinian's actual authority in other respects, Euphemia obstinately refused to permit any kind of formal union of Justinian

2. *Anékdota*, chap. x, sec. 11. Compare to this Procopius' own comments on Theodora in a more deliberately flattering vein, in his official panegyric, *On the Buildings*, when he describes a statue of her: "The likeness was certainly handsome, but it fell much short of the Empress' own beauty, inasmuch as to describe her beauty in writing or to copy it in some representation was altogether beyond human possibility" (Book I, chap. xi, sec. 9).

3. Compare the comments of Vasiliev, *Justin the First*, pp. 96–99.

4. *Anékdota*, chap. xi, secs. 27–28.

with a girl of such a shady past. Only after Euphemia's death could Justinian, with his uncle completely under his influence, clear away all social obstacles and marry Theodora. When Justinian was made co-Augustus by Justin in 527 she became his Augusta, and was thus his Empress when his sole rule began. Her rise from a youth of degradation to become a partner in the rule of the Roman world was certainly no less spectacular than that of the former swineherd, Justin I himself.

Theodora's detractors, particularly Procopius, go to the greatest lengths to portray the wild excesses she supposedly committed once power was hers. Significantly, no one could seriously accuse her of faithlessness to Justinian. So far as morality was concerned, her new life with her husband was as utterly transformed as her social status. In modern terms, the former showgirl, once her exploited youth was past, settled down to respectable married life. To be sure, she is portrayed as being power-mad, self-indulgent, intolerably arrogant, introducing new extravagances and ceremonials, demanding the utmost servility of all around her, dominating or manipulating her husband, advancing her creatures in office, pursuing implacably all enemies and rivals, engaging in unlimited intrigue and wire-pulling, and contributing mightily to the general disruption of the government and the Empire. Such charges may not be without some slight foundation. Socially, Theodora was, after all, a parvenue who could not but relish the unlimited glories of her new situation, with the memories of a past such as hers to goad her on. Certainly she was mindful of her past in other ways; even her worst enemies could not deny her benevolence and generosity in establishing pious foundations for wayward women, and her special care for her former sisters-in-sin in every possible way.

Moreover, Theodora was no mere frivolous ingenue who trod a boudoir path to power and then allowed her exalted position to turn her head. Use her power she did, to the hilt; but the extent to which she abused it may have been exaggerated by her critics. She was a woman of remarkable perception and of intellectual gifts in many ways not inferior to those of her husband. She was also a person of strong will, with ideas of her own, and with a force of personality to see them through to their fulfillment. It is true that many of her ideas and aims were not shared by Justinian, or ran diametrically opposed to his. It is also true that, partly as a result, the court became a hotbed of intrigue, double-dealing, backbiting, conspiracy, and suspicions. Yet, such conditions were not unique in Roman or Byzantine history, nor have they been in the histories of most other great monarchies. There is no doubt that Theodora was unscrupulous in her use of power and in her meddling in affairs both state and private. Certainly she could be implacable against any rivals or enemies in power; we will see how she might ruin those whom she opposed. Nevertheless her motives and accomplishments were often considerably more constructive than her detractors and her reputation might lead us to believe.

Above all, however much she abused Justinian's confidence or dependence, her contribution to his reign easily counterbalanced what harm she did. Justinian was a talented ruler, but his personality was often unstable and vacillating. With her indomitable willpower Theodora more than once gave Justinian backbone. Not only did she bring him a stabilizing, clarifying influence but she also helped him shape his policies more firmly and practically. Even her contrasting personality and activities often complemented his in ways which were obviously of great use to him.[5] How much Theodora meant to Justinian can be inferred in particular from the changes in Justinian's reign after her death. Whatever their several faults, then, together they made one of the most extraordinarily gifted pairs of rulers the world has ever seen.

Advisers and Courtiers

There is no doubt that much of Justinian's life and reign can be understood only in terms of the influences to which he was subjected by those around him. The influence of his wife,

5. So much so, that Procopius (*Anékdota*, chap. x, secs. 13 ff.) claimed that Justinian and Theodora secretly arranged to follow simultaneously opposite courses to keep their subjects confused and at variance, and to allow the one to do what the other could not. On this see the comments of Bury, *History of the Later Roman Empire* . . . (A.D. 395–565), II, 34.

the remarkable Theodora, was itself enormous and all-pervasive, but we must examine other personalities at Justinian's court.

In this category we may first consider three of Justinian's actual counselors and henchmen: Tribonian, John of Cappadocia, and Peter Barsymes. While any ruler with Justinian's responsibilities needed able subordinates, the vast projects he had conceived, beyond mere stewardship of the surviving Roman state, made his choices all the more important. Hence there is much insight to be gained into the kind of ruler Justinian was by familiarization with the kind of men on whom he relied, what he expected of them, what they accomplished, and what influence they exerted.

Ironically, the one of these three who perhaps contributed the most to Justinian's legacy to humanity is a man about whom we know relatively little. A native of Pamphylia in Asia Minor, Tribounianos, or Tribonian, was trained as a lawyer and rose through governmental service to the attention of Justinian. The Emperor, with his plans for the great legal projects to come, found in Tribonian precisely the man he needed and gave him the post of Quaestor, which made him in effect the chief of the Empire's judicial and legal system. The choice was a typically shrewd one, for Tribonian surely had the finest legal mind of the day, with an extent of learning symbolized by his supposedly unrivaled personal library of books on law. Much of Justinian's accomplishment as represented by the *Corpus juris civilis* is undoubtedly owed to this matchless adviser. Yet, Tribonian was not without his negative side. He was infected with the diseases — so damaging to any legal officer, but so common to the age — of greed and avarice. Under him the Empire's judicial system is alleged to have become terribly corrupt, and he rapidly became a target of particular public hatred. Curiously enough, he was also a pagan, an indication of how tenaciously and how late the ancient beliefs lingered on among private individuals. His personal religious outlook seems to have been no obstacle for him in the sight of the fanatically pious Justinian; perhaps this is explained in part by Tribonian's reputation as an especially artful flatterer. He appears to have retained Justinian's favor throughout their association.

By far the most spectacular of Justinian's advisers was John of Cappadocia, for some time the Emperor's chief financial minister. The black portrait drawn of him by the malevolent Procopius is to a large extent corroborated by other sources. John was, at the very least, a vivid personality: of great physical strength, he was also bold, outspoken, shrewd, endlessly resourceful; but unscrupulous, cruel, ruthless, sadistic, depraved, and insatiably greedy. Nevertheless, these qualities were subordinate, or contributory, to the one essential virtue which commended him most to Justinian: he could raise money. This was a talent of which Justinian had vital need in view of his ambitious projects. It is true that the economies of Anastasius I had left an overflowing treasury. But these resources had been reduced by various strains such as the disastrous earthquake at Antioch in 526 and the ensuing phase of frontier wars with Persia. These specific financial burdens had been aggravated by incompetent administration of the revenue system during Justin's reign.[6]

In these circumstances, John's talents for handling money, which had been discovered early by the new Emperor, made him a pearl beyond price. He proved his merits as a subordinate supervisor of provincial tax systems, and by 530 was finally given the exalted status of Praetorian Prefect, one of the highest offices in the state. It is possible that his bad reputation can be leavened with credit for some constructive administrative reforms. Nevertheless, his ultimate goal was the rapid and extensive raising of revenues, by any means, fair or foul — usually the latter. He is reported to have reduced vital public services to save money. Worse, his rapacious and extortionate fiscal policies bore down mercilessly on the peoples of the Empire. In spite of the glory Justinian may have restored to the Roman Empire, he certainly imposed considerable oppression and misery on the subjects who were obliged to sustain it. We have a lurid account of the plundering of the province of Lydia in southwestern Asia Minor by one of John's agents. If the report is accurate, it would make a barbarian invasion seem mild by comparison.[7] There were those who, regard-

6. For Procopius' comment on this, see above, p. 57, and n. 10.

7. The account of this is given by an official of Justinian's government, John Lydus, in his treatise *De magistratibus* (in its original Greek title, *Concerning the Offices of the Commonwealth of the Romans*), III, 58–61, the author being himself a native of the province he claims to have been thus plundered. The episode is included in a bitter denunciation of John the

less of their personal dislike for the man, were aware of the damage John was doing; and the early excesses of John's administration were no small element in the underlying causes of the great insurrection of 532 against Justinian. Yet, the Emperor continued to cherish him, for John's proven capacities to squeeze out of the Empire the money Justinian so badly needed enabled Justinian to close his eyes to all of his minister's other faults and misconduct. He alone among the Emperor's advisers could speak out freely and forcefully against the reconquest projects which were so dear to Justinian's heart.[8] His influence over Justinian came to be second only to that of Theodora.

It was Theodora herself, however, who was to destroy the all-powerful Cappadocian. Inevitably, she hated him intensely as a rival to her own influence over Justinian, though such was the Emperor's need for John's peculiar talents that not even Theodora's word could alter his esteem for the powerful Prefect. Perhaps there was also an element of loyalty to her husband in Theodora's hostility to John, for she knew that John's activities were harmful to public interest; and, even more, she might well see John as a threat to Justinian himself. The shallow and ambitious Cappadocian had let power turn his head. It was thus an easy matter for Theodora and her helpers to spin a web of intrigue around John in the year 541, getting him to commit himself wholeheartedly to a pretended conspiracy against Justinian. Even amid these manipulations Justinian tried to save his needed favorite from ruin, but he had to bow to the course of events. John was disgraced and was for years pursued in exile by the Empress' relentless hatred: only after her death (548) was he recalled from exile. His power had by then vanished.

The fall of John of Cappadocia in 541 was a victory for Theodora's influence, but the victim was an individual not a policy. Justinian's need for a man of his kind was not ended. Rather, it was underscored by his choice of the man who became John's

Cappadocian and his conduct, complete with a lurid description of his savage cruelty and his debauchery, to all of which the author was to some extent apparently an eye-witness (III, 57–67, *et seq.*). Note the comments of Bury, *History of the Later Roman Empire* . . . (A.D. 395–565), II, 36–39.

8. Procopius, *Wars*, Book III, chap. x, secs. 7–18.

ultimate successor, Peter Barsymes. A Syrian by origin, Barsymes differed from John in lacking the latter's repulsive and obtrusive personal qualities; in addition, he had the favor of Theodora rather than her enmity. His career was uneven, but he long held the office of Count of the Sacred Largesses, which made him a kind of Secretary of the Treasury, and for a time he even occupied John's old post of Praetorian Prefect. His methods, if less sensational than John's, were apparently no less oppressive. He was as resourceful as his predecessor in finding new sources of revenue for his master. He seems to have achieved nowhere near the influence with Justinian that John had enjoyed, but he proved a dependable fiscal henchman of the kind Justinian had sought in John himself.

Beyond the specifically civil advisers of Justinian, there are four more individuals of the Emperor's circle who deserve consideration in this context. The first is perhaps the most celebrated figure of Justinian's reign, after Theodora, and to many the most sympathetic. This is Belisarius, the outstanding general of the age, and one of the remarkable commanders of history. He was an extremely able field commander, a skillful tactician and strategist, and a capable administrator. His particular genius lay in accomplishing maximum results with minimum resources. Though he shared an Illyrian peasant background with Justinian, he was quite different from his master in his simple and straightforward personality. As circumstances showed, he was capable of cunning and deception, but he had the advantages of an upright character, unimpeachable morals, and unwavering loyalty. For these qualities he was admired by everyone, friend and foe — save perhaps by Justinian, whose suspicions of Belisarius have reflected discredit on himself rather than on his great general.

Belisarius' one weak point was his exceedingly trusting and pliant nature, which was particularly revealed in his matrimonial situation. His wife, Antonina, was of the same background as Theodora. The friendship and general trust between the two women was often of great help to Belisarius when he fell under the cloud of Justinian's disfavor. Unlike Theodora, Antonina did not settle down after her marriage, which seems not to have altered her immoral behavior. Hence her intrigues at court apparently came to be rivaled by her intrigues in the boudoir. For the most part, Belisarius endured his wife's presumed unfaithfulness with sorrowful tolerance or, at worst, embarrassment and helpless frustration.[9]

It is also in connection with Belisarius himself that we can note another important figure of this period: not a minister or a general, but the man who was to become its principal historian. The student of the age of Justinian is fortunate to have as his most immediate guide a truly important master of the writing of history. By general agreement, Procopius of Caesarea was the last of the great historians in the Classical Greek tradition. He was even able to conform to the ancient presumption that the best historian will be a man of practical affairs and a participant in the events he describes. He was born in the Palestinian Caesarea in the late fifth century (we are not certain of the date), and began a promising legal career in Constantinople. His abilities and diligence attracted attention, so that by 527 he was appointed to the post of private secretary and legal aide to Belisarius, then just rising as a young and promising commander in Justinian's service. In this capacity he accompanied Belisarius on his campaigns, discharging vital functions. Thereafter he also followed a career of his own at court. He was thus ideally placed for observing and recording the events of his period. Moreover, he was well-educated and had a thorough sense of style. His prime model was inevitably Thucydides, whom he emulated in many ways; he could not even resist the opportunity which the plague of 542–543 gave him to parallel his prototype's classic account of the great plague in Athens.

9. The reader interested in music might be amused to hear that Belisarius is also the subject of an opera. This is *Belisario*, by Gaetano Donizetti (1797–1848), first produced in Venice (appropriately, a once-Byzantine city) on Feb. 4, 1836, and now all but forgotten, together with most of this composer's operatic output. Its libretto, incidentally, was by Salvatore Cammarano, who not only wrote the text for Donizetti's still-popular *Lucia di Lammermoor*, which preceded it (1835), but also later wrote several libretti for Giuseppe Verdi: *Alzira* (1845), *La battaglia di Legnano* (1849), *Luisa Miller* (1849), and *Il trovatore* (1853). Verdi himself composed about the only other important opera concerning events discussed in this book, his *Attila*, first produced — again appropriately, in Venice, the city according to tradition first settled by refugees from the Huns' invasion of Italy — in 1846.

Procopius' principal narrative account of Justinian's reign is his work which is properly titled *History in Eight Books*, but is more usually called *History of the Wars*. It covers its material by theater, rather than in a single continuous chronological narrative: the first two books on the Persian Wars, the next two on the Vandal Wars, and the remaining four on the Gothic Wars, covering events down to about 554. This work is, of course, primarily focused on the military and external aspects of Justinian's reign. It seems to have been composed as something of an official work, and hence a good deal of it is at least outwardly biased in favor of Justinian and his efforts, though occasional criticisms rise to the surface. More sharply biased, however, is another of Procopius' works, in this case frankly a panegyric of the Emperor. This is the treatise in six books, often given the Latin title *De aedificiis*, or *On the Buildings*. It is a systematic and extravagantly laudatory description of Justinian's building projects of all kinds, ornamental, functional, and defensive, throughout the Empire. Its date of composition is estimated at about 560, and in spite of its exaggerated tone it is full of valuable information.

Procopius did not carry his narrative into the last years of Justinian's reign. We do not know the date of Procopius' death, so that the reason for the lapse is not fully clear. It remained for other historians to continue his work, Xenophon-like, in an inferior fashion. Nevertheless, another work does survive which was apparently Procopius' attempt, not to extend his previous writings, but rather to add another side to them. This is the so-called *Secret History*, in thirty chapters, more correctly called the *Anékdota* (Greek for "The Unpublished Material"), so named from the fact that it was not intended for circulation during Procopius' own lifetime. There has been considerable dispute among modern scholars as to whether or not this is really an authentic work of Procopius. That question has largely been decided in the affirmative, and composition of the work is now usually dated about 550, between the writing of the seventh and eighth books of the relatively official *History of the Wars*. Its character has already been noted: it seems to have been the embittered historian's means of unburdening himself of all that he could not put in his other writings, and of all the hatred he had built up over the years

against his masters.[10] Procopius here has hardly a favorable word
about anyone. He is particularly eager to discredit the four people
who shaped his destiny most closely. Among them even his hero
Belisarius emerges as a fatuous cuckold, while Antonina is pilloried
for her treachery and licentious faithlessness. His principal targets
are the two sovereigns: he depicts Justinian as a tyrant and as an
inhuman, or rather non-human, monster, who committed the vilest
crimes and intentionally ruined the state; but his particular venom
is reserved for his unspeakable portrayal of Theodora. The hys-
terical scandalmongering, the unrelieved exaggeration of this
work repel the serious reader, discredit the reputation of the otherwise exalted historian, and compromise the value of at least this
book itself as a source. Nonetheless, used with caution and in careful relation to other materials, even the *Secret History* is of considerable value to the historian of Justinian. It is also an important
part of Procopius' total contribution, one which need not fundamentally alter his genuine status as a great historian.[11]

Finally, in relation to Belisarius again, we should take note of
his successor in command, Narses. In spite of the fact that they

10. P. N. Ure, in his admirable little volume *Justinian and his Age* (Pelican paperback, A–217, 1951), pp. 170 ff. and 184, suggests that Procopius'
bitterness may have resulted in part because the historian had originally
shared Justinian's great dream and had indeed approved the Emperor's
ambitious projects. As these floundered or went unfulfilled, says Ure, Procopius might then have been prompted to turn against their Imperial initiator
out of a sense of disillusionment.

11. These writings by Procopius are, of course, among the few sources
for Justinian's reign which are now available in translation. There are several
translations of various parts of Procopius in English, but the most accessible
integral one is that in the Loeb Classical Library series, giving both the
Greek text, in the Haury edition, with parallel English translation by H. B.
Dewing (together with G. Downey in the final volume). The distribution of
contents is as follows: Books I and II, on the Persian Wars, are in the Loeb
Vol. I (1914); Books III and IV, on the Vandalic Wars, are in Vol. II (1916);
Books V–VIII, on the Gothic Wars, are in Vols. III–V (1919, 1924, and
1928, respectively); the *Anékdota* or *Secret History* is in Vol. VI (1935);
while Vol. VII (1940) contains *On the Buildings*. For the general reader,
concise discussions of Procopius, and of other contemporary writers of this
period, may be found in the appropriate chapters of Ure's *Justinian and his
Age*, pp. 168–196, and in Bury's *History of the Later Roman Empire* . . .
(A.D. 395–565), II, 417–436.

disagreed with each other, that they were rivals in counsels and in intrigue, and that Narses often worked highhandedly against Belisarius, Narses has much in common with his colleague as one of the few genuinely attractive and admirable figures of the age. Narses was an eunuch, of Persarmenian origin, and he seemed destined for a career as a court and civil functionary. Certainly his talents appeared to lead him in that direction. He rose through the ranks of fiscal service to the office of Grand Chamberlain, highest of the palace officials. In contrast to most of Justinian's administrators, Narses seems to have earned a high reputation for honesty, uprightness, and benevolence. His fiscal responsibilities, however, involved him in the expensive campaigns in Italy. After the seeming collapse of the Roman reconquest effort there in the wake of Belisarius' final failures, Narses found himself advanced into a new military career. As we shall see, he pursued it with a distinction which belied, or at least complemented, his civil background, and completed the work begun by Belisarius in realization of Justinian's goals. In this fashion he served his master with at least as much loyalty as Belisarius had shown, and he maintained Justinian's confidence far better than his predecessor had managed to do.

This survey of course by no means exhausts the list of powerful or influential people around Justinian. We know of many other officials and personalities, of varying degrees of importance and commendability. Nevertheless, these few sketches may illustrate some of the chief human factors upon which the Emperor's reign was built. Without them that reign would have been quite different. Justinian was undeniably fortunate in having available to him the talents, admirable or otherwise, of such followers. Yet, it would be a mistake to assume that it was really they who were responsible for Justinian's accomplishments. Nor did Justinian simply find them ready-made and readily at hand for his immediate exploitation. If we consider at least the major personalities discussed thus far, including Theodora, we may note that none of them was of particularly exalted origin. Not that there were no officials and courtiers who were of the nobility or who had distinguished antecedents. Nonetheless, it is a fact that most of the principal people around Justinian, the ones on whom he relied most, were of backgrounds which were, like his own, humble or obscure, or at least uncertain; people who had risen on the basis of their merits or what we might call "lucky breaks." The "lucky breaks" were in most cases the opportunities deliberately provided by Justinian himself. Here, then, is the point: Justinian was constantly seeking out people of talent. It is self-evident that he had a sharp eye for such people, and a genuine gift for picking qualified subordinates, and this, after all, is a prime requisite for a successful sovereign.

The kind of court which ruled the despotic Later Roman state naturally prevented the Emperor's staff from always functioning smoothly, however carefully its members were chosen. Intrigue was taken for granted. The Empress connived against the individuals and officials she hated; the civil officials intrigued against each other, or against the military commanders; and the commanders themselves conspired against each other. One of Justinian's less admirable qualities was his extremely suspicious nature. Among the greatest blots on his record were his failure to recognize the selfless loyalty of Belisarius and his occasionally mean treatment of his great general. Part of this was the result of jealousy, in all probability. Justinian never sought glory in the field. Since the days of Theodosius I, the Emperor had remained at home, supervising the Empire as a whole and leaving direct military command to his generals. Perhaps Justinian, if he could not share the toils of compaigning, at least envied the glories with which the triumphant Belisarius covered himself. In all fairness, Justinian's treatment of his general was frequently liberal and just. Yet, one must acknowledge that no ruler of the kind Justinian was, and had to be, could rest easily while another man amassed a spectacular military reputation and vast popularity. Justinian's ungenerous conduct was thus not completely beyond understanding, even if it was sometimes ungrateful in the specific case of Belisarius.

Besides its suspicion and ingratitude, Justinian's personality was also marked by frequent vacillation. It has even been all too easy to picture Justinian as constantly swayed by those around him. Perhaps some of his vacillation was really the result of his being pushed and pulled back and forth by his advisers, who might play upon his fears or suspicions or jealousies — as in the case of Belisarius. Certainly he was subject to influence, and there were those whose influence was enormous.[12] On the other hand, while he undoubtedly heeded the advice of those around him, such as John of Cappadocia, Belisarius, Narses, and, of course, Theodora, he could by the same token often resist it. However great the power Theodora exerted over him, he could and did frequently oppose her; as witness, for example, his consistent favor to John of Cappadocia in spite of his wife's hatred for the man. His disregarding of Belisarius' advice ultimately hastened the ruin of that general. We have already noted the occasion when John of Cappadocia spoke out against the Emperor's conquest plans, as an indication of the great freedom of opinion and high position allowed to that minister by the Emperor. Yet, the fact remains that, despite his high esteem of John, Justinian ignored his advice on this occasion and did pursue these plans.

It seems plain, then, that Justinian was determined to be master of his own government. He sought out and highly prized the men whose talents he needed, and he was more than open to their influence. Yet, we may seriously wonder if their influence extended very far or very often beyond their own areas of competence. Even within these areas, also, Justinian kept constant watch over them. Some of his officials he seems even to have maintained simply to exploit. Procopius charges that Justinian consistently encouraged his officials to plunder his subjects, allowing them to build up outrageous wealth, and then disgraced them after a while so that he could confiscate for himself all they had accumulated — a fate to which even John of Cappadocia fell victim.[13] However much this was an actual basis of policy, it is certain that Justinian kept careful rein on his subordinates. He had much need for hatchet men to do the unsavory work his programs required, and he was not above using or abusing them when he could. He could cherish or abandon, trust or despise, such henchmen as he saw fit. Vacillating he may have been, and subject to influence, but he was also by

12. Procopius makes several malicious comments about Justinian's supposed readiness to accept blindly the advice or influence of others; see *Anékdota*, chap. viii, sec. 3 and 28; chap. xiii, secs. 10–11; chap. xxii, secs. 29–31.
13. *Anékdota*, chap. xxi, secs. 3–8.

nature an autocrat. No one was to be a rival to his power, and the will of no other would overshadow his. One of his greatest vanities was his minute supervision of all aspects of government. He even neglected his nightly rest to keep busy,[14] earning the nickname of "The Emperor who never sleeps," so diligently did he devote himself to his Imperial duties.

Such then, was the nature of this ruler, and such were the chief individuals around him. Their interrelated roles provided the strands of which the fabric of his reign was to be woven.

The Nika Riots

As we have seen, when Justinian ascended the throne in his own name, in 527, he had already been enjoying power and conducting the government for some time. He had also been formulating his policies and projects, although in many cases it was only upon his accession as sole ruler that he had the freedom to prosecute them.

It is not difficult to imagine the broad outlines of his plan or to understand the basic trends of his thinking. Four fundamental attitudes colored his entire outlook, and they must be seen as having shaped everything he did. First, he was convinced that as Emperor he was the ultimate sovereign, God's viceregent in this world, with a will to be challenged or flouted by no one on earth. Second, he was determined that he would be no mere clothes-rack for the Imperial robes he wore: he would not stand by and observe events passively, but would take the initiative in guiding them boldly by exerting his powers to the full. Third, he was a conservative in that he intended everything he undertook to help safeguard the heritage of power, faith, and culture which had become his responsibility as Roman Emperor. Finally, he saw that heritage as indeed a Roman one: that is, in accordance with his own Latin-speaking background, he recognized this very heritage as all that Rome had in fact represented as a world-state for cen-

14. *Anékdota*, chap. xiii, secs. 28 ff., though Procopius tries to portray even this as one of Justinian's evil qualities.

turies. Everything that was — or had been — a part of it belonged under him as its proper sovereign.

Within these frames of reference his policies readily took shape. Some of them dealt with old problems of long standing, which any ruler assuming power at that time would have had to face. Others were partly or entirely new ventures, inaugurated on his own initiative, although they were rooted in a fully traditional and conservative outlook. The distinction between these two categories should perhaps not be overemphasized; and though they will be discussed in their respective turns below, it is well that we review them succinctly at this point. As administrator Justinian was determined that the government of the Empire should be reformed wherever necessary to make it just and efficient, and, above all, revenue-producing to the fullest possible extent. As heaven's supreme viceroy on earth, he was dedicated to bringing peace and unity to the Church, by ending the Acacian Schism and the ill-feeling with the Roman See, and at the same time closing the problem of Monophysite dissent. As a diplomat and overseer of his realm's economic well-being, he wished to open new trade routes, to end unfavorable trade dependencies on the hostile Persians, and to strengthen important industries within the Empire. As guardian of the territories of his realm he wished to secure its wide frontiers against attacks from many quarters. But as heir to the traditions and authority of Augustus and Constantine, he had consecrated himself to recovering the Empire's rightful territories and subjects in the Western Mediterranean, the actual sovereignty of which had been usurped by alien peoples whose status had only the thinnest veneer of legality.

These were the plans which, with all their implications and interrelationships, filled Justinian's mind as he rose to supreme power. As we shall see, progress had been made in implementing them even before 527, and more definite steps were taken in the early years of his personal rule. Still, schemes of this magnitude required more than mere will power. Much was needed in the way of preparation, especially in terms of finances. Then, too, there were such annoying distractions as the Persian frontier fighting. Above all, however, it was only a near cataclysm that struck the final spark in Justinian, and prompted him to devote himself to his projects with the full energy and momentum which they required. This was the occasion when Justinian was very nearly toppled from his throne, in the event known as the Nika Revolt.

The unrest of the demes in Constantinople had not ceased after the terrible disturbances of Anastasius I's reign. That unrest had its deep social roots, as has been stressed, and not only in the discontent of the lower classes, but even in upper-class interests as well. The rise of Justin I and his family to power added further complications. Staunchly Chalcedonian in their views, the new rulers were naturally favored by the orthodox-oriented Blues. In addition, though the new sovereigns were of humble origins, they were supported initially by the nobility — whose interests also were reflected by the Blues — who hoped to win more influence under them than they had previously enjoyed in the government. This atmosphere of apparent favor for the Blues made the extremists in this faction increasingly arrogant in the early years of Justin's reign. They created violent disturbances in both the capital and the provincial cities. In 520 they were involved in riots in connection with the assassination of Vitalian. It was only in 523 that Justin and Justinian were obliged by the excesses of their Blue partisans to repress them forcefully. Disorders were firmly quelled, and thereafter the Blues behaved more discreetly. Nevertheless, the alliance of the new dynasty with the nobility and the Blues seems to have cooled thereafter.

Justinian issued ordinances of his own in 527 to curb the violence of both factions impartially, thereby extending the policy of his uncle's regime. The restless factions remained ready to break out into new disorder, however. The Blues were by this time smarting from what they considered the Emperor's callous abandonment. It should also be remembered that these circus factions provided the only means for expression of popular feelings or discontent. Thus, a frequent focus of their disturbances was a bill of complaints against unpopular officials. As the early years of Justinian's reign proceeded, the number of unpopular officials was bound to increase as a result of the growing ruthlessness and oppression of his government. This was the background to the outbreak of 532.

Typically, a trivial incident was the immediate cause of trouble. There had been one of innumerable minor riots in which some people had been killed. Rioters of both factions had been arrested, and a few were found guilty of murder by the City Prefect, Eudaemon. On the occasion of the culprits' execution, in the early days of January 532, the hanging of two of them was bungled by the executioners. These two men, one a Green and the other a Blue, were then whisked away still alive to sanctuary in a church. The Prefect cordoned off the church with a guard, but each faction was determined to rescue its member-in-distress. A few days later, on January 13, Justinian was presiding over the usual races in the Hippodrome when the factions appealed to him to pardon the two men. The Emperor ignored them. To everyone's amazement, the clamorous cry soon arose: "Long life to the benevolent Greens and Blues!" It was plain that, in a rare reversal of the usual situation, the two factions had buried their differences and had agreed to cooperate in pressing their mutual demands. The united factions also adopted as their joint battle cry the pregnant watchword "*Nika*" (Greek for "Conquer!"), from which the outbreak was to take its name.

The government at first attempted to stand firm against these demands. The faction mobs gathered at the building which housed both the Prefect's headquarters and the prison to demand the release of the two demesmen still in sanctuary. When no satisfaction was obtained on this count, the mob broke into the prison, released all of the criminals then in custody there, set fire to the building, and began a rampage of incendiarism through the city. Their burning of buildings continued on January 14, when Justinian attempted in vain to distract the rioters with new races in the Hippodrome. Pressing their advantage, the factions advanced more definite demands. Significantly, they now called for the removal of the three most unpopular government ministers: the rapacious Praetorian Prefect John of Cappadocia, the learned but corrupt Quaestor Tribonian, and the City Prefect Eudaemon himself. The situation had become serious. Justinian decided to placate the factions by agreeing to the dismissal of the three officials, and replaced them with more popularly acceptable men.

The concessions had come too late. However mollified the faction leaders themselves might have been, the control of events had now passed out of their hands. The city was at the time full of impoverished provincials who had been the particular victims of the government's fiscal oppression. Their role had doubtless been decisive in the factions' move to take advantage of the disturbances by demanding a purge of the most hated officials in the administration. Still another factor was now emerging. The nobility, already identified to some extent with the Blue faction, had its own interests to pursue. The Senatorial aristocracy of the capital deeply resented its failure to dominate Justinian; worse, its members now feared, and were outraged by, Justinian's growing personal autocracy and independence of any traditional checks on the Imperial authority. A chance to unseat Justinian and to clear the throne for a more amenable candidate of their own would not be wasted by them. It was the interplay of these additional elements that helped turn an incidental riot into a class protest movement, and then into a revolution.

The mob was now completely out of hand. It roamed unchecked through the city, pillaging, ravaging, and burning. It even began looking for a candidate it could place on the throne. The most popular choice seems to have been one of the nephews of Anastasius I, Hypatius. Any claim he may once have had to the throne had been swept aside by the unexpected and sudden emergence of Justin I in 518. Since then he had remained loyal to the new ruling house and at peace with it, a man apparently devoid of active ambitions. For the moment, too, he was out of the mob's reach, since he was in the palace with Justinian and the other leaders of the aristocracy. Virtually besieged by the mob, Justinian was in a grave position. He was unable to trust the wavering loyalties of his palace guards and of the city troops. He did have at hand, however, the largely barbarian forces of two of his loyal commanders, recently returned from the frontiers: the Danubian commander Mundus, and Belisarius himself, then back from the Persian fighting. With these troops Belisarius sallied forth about the middle of the month to try to quell the rioters. Little was accomplished and the mob, thoroughly antagonized, carried its incendiarism even further. As the danger deepened, Justinian suspected that the nobles who attended him in the palace could not be trusted. He was probably correct in some cases, but his dismissal of them on January 17, including the protesting Hypatius and Pompeius, Anastasius' nephews, was an imprudent step.

On the next day, January 18, a Sunday, Justinian made one last desperate effort at placating the rioters. As they gathered in the Hippodrome he repeated something of the performance Anastasius I had once given. Entering the *Káthisma* with a copy of the Gospels in hand, he promised under oath to grant amnesty and to heed the rioters' demands, but the mob would have none of him. With the news that Hypatius was now at large, the populace rushed to his home and compelled him to accept the Imperial office. By this time the aristocratic element was taking charge. Hypatius was plainly the nobles' candidate, and their leaders promptly closeted themselves with him to decide on the means of completing Justinian's overthrow. It was agreed to storm Justinian in his beleaguered palace. In the meantime, the newly proclaimed Hypatius was installed in the *Káthisma* to receive the plaudits of the mob.

The climax was now at hand. Vacillating as never before, Justinian — a man of bold vision but apparently limited personal courage — was terrified. Swayed by the advice of John the Cappadocian, who had as much to lose as his sovereign, Justinian and his advisers decided upon flight. Justinian ordered an escape fleet to be readied and to be loaded with treasure and other necessities. At this crucial juncture Theodora made her famous intervention. It is true that it was traditional for Classical historians to season their writings with speeches put into the mouths of their personages, which perhaps reflected their thoughts of the moment, but in final form were entirely the product of the author. Mindful of his models, Procopius did not fail us here. To whatever degree the speech he ascribes to Theodora is the work of the writer's own hand, however, it suggests vividly just the sort of thing she must have said. Here are the passionate sentiments of a woman who had clawed her way up from a life among the dregs of human society to the peak of human ambition, and who was determined not to lose in the panic of a moment all she had won:

While it is not proper for a woman to be bold or to behave brashly among men who themselves are hesitant, I think the present crisis hardly permits us to debate this point academically from one perspective or another. For, when people's interests have reached the greatest peril, they consider nothing more vital than to settle matters in the best possible fashion. For my part, then, I consider flight, even though it may bring safety, to be quite useless, at any time and especially now. Once a man has come into the light of day it is impossible for him not to face death; and so also is it unbearable for someone who has been a ruler to be a fugitive. For, let me never be without this purple garment, and let me never be alive upon that day when all those who encounter me do not greet me with the salutation of "Your Majesty." So now, if it is still your wish to save yourself, O Emperor, there is no problem. For we have plenty of money, the sea is there, and here are the ships. Nevertheless, consider whether, once you have managed to save yourself, you might not then gladly exchange your safety for death. But as for me, I take pleasure in an old expression that royal rank is the best burial garment.[15]

Whether this bold speech was the result of simple courage, or pride, or intuition, or else of some particular shrewdness, one can only speculate, but it did mark the turning of the tide. And, as events proved, it was more than justified by the outcome. For in fact the mobs were now just where Justinian could at last deal with them. They were packed in the Hippodrome, acclaiming Hypatius and denouncing the supposedly doomed Imperial couple. Hypatius for his part seems even then to have tried to warn Justinian and have him strike while the rioters were in the Hippodrome. But he was deceived by reports that the Emperor had indeed fled, and so he surrendered himself to his newly imposed status. After the fresh courage which Theodora's brave stand had given Justinian, however, the Emperor and his advisers had decided to remain and take action. Narses, emerging to prominence for the first time as a court official, was sent out to sow rumors and money among the Blues, to discourage their full support of Hypatius — who, after all, was but a kinsman of the late Emperor Anastasius, the Green's old partisan. Meanwhile, Belisarius and Mundus again prepared their loyal troops, mostly Goths and other barbarians. These forces were unable to effect an

15. Procopius, *Wars*, Book I, chap. xxiv, secs. 33–37. The "old expression" which Theodora quoted is derived from Isocrates' *Archidamus*, sec. 45.

entry directly into the *Káthisma* and thus disable the revolt at its head by seizing Hypatius, but the two commanders did manage to make their way into the Hippodrome itself at roughly opposite places. Belisarius decided there was no choice but to turn on the rioters themselves, and Mundus in due course followed his example. Disunited now, poorly armed, and no match for the cold discipline of alien professional soldiers, the rabble was mercilessly slaughtered. The number of the slain is reported to have reached more than 30,000 before this frightful carnage was ended.

The Emperor could finally dispense justice. Hypatius and Pompeius and the rebellious aristocrats were seized and brought before the Emperor for judgment. Hypatius argued with reason that he had been compelled to accept the diadem offered him, and that he had really been trying to work loyally on the Emperor's behalf to quell the riot. Justinian may have recognized an element of truth in this defense, but Hypatius and his brother were by now too clearly compromised, and their potentialities as rivals to Justinian were too great to be suffered; the pair was executed and their bodies cast into the sea. The leading aristocratic conspirators were spared, though they were deprived of their properties and exiled. After a few years, when the last embers of rebellion were long extinguished, Justinian could afford to be moderate: he made some restitution of properties to the surviving conspirators and also to the innocent children of Hypatius and Pompeius. Nevertheless, any hope of further aristocratic action against Justinian was now doomed. The nobles were thoroughly under his thumb, and he was merciless in his confiscations and repression thereafter. In addition, his independence of action and his autocracy could now flourish without any check.

As for the demes themselves, there was no question of destroying them. They were too much a part of the whole fabric and basic organization of urban society in the Empire to be eliminated. Nor was it completely possible to end their restlessness. They could still make their complaints known to the Emperor. And though they seem to have been quiet for some years, they were to resume their rioting in the later part of Justinian's reign. Afterwards, they even continued to play an important role in politics, especially in the late sixth and early seventh centuries. Nevertheless, Justinian had at least broken the one major attempt of the two factions to join forces against the government. They would never make such an attempt again. The Emperor had also taught the populace of the capital a grave lesson in the perils of trying to take power into its own hands.[16]

Constantinople itself was, of course, a shambles. Large sections of it had been gutted by fires and the destruction which the rioters had wrought. Another new burden was thereby placed on Justinian's finances, but it also gave him an opportunity to rebuild the city in his own way, beautifying it lavishly. This opportunity fitted in quite well with his ambitions, and it actually served as an inspiration for some of his most notable contributions to the world of art and architecture. Nor were his fiscal policies much hampered by the concessions he had been forced to make. John of Cappadocia's successor as Praetorian Prefect, appointed during the riots, was a popular and moderate official named Phocas. He was unable to keep abreast of the Emperor's financial needs, so by the beginning of 533 Justinian removed him and without the slightest difficulty restored John to his old post, thereby assuring himself of more revenue. Tribonian, too, was soon returned to his post as Quaestor, so that the Emperor's legal work, as well as this official's peculations, could continue.

On balance, then, once the Nika Revolt was put down, Justinian emerged the stronger for it. The principal outburst of internal opposition to his regime had come and had failed. Justinian's hands were freer than ever, especially since the Persian menace was also ended for the moment. Theodora's influence was confirmed once more. Such supporters as Belisarius, already the outstanding general in the Emperor's service, had proved their loy-

16. Compare the comments in the provocative little book, *Constantinople in the Age of Justinian*, by Glanville Downey (Copyright 1960, University of Oklahoma Press), p. 42: "Justinian punished the senators less severely than he might have, and the whole episode served to establish his power more firmly. To the people of Constantinople this story was a sad reminder for many years. The citizens of the great capital, many of them prosperous and fortunate, had felt their power and had tried to use it. One part of the living city had attempted to assert its supremacy. But it was really the emperor — one might say the imperial office — that was supreme. The city and its people must not forget this."

alty. The danger and the triumph which the revolt had involved brought Justinian a measure of rejuvenation and enabled him to release at last the energies he had been developing. It is no coincidence that Justinian's most ambitious steps were taken only after the Nika outbreak. The last obstacles to his bold schemes were now removed. It is from the quelling of this revolt that we can most decisively date the full-scale blossoming of the era of Justinian.

III   THE OLD PROBLEMS

The View from the Throne

We have traced thus far the evolution of the Later Roman world into the sixth century, and we have followed the emergence of Justinian himself as ruler of that world. We may now examine his policies and activities amid the circumstances which had been given their final form in the hectic reign of Anastasius I, but whose roots went so deeply into the previous century and beyond.

In the previous chapter we noted cursorily the barest lines of Justinian's policies and ambitions. We might recapitulate here, under six rough headings, what he seems to have intended to do: first, to reestablish peace in the Christian *oikouméné* by ending on the one hand the so-called Acacian Schism between Constantinople and Rome, and on the other hand the disruption caused by the Monophysite problem; second, to secure the Empire's current frontiers, primarily the European northeast and the Asiatic southeast, from the dangers of various attacks; third, to win back the Western lands, then in the hands of the German barbarians; fourth, through diplomatic or other means, to secure more favorable trade opportunities in order to rectify certain imbalances in the Empire's commercial position; fifth, to overhaul the administrative and legal system of the Empire, in accordance with traditional precedents and current needs, for the purpose of providing the Empire with a just, efficient, and revenue-producing govern-

ment; and, sixth, to adorn his empire with new and glorious buildings of all kinds, especially in the capital, in order to heal the
scars of the Nika Riot, though also for other reasons.

The sequence in which these intentions have been set forth
need not itself be taken as significant, since it implies no necessary
order in the development or the precedence of his schemes. Indeed, the bulk of Justinian's plans seems to have evolved in his
mind as an entity, as a coherent program, all the time his prospects
of supreme power were dawning. These plans were often closely
related to each other, and all were the product of the Emperor's
understanding of his times, of his responsibilities, and of his
powers. Some do, of course, deal with essentially internal affairs
and others with essentially external ones. Viewed from another
perspective, however, some reflect efforts to face existing problems, which any emperor of Justinian's time would have had to
deal with, while others are the product of bold new initiative on
his part.

Again, either attempt to categorize Justinian's policies — as internal and external efforts, or old problems and new projects — is
essentially artificial. Justinian's activities were demonstrably all
of a piece and were consistently interrelated and interdependent.
In addition, Justinian himself would surely have rejected the
slightest insinuation that anything he was doing represented a
new element. "Innovator" would have been an insulting appellation to him. For this Emperor, all that he did was in a direct
and conscious line of tradition, devotedly concerned with preserving or reviving elements of the past; he undoubtedly thought
of himself as a conservative par excellence. There is no denying
that from his point of view he was right, as we shall see. It is
equally true that there are some aspects of his reign which would
have been paralleled by any ruler who had to fill his purple
shoes at this time, however much the details might have differed.
Yet, by the same token, there are aspects which are uniquely credit-
able to him, ones which would have been utterly different, or which
never would have existed had the throne been occupied in his
time by a different man — especially a man of lesser energy and
imagination, and of more limited perspective.

It is therefore the distinction between old problems and new projects which will give this and the following chapters their shape. Again, it is admittedly an artificial distinction. But the reader will do well to keep in mind the broad, unifying themes of all that Justinian undertook during the ensuing consideration of these two categories and their respective components.

The Religious Problems

Before one can follow the intricacies of Justinian's continuous preoccupation with ecclesiastical and theological affairs, something must first be said regarding the relationship of the sovereign to the Faith and of the State to the Church as it had developed up to his time.

The involvement of the sovereign in the religious life of his subjects was hardly a novelty by the time Christianity conquered the Roman world. In virtually all societies one of the ruler's prime responsibilities was to secure through his right conduct the favor of heaven for his realm. In the religious traditions of Near Eastern civilizations the ruler was himself actually regarded as a living manifestation of divinity, or as a semi-divine link between his people and the celestial powers. The Eastern custom of ruler-worship had strained and antagonized the blunt Macedonian soldiers of the visionary Alexander the Great and likewise the austere commanders of republican Rome. It nevertheless became a strong prop in the establishment of Roman Imperial authority from the time of Augustus and throughout the Empire's subsequent history. The Imperial cult, the ceremonial worship of the Emperor as a quasi-divinity and as a divine manifestation of earthly authority, personified in his image, was an act of political loyalty not very far removed from the modern practice of saluting the flag. It was, however, repulsive to the early Christians, who could not appreciate the fact that the religious element was merely superficial and that its essence was political, because they completely rejected all outward forms of image worship — much as some modern religious sects have resented or resisted saluting a national flag.

Despite its initial sentiments, the early Church was obliged to come to terms with the Imperial cult when relations with the sovereign changed. It was, after all, through the initiative of the Emperor in the fourth century that the situation of the Church was drastically altered and its triumph achieved. Constantine I (306–337) had adopted Christianity as his own faith, had made it suddenly more attractive to his contemporaries, and had laid the foundations for its favorable incorporation into the full fabric of the Roman world. Another Emperor, Gratian (375–383), first began to persecute paganism openly, paving the way for the natural final steps of Theodosius I (379–395), who established Christianity categorically as the only acceptable religion.

The Emperors were, however, more than benevolent sponsors of the new faith. Their conception of their responsibility to secure heaven's favor for their realm made it essential that they involve themselves actively in religious affairs — not only in the external circumstances of support and administration, but also in the fundamentals of actual doctrine. Religious controversy threatened the unity of the Empire and made the disposition of the Deity uncertain, and was therefore intolerable to the sovereign. Constantine's prompt involvement in the Donatist controversy in North Africa reflected this line of thinking,[1] and it was followed by his even more extensive involvement in the Arian controversy. His successors could not avoid further interference in the doctrinal concerns of the day. In succeeding generations Theodosius I and Marcian (450–457) followed in Constantine's footsteps by calling ecumenical councils to resolve vital issues of theological dispute, and made the Imperial will very much felt in the process.

What then was the proper relationship of the Emperor to the

1. The Donatist controversy involved certain clergymen and hierarchs of the Church who had yielded to pressure and betrayed their Faith during the last of the persecutions under Diocletian and Galerius, which ended in 311. One faction, lead by Donatus, maintained that by their misconduct these leaders had forfeited their positions in the Church and could no longer be accepted as valid ministers to the faithful. The entire question thereby involved also a denial of the efficacy of a sacrament of the Church regardless of the character of these ministrants, and caused violent controversy. In attempting to end the controversy (with only limited success, as it proved) Constantine was prompted to make his first intervention in Church affairs. In the process he made the first formal assertions of the Emperor's right and duty to act in this manner.

Church? The question seems particularly urgent when we recall the celebrated incident of Theodosius I's massacre of the Thessa-lonians. Provoked in the year 390 by unrest in Thessalonica, particularly against the Emperor's unpopular German troops stationed in the city, Theodosius had given way to a fit of anger. From his headquarters in Milan he had ordered a cold-blooded slaughter of the body of Thessalonian citizens gathered in their stadium. The Emperor was brought back to his senses by the forceful Bishop of Milan, St. Ambrose, who obliged Theodosius to acknowledge his terrible sin and to do public penance for it. While this incident demonstrated forcefully the fact that the Emperor was indeed a man subject to the laws of God, it has often been unduly inflated as a precedent for the principle, at least in the West, of the supremacy of the *sacerdotium* over the *regnum* — of the priesthood over the temporal sovereignty.[2] Generally the lines were drawn in the other direction: that is, what were to be the powers of the Emperor in the Church and the nature of Imperial sovereignty in a new Christian context?

The basic answers to these questions were emerging in the time of Constantine himself. The Christian was still, of course, ultimately concerned with the empire of heaven, not that on earth; that is, with the Christian commonwealth of the next life and salvation, rather than with mere terrestrial authority. As that distinction was drawn more clearly by the early Christian apologists to persuade the earthly Emperor of the Roman state that there was no conflict between him and the heavenly Emperor, their Lord and Savior, it became increasingly possible for the Christians to compromise their old militance against the principles of the Imperial cult. From compromise it was but one step to capitulation to the essentials of the old pagan concepts. The prime formulator of the Christian theory of Imperial sovereignty was the early fourth-century Church Father and historian, Eusebius of Caesarea, one of Constantine's counselors and confidants. His interpretation of the problem represents a fusion of Christian and

2. See, for example, the comments of N. H. Baynes in his chapter "The Dynasty of Valentinian and Theodosius the Great," in *The Cambridge Medieval History*, I (Cambridge, 1911), 244–245. Baynes regards the incident essentially as an encounter between two noble and powerful personalities.

traditionally pagan ideology, partly indeed as a surrender of the Church to the State which it had once opposed, partly as a gesture of deference to the ruler who had so altered its fortune. The old oriental and Hellenistic tradition of the sovereign as the representative, agent, and interpreter of Divine Will on earth was thus also applicable to the Imperial deputy of the Christian God, the custodian of His wisdom, and exemplary paragon of His virtue and benevolence. The stage of mere rhetoric was left behind, for the Emperor was now represented in sacrosanct images and by other forms of iconography as a supra-human and exalted figure with quasi-divine and hieratic attributes. Constantine himself was hailed as *Isapóstolos*, the "Equal of the Apostles," or sometimes also as the "Thirteenth Apostle." By natural extension, the Emperor assumed a unique status not only in the secular affairs of this world, but in the spiritual as well.

It was in accordance with such theocratic Imperial conceptions that Justinian formed his ecclesiastical policies.[3] As no will could be allowed to oppose his will in governing the Empire, so, too, would his will be supreme in matters of faith. His deportment in this respect has been taken as a very model of the principle which we call "caesaropapism" — the rigid control of matters spiritual and ecclesiastical by the temporal ruler. Nor would his example be lost on subsequent rulers. A later Byzantine Emperor could emulate him with the assertion that "I am Emperor and Priest" to justify his interference in doctrinal matters. To be sure, it is perhaps easy to overstress the extent of caesaropapism in Byzantine history. Without doubt, strong Emperors would seek to dominate the Church, often to the extent of deposing independent-minded Patriarchs and installing more docile candidates of their own. Yet the relationship often depended much on the personalities of the respective occupants of the Imperial and Patriarchal thrones at a given time. For certainly there were many over-

3. We have an interesting exposition, written in Justinian's reign, of what the Christian Emperor's powers and responsibilities were conceived to be and one which certainly reflects Justinian's own attitudes, whether or not it was composed at his order or for his eyes. This is the short treatise called the *Scheda regia*, or "Mirror of Princes," by Agapetus, a Deacon of the clergy of Haghía Sophía. For a good summary of its ideas, see Downey, *Constantinople in the Age of Justinian*, pp. 49–53.

weening and powerful Patriarchs. The relationship between Emperor and Patriarch came to be viewed in theory — a theory which was officially stated in the ninth century — as that of two interdependent embodiments of the same fundamental power and Divine Will. The secular and ecclesiastical authorities were but overlapping and harmoniously linked aspects of a basic entity — independent, equal, parallel, and inseparable. And in the centuries after Justinian, the Emperor's right to meddle actively and on his own initiative in matters of Church affairs and doctrines would be challenged bitterly in some conservative quarters of the Church. Nevertheless, whatever the practical or variable limitations on Christian Roman "caesaropapism," there is no doubt that Justinian came as close as any Emperor to the actual exercise of such power in Later Roman and Byzantine history.[4]

As the Lord's Anointed and the conscious overseer of his subjects' welfare, temporal and spiritual, Justinian concerned himself with all aspects of religious problems. He stated repeatedly in his enactments the government's responsibilities in this sphere, and he strove beyond all previous example to fulfill them.[5] His

4. Note the comments on the problem by J. M. Hussey in her valuable survey, *The Byzantine World* (London, 1957; reissued as a Harper Torchbook paperback, TB–1057, New York, 1962), pp. 91–92. But even she cannot deny elsewhere (p. 21) that "Justinian however went his way and exercised firm control over the Church; he is one of the few Roman Emperors to whose religious policy the much abused word 'caesaropapism' may fairly be applied." In G. Every's stimulating survey, *The Byzantine Patriarchate, 451–1204* (revised edition, London, 1962), may be found some good background material, and on pages 39–54 there is a useful summary of Justinian's ecclesiastical policies.

5. Compare the characterization by Bury, *History of the Later Roman Empire* . . . (A.D. 395–565), II, 360–361: "Justinian took his responsibilities as head of the Church more seriously than any Emperor had hitherto done, and asserted his authority in its internal affairs more constantly and systematically. It was his object to identify the Church and State more intimately, to blend them, as it were, into a single organism, of which he was himself the controlling brain. We must view in this light his important enactment that the Canons of the four great Ecumenical Councils should have the same validity as Imperial laws. And we can see in his legislation against heretics and pagans that he set before himself the ideal of an Empire which should be populated only by orthodox Christians. He determined 'to close all the roads which lead to error and to place religion on the firm foundations of a single faith' [Procopius, *Buildings*, Book I, chap. i, sec. 9], and for this purpose he

legislation teems with regulations of all the minutiae of ecclesiastical administration. He was especially benevolent to the growing number of monastic institutions, which received particular impetus to multiply and prosper under him. Beyond tending the affairs of the pious, there was a further obligation upon Justinian, of course, to protect them from the errors of the misguided. Persecution of unbelievers and dissenters was a constant theme of his reign. Though the Palestinian Samaritans were harshly treated and though their resulting revolts were severely put down, the Jews in general, however, seem to have been treated with only moderate abuse.

More rigorous were his dealings with the remnants of paganism which still flourished among private individuals, especially in Hellenic intellectual circles. Justinian on several occasions rounded up notable pagans, including many aristocrats and officials. He punished them or obliged their conversion, but pagan beliefs still lingered on weakly among them thereafter. Nevertheless, centers of pagan worship in the provinces were destroyed, and remaining cults forcibly extinguished. The real deathblow which Justinian dealt paganism, however, was that directed against its strongest remaining bastion, the Classical educational system and institutions. Formal adherence to orthodox Christianity was made a necessary prerequisite for teaching, and thus the remaining exponents of the old pagan philosophical and rhetorical traditions were deprived of their livelihood. Even more specifically, in 529 Justinian closed the schools of higher learning at Athens, thus killing the last traditions of the Platonic Academy. As a result, there was a great exodus of pagan scholars beyond the Empire's frontiers, most notably to Persia. The Empire thus lost a large body of learning and a good deal of its link with the cultural life of Antiquity. Such blows against the old pagan centers of learning did, nevertheless, serve to exalt by contrast the

made orthodoxy a requisite condition of citizenship. He declared that he considered himself responsible for the welfare of his subjects, and therefore, above all, for securing the salvation of their souls; from this he deduced the necessity of intolerance towards heterodox opinions. It was the principle of the Inquisition. None of his predecessors had taken such a deep personal interest in theology as Justinian, and he surpassed them all in religious bigotry and in the passion for uniformity."

importance of the great school of higher learning in the capital, founded a century earlier by Theodosius II, as a more vital center of distinctly Christian scholarship and education. In addition, by this time, the identification of "Hellene" with "pagan" and "paganism," which was to characterize the thinking of generations to come, was made more definite among those who regarded themselves as "Romans," that is, citizens of the Christian (Roman) Empire.

Among all the targets of Justinian's persecutions, it was those classified as heretics who suffered most. Already the medieval conception of the heretic, the religious dissenter, not only as an enemy of Divine Truth, but also as a social menace and a political traitor — the community, the state, and the Faith being inextricably bound together — had clearly taken shape. No one who was not an orthodox Christian should properly enjoy the blessings of this world. Proven heretics were at the very least subject to loss of all civil and property rights. In cases of large heretical communities in various localities, forcible conversion or repression was in order. Some dissenters, such as the dualistic Manichaeans and relapsed heretics in general, were subject to capital punishment, often of the most gruesome sort. The government felt itself free to apply its chastisement flexibly to particular heretical groups, as it might see fit.

Of course, the definition of heresy could be flexible also, and so likewise the actual degree to which heretics would be prosecuted. Inevitably the chief body of religious dissent with which Justinian was concerned was Monophysitism. Here we must return to one of the major problems bequeathed to him by the fifth century and particularly by the reign of Anastasius I. Its significance cannot be overemphasized. On the one hand, it involved a rent in the unity of the Church as a result of a fundamental and bitter theological dilemma. On the other hand, its link with national sentiments and local dissatisfactions imparted to it grave political implications which menaced the unity and viability of the entire Empire. In addition, the central government's need to resolve this issue affected its position in many other spheres. Any emperor would have had to do something about it. No one can accuse Justinian of not having tried.

As has already been noted, the reign of Justin I and his nephew represented, among other things, a reaction to the overtly pro-Monophysite position of Anastasius. The experiment of attempting, as it were, to beat the Monophysites by joining them was at an end. Out of staunch personal convictions, as well as out of regard for the orthodox elements among the nobility and others from which the new house drew support, the government adopted a firmly Chalcedonian policy. In the middle of July of 518, within days of Justin's accession, amid stormy scenes of popular insistence, the Patriarch anathematized the Monophysite position. More formal ecclesiastical reaffirmation of Chalcedonian allegiance was made in a synod on July 20 of that year. The change in policy was promulgated in synods and gatherings throughout the provinces. The removal of the Monophysite faction from its position of power was accompanied by violent and ruthless persecution of the Monophysite sectaries. Nevertheless, however concentrated the effort, it was impossible as yet to scour out systematically all of the centers of the dissenting creed, especially in Syria and Egypt. There appears to have been a slackening in the pace of persecution a few years after the assassination of the more fanatically Chalcedonian Vitalian in 520. Perhaps partly as a result of the temporary suspicion that uncompromising repression might not be the most effective course, this slackening continued until Justin's last year. But a renewed application of stringent measures against the Monophysites was apparently made in 527, during Justin's and Justinian's joint rule. This policy continued into the initial years of the latter's sole rule.

Closely linked to the Monophysite question was, inevitably, that of relations with Rome. The so-called Acacian Schism, dating from the days of Zeno's *Henōtikón* (482), had never been healed under Anastasius. Indeed, it had only worsened, since that Monophysitically inclined Emperor had stubbornly retained as an article of policy the very *Henōtikón* which was so hateful to Rome. As a result, the last contacts with Pope Hormisdas in Rome were broken off in 517. A year later, the new regime of Justin I and Justinian made it a primary policy to renew relations with Rome. Messages of goodwill were exchanged, and the Pope was even invited to come to Constantinople to preside over the liquidation of all disagreements. This was a difficult point, however, for the Roman Pontiff was, after all, under the immediate authority of Theodoric, the Ostrogothic King of Italy, who would have some voice in any such plans. Theodoric was, to be sure, theoretically a subordinate of the Emperor; but Constantinople's actual power over the King was all but nonexistent. Theodoric was, moreover, an Arian Christian whose attitude towards the reestablishment of orthodox accord between Rome and the Empire would have to be taken into account.

Pope Hormisdas therefore chose to send legates to Constantinople in the early months of 519. They brought with them the Pope's *Libellus*, the formula reaffirming Chalcedonian orthodoxy to which the Patriarch and his hierarchy were to subscribe. In due course this document was signed, on March 28, 519, though the circumstances of the proceedings were manipulated so that the Emperor's position in religious affairs was in no way prejudiced or undercut by the victory of Rome as the champion of Chalcedonian orthodoxy.

This reconciliation was diligently promoted by Justinian, who was beginning to emerge more definitely as the power behind his uncle's throne. Hormisdas died shortly after these events (August 6, 523), and his successor, John I (523–526) took up the scheme of a personal visit to the Eastern capital. The plan now received definite encouragement from King Theodoric. The Arian monarch was beginning to feel dangerously isolated among the non- or anti-Arian powers around him in the West. He had decided to seek closer ties with the Emperor in Constantinople, and he hoped that a visit by the Bishop of Rome to Constantinople would be to his benefit. And so in the early spring of 526 Pope John traveled eastward. When he arrived in the capital he was received magnificently; showered with honors, he was required by Justin to recrown him personally as Emperor. In spite of the festivities of the first visit of a Roman Pontiff to Constantinople, and for all the significance of the celebrated accord between the two powers, the episode ended tragically. When the Pope returned home after a very brief stay he was faced with the wrath of Theodoric, whose hopes in the embassy had not been fulfilled to his satisfaction. Pope John died on May 18, 526, under the shadow of the King's disfavor and mistreatment.

This reconciliation was, however, only a start in the right direction. If Rome and Constantinople were once again united in the Chalcedonian creed, the Eastern Church elements represented by Alexandria and Antioch had yet to be brought back into harmony. The problem of ending the Monophysite dissent had not been solved by persecution, as Justinian recognized again in the early years of his independent rule. Consequently, before the third decade of the century had ended, Justinian began to consider seriously the possibilities of a conciliatory policy. A new and complicating factor was already making itself felt as well, for within the Emperor's own circle there was a powerful pro-Monophysite force. Its source was no less than the Empress Theodora herself. Whether from her own upbringing or from the time spent in the Eastern provinces, Theodora had become devoted to the Monophysite doctrines. She was determined to assist her co-sectarians, and her perseverance and machinations to this end, before Justinian's eyes or behind his back, constituted the principal area of her divergence from her husband's aims. She was ready to resort to deceit and intrigue when necessary, but she was able at times to soften Justinian's zeal, encouraging his schemes of reconciliation. Perhaps we may detect her influence to be behind Justinian's suspension, by 529, of his persecution of Monophysites and his encouragement of their exiled leaders to return. He even had hopes of effecting some kind of understanding between opposing religious leaders through conferences which were held in the capital under his sponsorship in 531. These produced no more than debates and an exchange of ideas, but failure did not deter Justinian from continuing to seek a basis for understanding.

By this time he had found what promised to be just such a basis. Early in Justin's reign, in 519, some Scythian monks had developed a compromise theory that, after his initial opposition, had won Justinian's favor. This was the so-called Theopaschite theory, the first of a long line of attempts to put the number "one" in a statement of belief in such a way as to satisfy the Monophysites without entirely destroying the Chalcedonian position. This particular formula stated that "one of the Trinity suffered in the flesh." In other words, though the manifestation of Divinity (*theós*) in Christ was an entity, it was in Its incarnate human form that It could be brought to suffer (*páschein*). Thus, even though Christ's suffering was human, fleshly suffering, He was still a Divine Entity. Justinian had sought in vain to have the skeptical Pope Hormisdas approve this doctrine in 519. Now, in the early 530's, he sought to promote it on his own initiative as *the* compromise formula. In 533 an edict embodying this doctrine was issued, and it even received endorsement from the current Pope, John II (533–535), who was eager to extend the cooperation between Rome and Constantinople.

As might have been expected, this latest compromise attempt was a failure, since it satisfied the basic requirements of neither side. The extremists of both factions rejected the Theopaschite formula outright, oblivious of any pressure from Justinian. Undaunted, the Emperor proceeded to sanction even further compromise of his orthodox goals. Theodora's influence seems now to have triumphed, and the ensuing developments are credited to her Monophysite initiative. The Patriarchal throne of Constantinople had become vacant with the death of Epiphanius (520–535). Under Theodora's influence, Anthimus, Bishop of Trebizond, was chosen to succeed him. Since Anthimus was pro-Monophysite in sympathy and opinion, he initiated an open policy of friendship and cooperation with the leading Monophysite prelates. It was to such a relaxation of standards as this that Justinian had been brought by his desire to smooth over the disrupting religious dissent posed by the Monophysite problem.

So drastic a relaxation soon provoked mounting opposition among the Chalcedonian adherents. Justinian was finally moved to abandon the conciliatory program by a dramatic intervention from Rome. The new Gothic King, Theodahad, followed in Theodoric's footsteps by sending the Pope as his intermediary in current negotiations with the Emperor in hopes of staving off Justinian's plans to attack the Ostrogothic kingdom. Therefore the new (since May 535) Pope, Agapetus, was dispatched to Constantinople. Again a Roman Pontiff was welcomed cordially by the Emperor. The Chalcedonian party in the East seized this opportunity to persuade Agapetus to act forcefully in their interests and curb the current Monophysite drift in the Patriarchate of the capital. Agapetus thereupon deposed Anthimus in March of 536 and personally consecrated his orthodox successor, Menas

(536–552). The Pope himself died in the capital during the following month. Menas called a synod in Constantinople in May of 536, which decreed a forceful reversal of the recent pro-Monophysite developments. Since Justinian was in need of good standing with the orthodox Chalcedonian peoples in the West to further his plans against the Ostrogoths in Italy, he decided to suffer this rejection of his program. It was to be the last time he would follow the leadership of a Roman Pontiff. He nevertheless endorsed the new Patriarch's policy by instituting a new persecution of Monophysites throughout the East. Later, the Papal legate Pelagius spent some time at the court to serve as the Emperor's Chalcedonian conscience.

With Justinian's return "to the right" in his religious policy, the pro-Monophysite interests of Theodora went underground. What she had failed to win by influence over the Emperor she now sought to achieve through intrigue. A number of Monophysite leaders, including the deposed Patriarch Anthimus, were concealed within the safety of the apartments of Theodora's palace. More directly, she found an opportunity to wreak her vengeance on the Roman See itself. On the death of Agapetus in Constantinople, the Gothic King Theodahad had secured the election (June 536) of Silverius, the son of the late Pope Hormisdas, as the new Pontiff. This impolitic dependence of the new Pope upon Gothic support was his undoing. Theodora had been hoping to install her own candidate on the vacant throne of St. Peter. The Papal *Apokrisiários* (Nuncio) to Constantinople was then a prominent Roman deacon named Vigilius, who had for some time nourished ambitions of becoming Pope. He convinced the Empress that he would be her willing agent in fostering Monophysite interests, and so she sent him back to Rome with liberal support and endorsements to secure the Papacy. By the time he reached Italy, however, Silverius was already installed. Thus checked, Theodora first tried to do business with Silverius, but he refused her demands for the restoration of Anthimus. This bold stand determined her to have him deposed and replaced by her favorite, Vigilius.

In that goal Theodora was amply supported by circumstances. At the end of 536 Belisarius had taken Rome from the Goths, and his first occupation of the city had begun. Silverius had done his best to welcome Justinian's armies and to dissociate himself from the Goths, but he was in an exposed position now. Theodora connived with Antonina, who was with her husband in Rome, to frame a case against Silverius as a pro-Gothic traitor. Whatever the Monophysite intentions of her action, Theodora could expect anything but opposition from Justinian in this matter. The Emperor himself was angered over the appointment of Silverius by Gothic influence, and wished to secure for himself the power to confirm, if not also to choose, the Roman Pontiff. Therefore Belisarius began a process of alternate cajoling and intimidating of the innocent but compromised and adamantly anti-Monophysite Pope, whom he finally deposed. Silverius was sent into exile, and died shortly thereafter. Meanwhile, on March 29, 537, Vigilius was safely installed as Pope.

Theodora was, however, to be bitterly disappointed in her hopes for manipulating the Roman See to Monophysite ends. Out of her sight, Vigilius proceeded to take a firmly Chalcedonian position. His legate Pelagius managed to keep peace between the courts, but Theodora now had a new grudge to nourish against Rome. Even so, this setback by no means hindered her zealous furtherance of the Monophysite cause. The many Monophysite leaders who had been brought to Constantinople to be kept under surveillance used their situation to spread their creed in the capital itself. With Theodora's help, some of them even obtained favor at court. She already had sponsored the election of the pro-Monophysite Theodosius as Patriarch of Alexandria. But he had had to be imposed by force upon the strife-torn city in 535 with the aid of Narses. Theodosius was soon deposed from his See, in 537, amid a reaction against his views and in the wake of Justinian's reversal of policy after Agapetus' visit in 536. One result was the creation of a divided succession to the Patriarchal throne of Alexandria, as the Monophysites continued to recognize Theodosius and his line instead of the sequence of Imperial appointees. Nevertheless, Theodosius himself was not harshly treated, since Theodora kept watch over the Monophysite prelate's interests. She even managed to have him and some of his followers provided with a monastery in Sycae, directly across the Golden Horn from Constantinople in the area later to be called Galata. Here they were left largely unmolested by the Emperor as long as they did not parade their sentiments openly. This monastery became one of the principal centers of clandestine Monophysite enterprise thereafter. From it emerged missionaries who were sent to undermine the Emperor's own missionary work in Nubia, and who aided the spread of Monophysite Christianity among the Ghassanid Arabs. Perhaps Theodora's greatest success in this regard was the dispatch of Jacob Baradaeus (Barad'ai or Baradai) as the underground leader of the oppressed Monophysites of Syria. She had this monk of Sycae secretly consecrated Bishop of Edessa in 543 by the former Patriarch, Theodosius. For some thirty-five years this dedicated and resourceful man evaded all obstacles and danger of capture to preserve his flock in Syria and beyond, winning new converts and maintaining the essential structure of a secret clergy. In token of his achievement, the Syrian Monophysite Church became known thereafter as the Jacobite Church. Through such activities Theodora could congratulate herself that the fire of the Monophysite heresy was kept burning throughout the Eastern provinces of the Empire, whatever efforts her husband made to extinguish it by force.

Theodora's grudge against the treacherous Vigilius still remained to be settled. Her opportunity for retaliation came in a controversy which arose out of new ecclesiastical intrigue. About this time Palestine was the scene of a revival and elaboration of some ideas of the early Christian Church Father Origen (A.D. 182–251), a brilliant Alexandrian theologian whose ideas had nonetheless come to be considered heterodox. There was extensive opposition in the Eastern churches to the spread of these suspect ideas. Even so, one of the principal exponents of them, Theodore Askidas, for a time won the respect and favor of Justinian, and was even given the episcopal See of Caesarea in Palestine. Resenting his influence with the Emperor, the Constantinopolitan Patriarch Menas and the Papal legate Pelagius joined forces to arrange the condemnation of the Origenist doctrines. Justinian was won over to their point of view, and in 543 he promulgated an edict proscribing the doctrines as heresies. Pope Vigilius was persuaded to endorse this move, while Theodore Askidas himself, as Bishop of Caesarea, was obliged to accept defeat and sign his own endorsement of the edict.

Determined to have his revenge for this humiliation, and to regain his position of influence at court, Askidas provoked a new controversy which was to have prolonged repercussions. Himself an Origenist and apparently also a crypto-Monophysite, Askidas chose as his target certain theologians of the past whose views offended him. He directed the Emperor's attention to their writings, in particular those of Theodore of Mopsuestia, which had long been hateful to both Origenists and Monophysites alike as associated with Nestorianism. The writings of Theodore of Mopsuestia, plus some by Theodoret of Cyrrhus and Ibas of Edessa, were at odds with but not flatly condemned at Chalcedon. Askidas suggested to the Emperor that by condemning their writings he could cleanse the Chalcedonian position of features which still offended the Monophysites as tainted with Nestorianism. This proposal attracted Justinian. Here was a new method — imposed by Imperial fiat, which itself would especially appeal to the autocratic Emperor — that promised to reconcile the Monophysites to the Council of Chalcedon. Wiser heads were skeptical, knowing the likelihood that compromise would please extremists of neither side. Many Monophysite spokesmen, eager to see any compromise of the Chalcedonian position, indicated approval of the plan, and Theodora rapidly threw her support behind it. Pelagius was no longer in Constantinople, so that his stabilizing influence was unavailable. The arguments of Askidas were convincing. When the Imperial theologian studied the texts himself, he agreed, and whole-heartedly fell in with the scheme. Therefore he prepared his "Edict of the Three Chapters," condemning the works of the three disputed theologians.[6] The Eastern Patriarchs were persuaded to endorse the edict, which was finally promulgated in the year 546.

6. The expression "The Three Chapters" must be used with caution, for it has often been applied carelessly to the proscribed writings of the three theologians, Theodore of Mopsuestia, Theodoret of Cyrrhus, and Ibas of Edessa, themselves. It is, on the contrary, the proper designation for Justinian's own edict of condemnation, and for the position which the Emperor took on the issue, see Bury, *History of the Later Roman Empire* . . . (A.D. 395–565), II, 384.

It now remained to secure Papal support. Justinian felt that by bringing the Pontiff personally to Constantinople he could remove him from any hostile Roman influence and bend him to the Imperial will. Theodora readily encouraged any plan likely to humiliate Vigilius. It was arranged to carry off the Pope abruptly in November of 545 as he was officiating in a ceremony, amid a great show of military force by Imperial troops. It is not entirely clear whether or not Vigilius left against his will, but he did tarry in Sicily on his journey, and there he acquainted himself with the tenor of opposition to Justinian's intentions among Western ecclesiastical leaders. The Latin prelates saw no reason to condemn the three long-dead theologians. They could not but recognize the dangers of adjusting the Chalcedonian position. Vigilius decided to oppose the edict and continued his eastward journey slowly, arriving in Constantinople only in January of 547. Although received with cordiality by Justinian, he was presently subjected to extreme pressures intended to make him yield to the Emperor's wishes. Since he was a shallow and vacillating person, Vigilius' determination gradually crumbled. He finally yielded in substance, though he attempted to salvage something of the Papal dignity by preparing an affirmative opinion of his own, rather than simply subscribing to the Emperor's decree. Therefore, at the end of 548 he published his *Judicatum* or "Pronouncement," agreeing with the condemnation of the disputed writings, though he insisted on the continued validity of the decisions of Chalcedon.

For all his efforts at saving face, Vigilius had bowed to the Emperor in matters of policy. Theodora could breathe her last in June of 548 with the feeling that something of her old hatred for the unreliable Pontiff had been vindicated. Perhaps she might even have been able to die anticipating that for him the worst was yet to come. For Vigilius was promptly greeted by a storm of protest from the clergy in the West. Stunned and frightened by the bitterness of this reaction, Vigilius wavered in his new course. Now insisting on abrogating his own *Judicatum*, he asserted that only a new ecumenical council could pronounce the formal adjudication required. Being assured of the Pope's support for the Imperial policy nonetheless, Justinian yielded to this demand. The Pope continued to reside in the Eastern capital as preparations for the council were undertaken.

Opposition continued to mount, in the East as well as in the West. Justinian beat it down as best he could, issuing a renewal of his "Edict of the Three Chapters" in 551. When the Pope's support was again sought, Vigilius refused to take a stand on the Edict before the meeting of the council, which Justinian was increasingly reluctant to call formally. The Pope was soon moved to excommunicate the Patriarch Menas and Justinian's henchman Theodore Askidas for their support of their sovereign. Relations between the Pontiff and the Emperor deteriorated. Soon fearing for his safety, Vigilius took refuge in a Constantinopolitan church in August of 551. Soldiers were sent to remove him by force. Vigilius clung to the heavy marble altar for dear life and was all but crushed when it collapsed in the scuffle. Even his tormentors were abashed and withdrew, but the Pope was soon secured under house arrest. In December 551 he escaped from the capital to Chalcedon. A prolonged phase of bickering and haggling between Justinian and Vigilius ensued. Only with the Emperor's renewed assurances of deference to the Pope, loyalty to Chalcedonian doctrine, and a genuine summons of a new council, was Vigilius sufficiently mollified to return to Constantinople.

Fully committed now to the council he had never really wanted, Justinian actively began to make arrangements for it. As its opening in Constantinople drew near, it was the turn of the Pope to hold back. He feared he would compromise Papal authority by participating, and he still resisted yielding to the Emperor's wishes as far as the three disputed theologians were concerned. The council finally convened without him in May 553. It had been carefully packed to favor Justinian's program, and it wasted no time. In a rubber-stamp action, it rejected Vigilius' recantation of his earlier decision to condemn the three theologians, who were forthwith formally anathematized. For his vacillation and obstinacy the Pope himself was denounced and his name was removed from the diptychs of the Church as a recognized Pontiff. Within a month, in June 553, the Fifth Ecumenical Council ended.

As regards the Papacy, Justinian was soon able to seal his triumph. Vigilius was under arrest and powerless in Constantinople. As a result of the conquests by Narses, meanwhile, Italy was fully in the Emperor's hands. The Pope's only hope of recovering his position was to yield. Therefore Vigilius made his final doctrinal rotation: by December 553 he indicated his acceptance of the Fifth Council's decrees, and he issued a formal statement to that effect in the following February. Accepting his submission, the Emperor sent him back to Rome. Ironically, the pathetic Vigilius died on the way back (June 7, 555), and reached Rome only as a corpse for burial. Justinian next played his trump card. The leader of the opposition in the West to the condemnation of the three theologians had been the archdeacon, and former legate, Pelagius. His continued resistance had earned him incarceration. He was nevertheless a man of integrity and ability who could be used to advantage. With Italy now firmly in the Emperor's power, the Papacy was his pawn and his gift. Justinian offered Pelagius the Papal tiara in return for acceptance of the Council's decrees. As Paris was worth a Mass, Rome was worth a signature: following his late master's example, Pelagius yielded. He was straightway enthroned as the new Pontiff (556–561).

With this sordid episode Justinian had clearly won a triumph over the Papacy. Humiliated and thoroughly under the Emperor's thumb in all matters, from election to doctrine, it had been brought by Justinian to a new low as a dependency of the Emperor in Constantinople. So it was to remain in one degree or another for more than a century. For what it was worth, however, this was perhaps Justinian's only profit from the affair of the Three Chapters and the Fifth Ecumenical Council. Rabid opposition in the West continued, even if it was largely silenced in the East. What was worse, these authoritarian actions by no means removed the problem they were intended to solve. The opposition had been right: by his Three Chapters scheme Justinian had tinkered with the Chalcedonian stand without providing any genuine basis for appeasing the Monophysites. The latter sect's extremists would still accept no compromise short of full capitulation, complete abandonment of Chalcedon. Oppressed by persecution and disfavor, they still doggedly persisted — and survived — in their dissenting creed. In 553 the gap between Chalcedonian orthodoxy and Monophysitism yawned as widely as ever.

Though Justinian's religious preoccupations by no means ended in 553, the Fifth Council may be regarded as the terminus of his major activities in this sphere. His very last involvements in ecclesiastical affairs belong more properly to our subsequent consideration of his final years.

The Persian Problem

The allure of explanations in which the East is pitted against the West, Asia against Europe, as a consistent theme in history is always to be guarded against. Yet, it remains true that much of the history of the Mediterranean world must be read with this point of view at least partially in mind. Such a polarization began in the days of Classical Greece: every schoolboy knows (or should know) the epic story of the heroic Greek resistance to the Persian aggressors from Asia. The polarization, thus begun, was to continue in one form or another for centuries thereafter, not exempting the age of Justinian.

The Persians emerged in history as the last great heirs of the imperial tradition in the ancient Near East. Out of the Iranian plateau they pushed westward and under Cyrus the Great (550–530 B.C.) occupied the remnants of the last Babylonian Empire. Led by Cyrus and his successors, the Achaemenid Persians came to rule not only Persia itself and the Mesopotamian valley, but most of Asia Minor, Syria-Palestine, and Egypt. Though an oriental despotism in the best tradition, the resulting Persian Empire was in its way a remarkably effective multi-national state, serving as no small example to the Romans themselves in the techniques of imperial rule. Such was the mighty empire which received its astonishing rebuff from the Greeks in the successive Persian efforts under Darius in 490 B.C. and Xerxes in 480–479 B.C. The Persian menace gradually shrank for the Greeks until the situation was reversed during the fourth century B.C. In the fantastic campaigns of Alexander the Great of Macedon (337–323), the Persian Empire crumbled before Macedonian valor, and Alexander himself became the heir and successor of the Persian Great King, King of Kings. During the scramble for succession after Alexander's death in 323 B.C. his diverse empire was broken up, and the old Persian realms failed to survive as an entity amongst the various Hellenistic dynastic states.

Amid the rubble of the late Hellenistic Age a new Asiatic force gradually did assert itself in this area as the avowed heir to Achaemenid Persia. This was the people known as the Parthians. Rather wild in nature, they were spendid horsemen and they did have an energetic native dynasty, the Arsacids. Under them an impressive, partly Hellenized, Parthian state was developed. The remnants of the Hellenistic Seleucid kingdom were beaten back, and by the end of the second century B.C. the Parthians were in a good position to attempt a restoration of something of the old Achaemenid Persian realm. At this point their advances were opposed by the countervailing expansion of Rome. As Roman authority spread more thoroughly into the East, the united Mediterranean world was again marshalled against the new "Eastern problem" in the form of the Parthians. Crassus, the wealthy and vain colleague of Julius Caesar and Pompey in the First Triumvirate, sought to win military laurels for himself against the Parthians: instead, he lost his life as a result of the terrible disaster for Roman arms in the Battle of Carrhae (53 B.C.). Caesar himself was making preparations for a great expedition to avenge this defeat and to settle the Parthian question when he was assassinated in 44 B.C. Under Augustus the frontiers shared with the Parthians were fairly well stabilized, largely confining their empire east of the Euphrates River. In the early Imperial period Rome was even able to intervene in Parthian internal affairs and to exert some control over the Arsacid rulers at times. One Emperor, Trajan (A.D. 98–117), decided to take the bull by the horns and annex Parthia. His ambitious campaigns met with some success but were terminated by his death, and some of his conquests beyond the Euphrates were abandoned by his more prudent successor, Hadrian (A.D. 117–138). Though frontier irritations continued, Parthia lingered on as either a vassal or a generally inferior power for the next century.

Thereafter, however, the Eastern problem was given new point. Simultaneously with the decline of the Arsacid Parthian power, the Persians themselves underwent a new national revival in

their Iranian homeland. Under the leadership of the noble, Arde-
shir, the Persians began to challenge Parthian overlordship. The
inevitable clash (A.D. 226 or 227) was won resoundingly by the
Persians. The Arsacid Parthian state was replaced by that of
the new Persian house of Sassan. The Sassanids revived the old
Achaemenid title of *Shahinshah*, "King of Kings," sought to renew
the old Achaemenid pretensions to vast empire, and moved the
capital from Iranian Persepolis to Parthian Ctesiphon on the Euphrates. Under them Persia enjoyed a great new resurgence of its
culture and especially of its fire-worshiping Zoroastrian religion.

The emergence of Sassanid Persia quite altered the border
situation in the Near East. Rome very soon felt the weight of
aggressive Persian arms pressing on its frontiers. When the Emperor Valerian (253–259) led his army against the Persians he
was initially successful against them, but he was taken captive
by treachery and was submitted to a humiliating imprisonment
and ignominious death. The Roman frontiers continued for the
next century to resist fulfilling the Sassanid dreams of Achaemenid revival. Nevertheless, the military Emperors during that
period had to devote their efforts diligently to maintaining these
frontiers. A favorable stability was achieved under Diocletian
(284–305). Renewed war broke out seriously in the reign of Constantine the Great's son and principal successor, Constantius II
(337–361). So serious a menace to the Empire were the Persians
deemed that Constantius' successor, Julian the Apostate (361–
363), fired by the example of Trajan and the glory of Alexander,
was inspired to undertake a bold but probably reckless campaign
across the Euphrates. After some initial progress the campaign became bogged down, however, and it then disintegrated with
the premature death of the young Emperor. His shallow successor,
Jovian (363–364), made a necessary but humiliating treaty with
Persia which provided for Roman withdrawal and territorial
concessions. This ended the last actual attempt by Roman rulers
to wage a war of conquest against Persian lands. Henceforth the
Empire's stance was largely defensive in this area.

The nature of the relationship between the Romans and the
Sassanid Persians requires one clarification. The Persians posed a
very different problem from what Rome faced on its other frontiers

during and after the third century. Unlike the Germans and other such peoples, the Persians were not barbarians in the modern sense of the word. They were a civilized and sophisticated nation with a long cultural tradition of their own. Their government was a generally honorable one with which the Romans could deal on terms of equality and mutual respect. The Near Eastern situation up to and beyond the age of Justinian was therefore one dominated by two great powers, now friendly, now hostile, but neither expecting the other to disintegrate or disappear. They could coexist on terms of outward courtesy and respect. They could also cooperate on mutually beneficial projects, as they did in 387, when Theodosius I made a treaty with Persia by which Armenia, then ruled by a native line of the old Parthian Arsacid dynasty, was partitioned; a portion of Armenia was absorbed into the Roman Empire, and the remainder continued on as a Persian vassal state under the Arsacid house until that dynasty was deposed in 428, and replaced by a line of Persian governors.

Besides the conflicts of policy and culture, an ideological element was added to the rivalry of the two powers by the triumph of Christianity throughout the Roman world. Across the frontiers of Rome and Persia, Christianity and Zoroastrianism confronted each other, both exclusionist, proselytizing, and, all things considered, equally fanatical. The competition between the two powers was not only political but also religious. Indeed, much of the conflict between Persia and the Empire in the fifth century was over questions of Persian persecution of Christians within Sassanid territory. Actually, there were only very rare hostilities between the two powers during this period, and relations were at times decidedly friendly. There is even a report that in 408 the dying Emperor Arcadius commended his child-successor, Theodosius II, to the Persian King's good will and protection under a kind of guardianship. A treaty was framed in 422 which established a "Hundred Years' Peace."

One reason for the era of general peace during much of the fifth century was the combination of internal and external pressures to which Persia was then subjected. Internally, the Persian kingdom was rent by religious dissensions and unsettled by encroachments of the Magian priesthood upon the royal authority.

Externally, the Persian rulers were struggling against a new threat to their northeastern frontiers, the Ephthalite or "White" Huns, who had established a menacing power between the Oxus and Jaxartes rivers. In the light of such Asiatic threats the Persians and the Romans worked out arrangements for joint frontier fortifications in the Caucasus passes, in the area of the so-called "Caspian Gates." The original provisions for such an arrangement dated from the treaty of 363, but, as direct Roman authority had since been withdrawing from the areas, it was agreed in the treaty of 422 that the Empire should provide annual payments to help finance the Persian defense of the passes.

The question of annual payments became a cause of contention thereafter, with occasional friction resulting. When in 483 the Persians refused to return the Mesopotamian frontier fortress of Nisibis to Roman authority, as they were supposed to do by the 120-year-old treaty with Jovian, the Emperor used this as a justification for refusing to maintain the Caucasus defense payments. The Emperor Zeno maintained this excuse successfully, and when the able Persian King Kavadh I (or Kobad, or Cabades: 488–498, and 501–531) revived the demand in 491, Anastasius I also continued the policy. Kavadh renewed his claim in 502. To press his point, the Persian King invaded Roman Armenia at the end of the year, and then turned his arms against Roman Mesopotamia, seizing in January 503 the Imperial frontier fortress of Amida. Anastasius' armies fought back unsuccessfully, owing partly to the mismanagement of such commanders as his nephew Hypatius. Later in 503 Kavadh blockaded Edessa unsuccessfully, while in 504 the Romans were able to recover Amida. By this time, however, the Persians were distracted by the latest threat from the Ephthalite Huns, and so in 505 Kavadh was obliged to agree to a seven-year truce. Though it was never officially renewed it remained in force for the next two decades, during which time Kavadh was involved in putting the Ephthalites down once and for all, and in various internal preoccupations. In the interval Anastasius strengthened the Roman frontier position by building an important outpost at Daras (or Dara) near Nisibis. Kavadh protested, but he was not free to retaliate until some five years after Anastasius was dead.

The latest renewal of Kavadh's hostilities with the Empire brings us at last to the era of Justinian's dealings with Persia. In addition to Persian irritation at the Roman fortification of Daras, difficulties arose also from Roman and Sassanid competition in the Caucasus region. Here there flourished various peoples and states upon which this rivalry was focused, most particularly Iberia (Georgia), and the kingdom of Lazica (ancient Colchis) at the eastern end of the Black Sea; the latter had already become a vassal state of the Empire. A further incident added to Kavadh's resentments. Impressed by Justin I's personal fairness and frankness in their dealings, Kavadh hit upon an idea to bolster his plan to win succession for his favorite son, Khusru (or Chosroes), who was only the fourth in line for the throne. He invited Justin to adopt Khusru as his son. Justin and Justinian favored acceptance of the idea, but advisers pointed out that, as Justin's adopted son, Khusru might then be in the position of heir to the Roman throne, which would never do. Further complications arose over the Persian claims to Lazica, and so the whole project came to nothing, much to Kavadh's resentment. Determined also to pursue his interests in the Caucasus, Kavadh decided to break the treaty of 422, supposedly still in effect.[7] In 524 his forces invaded Iberia, overran it, and brought Roman influence there to an end. The Emperor's forces struck back from their Lazian bases. Counter-efforts against Persian Armenia were attempted in 526 under the command of Theodora's brother-in-law Sittas, and another commander who appears for the first time here: a young man named Belisarius, still in his twenties. Nevertheless, renewed offensives by the Persians prevented any substantial Roman gains.

The scene of conflict was soon expanded to include Mesopotamia, however. Operations against the Persians were opened inconsequentially in 527. By the following year the command there had been given to Belisarius, who now emerges as the leading general in this conflict. An attempt to extend the fortifications at Daras in 528 brought a Persian attack. The next year or so was

7. Vasiliev, *Justin the First*, p. 269, notes the claim of Procopius that the breaking of the Roman buffer zone in Lazica was to be the first step in an ambitious Persian plan to conquer Constantinople and the whole of the Empire by working westward from this base along the Black Sea.

consumed in fruitless fighting. The first major battle of the war, and Belisarius' first great personal triumph, came in June of 530, when his force met a Persian army about twice its own size, and defeated it brilliantly. There was talk of negotiation, but hostilities continued. The Persians moved on Antioch and were intercepted by Belisarius in April 531 at Callinicum. The battle there went against the great general, and caused his brief replacement by Mundus.

The Empire's forces continued to be successful, however, and the death of Kavadh, who was succeeded after all by his son Khusru (September 531), prepared the way for genuine negotiations. Justinian himself was more than ready for them. The wasteful preoccupations on the Persian frontier were a great irritation to him. They were tying down his military forces and had already consumed much of the treasury surplus accumulated in the days of Anastasius I. With his dreams of great things westward, Justinian welcomed an end to these distractions. After much negotiation, the avowed "Perpetual Peace" was settled in the spring of 532. By its terms of friendship and alliance the Persians were left with Iberia, but respective conquests in Lazica and Persarmenia were returned; the Empire retained Daras, though this fortress was not to be the actual seat of the Roman commander in Mesopotamia; finally, Justinian agreed to pay an annual sum of 11,000 pounds of gold, which was supposedly in payment for the Caucasus defenses, but which smelled faintly of tribute, however politely perfumed.

Though far from "perpetual," the peace was an immediately workable one which untied Justinian's attentions, arms, and war chest. In Belisarius he now had a gifted general who had further proved himself in the Nika Riots. After that catalytic episode Justinian's master projects were set fully in motion without the distraction of any second-front hostilities with Persia.

It was a situation which was, however, not to last. The new Persian King, Khusru I, surnamed "Anosharvan" ("Of Immortal Spirit"), was one of the greatest of the Sassanids, whose reign (531–579) was a period of particular glory, might, and internal reorganization for Persia. This brilliant monarch soon came to view with increasing chagrin the grand accomplishments which

Justinian was now free to pursue in his great Western projects. He even sent a sardonic message to Justinian demanding a share in the spoils of the conquered Vandal kingdom, since its conquest by the Empire had really been made possible only by the peace which the Persian King had granted Justinian; a suggestion which Justinian actually took with some seriousness.[8] Indeed, the expansion of Justinian's power and influence in many directions began to alarm the King of Kings. Even during the years of peace between the Empire and Persia, Justinian had been diligently strengthening the Roman frontier position in Mesopotamia and elsewhere. There were many interests of his own which the Persian King could further in renewing hostilities. Also, in 539 there were urgent communications from the Gothic King, Wittigis, then falling back before the victorious Belisarius in Italy, which asked the Persians to renew war with the Emperor who was, after all, their common foe. Similar pleas and encouragements were contributed by Justinian's restless Armenian subjects. There was also a final incident in the controversy between the respective Arab vassal states of Persia and the Empire, the Lakhmids of Hira and the Ghassanids, of whom we shall have more to say shortly. Thus, by the end of 539, sufficient irritations had accumulated to provide Khusru with pretexts for breaking the peace in the following year.

With the King in personal command, the Persians invaded Syria in the spring of 540, taking Sura, and menacing Antioch itself. This great metropolis was inadequately defended. The Emperor's cousin Germanus was sent to look to its fortifications and, despairing of their weaknesses, he withdrew from the city with the explanation that his own presence there might only further tempt the Persian King to take it. But Khusru did not require the inducement of capturing a member of the Imperial house to lure him against one of the Empire's richest cities. Antioch, exposed as it was, gave the Persian King an opportunity to deliver to the Empire a humiliating blow. The city was stormed and subjected to all the horrors of massacre, pillage, and destruction. Even while negotiations for peace were being opened, Khusru continued his campaign of devastation. Along his march northwards

8. Procopius, *Wars*, Book I, chap. xxvi, secs. 2–4.

he extorted ransoms from those cities he deigned to leave untouched. Then, turning eastward, he made a vain attempt to seize
Daras, and he finally abandoned his siege of it only on payment of
further ransom. Justinian had been willing to accept Khusru's
heavy peace terms, but in view of the King's continued rapacity in
the midst of truces and talk of peace, all dealings were angrily
broken off. Justinian hardly wanted a major new Persian conflict
on his hands. At this time, however, by 540, the conquest of Italy
seemed complete and Belisarius was available for the Persian
front once more. If Khusru wanted war, war he would have.

As the conflict that would last another twelve years formally
commenced, the theaters of action were expanding. In the wake
of their successful annexation of Iberia, the Persians turned their
attention towards Lazica, to extend westward, to the Black Sea
coast, their conquest of the lands south of the Caucasus Mountains. The disaffected Lazian King provided the pretext by invit-
ing in the Persians. Khusru led the new Persian effort here in
person. The Lazi submitted to Persian rule and Khusru proceeded
to capture the principal Roman outpost in Lazica, Petra. But
further operations were cut off in this area. News reached the
Persian King that Belisarius was, in the spring of 541, back in
command in Mesopotamia. Justinian's great commander had
marched boldly into Persian territory; while his Arab auxiliaries
raided freely if independently, Belisarius himself took and destroyed the Persian fortress of Sisaurana. Circumstances then
obliged him to withdraw without accomplishing much else, save
to direct Khusru's attentions back to this area. Khusru now contemplated a descent upon Palestine in 542, with sacred Jerusalem
itself as the main goal. Belisarius was sorely lacking in adequate
forces, but with the use of clever bluffing, and aided by the outbreak of plague in Persia, he induced the King to return across
the Euphrates, to plunder his way home to Ctesiphon. This was
Belisarius' final performance in Justinian's Persian wars, for the
Roman position in supposedly conquered Italy had collapsed, and
the general was now recalled to attend to the fighting there.

The wars with the Persians dragged on. In the spring of 543
Khusru made an abortive attempt to attack Roman Armenia. Justinian countered by ordering Roman commanders to attack Per-

sarmenia, but there the Imperial efforts only encountered defeat. In 544 Khusru returned to Mesopotamia and mounted a fierce attack on Edessa; it failed, and the King of Kings was obliged to content himself with a ransom. By 545 both sides were ready for a truce. A five-year term was formally agreed upon, in exchange for payment by Justinian of 2,000 pounds of gold — plus the services of a distinguished Palestinian physician whom Khusru admired.

Justinian would have welcomed an end to Khusru's aggressions: the Empire was committed on two fronts, now that war was renewed in Italy. His best troops and Belisarius, his best commander, were required there. But even the truce was not to bring much respite on the Eastern front. In the very process of implementing it, the perfidious King made an attempt to seize Daras by ruse — unsuccessfully, as it proved. Above all, determined to press their advantages there, the Persians had insisted on excluding Lazica from the terms of the truce. It was to be their loss, for, in spite of elaborate Persian efforts to strengthen their hold on the land, the fanatic zeal of the Magi in attempting to spread Zoroastrianism had antagonized the Christian Lazi. The latter now turned to the Empire once more, and the rival interests of Persians and Romans again brought turmoil and bloodshed to the Caucasus realms. The Romans continued to command the sea. An Imperial force was sent, and after some reverses it was put under the command of the aged general Bessas, who was anxious to redeem his recent poor performance in Italy. He first suppressed a revolt by the vassal state of the Abasgians, to the north of Lazica and just south of the Caucasus Mountains on the Black Sea coast. By 550 the general truce was ended, and while negotiations proceeded to renew it, Bessas pressed the Imperial advantage in Lazica by besieging the cream of the Persian occupation forces in the stronghold of Petra. By spring of 551 this fortress was taken, amid displays of great heroism on both sides. When the truce was renewed in the fall of 551, at a cost of 2,600 more pounds of gold paid by the Emperor, the Lazian theater was still excluded from its terms.

Hostilities continued inconclusively and amid increasing complications. In 555 some of the Imperial officials became embroiled in a dispute with the Lazian King and high-handedly murdered him. This blunder threatened to poison Lazian loyalty until, with a great display of Roman justice, the guilty officials were finally punished in 556. As for the fighting itself, in the course of these operations another of Justinian's kinsmen-commanders, Justin, son of the Emperor's cousin Germanus, emerged in prominent command. Eventually, in 556–557, the truce was due for renewal again. Both sides were exhausted, and so the Persians this time conceded the extension of the truce to Lazica, on a status quo basis, and with neither time limit nor exaction of money from the Empire. The Persians thus had not been driven out of Lazica, where the last phases of the war had been concentrated; but at least the Romans had successfully checked the intended advance of Persia to the Black Sea, thereby preserving their own freedom and control of that waterway.

Arrangements for a final peace on the basis of the 557 truce were delayed another five years. After much haggling, it was eventually agreed in 562 that there should be a fifty-year peace. By its terms the Emperor had to pay an annual sum of 30,000 gold pieces, a part of it in advance, but the Empire was allowed possession of Lazica, and of Daras as well. Elaborate provisions were also made for frontier defenses, for commercial and frontier regulations, as well as for protection of Christians within Persia from Magian persecution.

Thus ended Justinian's Persian wars, a scant three years before his death. Occasional successes aside, they had brought him only irritation, distraction, ruinous expenditure of money and resources, and humiliation. Unlike his own ambitious projects elsewhere, these wars were plainly not ones of conquest. They were provoked by the aggressions of the Persian kings themselves, and were fought by Justinian essentially to protect his frontiers in Syria, Mesopotamia, and Armenia, and to secure Imperial interests in the Caucasus and Black Sea areas. Probably nothing had been less welcome to Justinian, among all his other problems, than these Persian conflicts. In point of fact, they should be considered not so much as an integral part of Justinian's activities — which they really were not — but, instead, simply as his unwilling involvement in the much broader process of the great East-West duel between Imperial Rome and Sassanid Persia, an independent story in its own right.

Before we leave the Persian wars, however, we should note the significance of one related aspect. This is the development by Justinian of an Arab vassal power under the Ghassanid house. The pagan Arab raiders from the deserts beyond the frontier of Mediterranean civilization had long been a danger for Roman frontiers. At times the more civilized Arab tribes had been able to organize important political entities. Most notable of these was the third-century Arab power of Odenathus and his famous Queen Zenobia (to use their Latinized names), centered in the great caravan city of Palmyra (Tadmor), which even challenged Rome and had to be destroyed by Aurelian in A.D. 272. In the late fifth century a central Arabian power, Kindah, became involved with the Empire, and Justinian himself had some dealings with it in the sixth century. The most important of these Arabian powers for our purposes were two great rivals, the Ghassanids and the Persian client state of the Lakhmids.

The Lakhmid power was the elder of the two in order of organization. Of southwest Arabian origin, this house emerged to rule over the tribes that had been migrating to the Euphrates area. The Lakhmid capital came to be Hira, in an area populated extensively by Nestorian Christians. The princes of the house of Lakhm, however, generally remained pagan. In view of their location and obvious dependency, the Lakhmids became a natural client and buffer state for the Persians. By the time of Justinian, the Lakhmids of Hira were reaching their peak under their greatest ruler, al-Mundhir III (ca. 505–554), the "Almoundaros" of Greek sources.

The Lakhmid Saracens served as ideal frontier raiders against Roman territory in Mesopotamia and even Syria. Al-Mundhir III made particularly devastating attacks in Kavadh's service in 523, and Justin I was forced to negotiate a special peace with him in the following year. To counteract such threats the Romans cultivated an Arab client state of their own, the Ghassanids, established in the frontier lands to the southeast of Damascus. The tribesmen under these princes had themselves long been raiders on the

Roman frontiers, but by the beginning of Justinian's reign they were firmly brought into the orbit of the Empire as a buffer to Bedouin attacks and as a rival power to the Lakhmids. Abandoning their original paganism they became Christians and were particularly zealous in their new faith. The greatest of the Ghassanid princes, al-Harith (Arethas to the Greek writers), was a contemporary of Justinian in rule (*ca.* 528–569), emerging as a worthy opponent of al-Mundhir III of Hira. In 529 Justinian gave al-Harith the rank of Patrician and the regal title of Phylarch. Al-Harith led his Saracen auxiliaries regularly in the Persian wars, under such Imperial commanders as Belisarius, with whom, however, he did not get along at all well. His greatest triumph came in 554 when he defeated and killed his old and bitter foe al-Mundhir III the Lakhmid.

Al-Harith's relationship to the Empire was somewhat complicated by the fact that the Christianity which he and his people had so ardently adopted was of the Monophysite brand. Since the Ghassanids were particularly eager to foster the conversion of their pagan Arab brethren in general, the sectarian factor raised problems. Not that Justinian was entirely loath to apply Monophysite zeal to the winning of the Arabs at large. Nevertheless, this Monophysite coloring often impelled Justinian and his successors to check what might have been a powerful force among the pre-Islamic Arabs at a crucial stage in their history. Apparently through Theodora's influence, however, al-Harith's request for a Monophysite bishop for the Syrian Arabs was granted about 542, and some organization of the heretical Church among them was possible, parallel with the work of Jacob Baradaeus. Al-Harith also managed himself to retain high favor with the Roman government. In 563 he was personally received by the aged Justinian at Constantinople, where his commanding appearance made a deep impression on the Emperor and his court. It was only later in the century that the important position of the Ghassanids was ill-advisedly allowed to deteriorate. While Justinian reigned, this significant Saracen state was carefully maintained. Nevertheless, as we shall see presently, this involvement with the Ghassanids was not the only impress the age of Justinian made upon the Arabs.

Diplomacy, Foreign Relations, and Trade

It is very easy to think of power politics and high diplomacy as functions of recent times. Nevertheless, the modern era has hardly had a monopoly on such activities. Whenever there have been states, and whenever these states have had to deal with each other, or with any external power, then there have been diplomacy and international politics. If many of the practices and standards of diplomacy are modern, there was still much scope to the diplomacy of ancient and medieval times. Through much of the medieval period the Byzantine Empire possessed, together with its unrivaled bureaucracy, a diplomatic and intelligence service which could be matched by few, if any states, certainly in Christendom. Byzantine agents ranged widely, and the authorities in the capital often knew more about other states or peoples than the latter knew about themselves. Byzantine diplomats were for centuries the smoothest, most cultivated, and most respected in the Christian world and were in addition usually at least a match for their counterparts in the Islamic world in its flourishing period. With such talents at his disposal, the Emperor in Constantinople was in an often unparalleled position to manipulate difficult circumstances to his advantage, in ways which even many modern powers might well envy.

Nevertheless, there is much that remains to be understood about Byzantine diplomacy. Occasional piecemeal investigations aside, its techniques, qualities, and achievements have yet to be submitted to a thorough examination. When an extensive study is made, the age of Justinian will assume particular significance for a number of reasons: in part simply because of the length of this Emperor's reign, partly because of our extensive information about it, partly because of what he attempted, and partly because of its place at a crucial juncture in the course of the Empire's history. For our purposes, therefore, at least a few cursory observations ought to be made on the nature and implications of Justinian's dealings with foreign powers.

Many of the techniques of Justinian's diplomatic relations were not unique to him, either in the context of his Empire's history or as against the history of any great state and ruler. Yet, his reign does serve as a kind of perfect textbook of their range, variety, and applications — and, to some extent also, of their fallacies. The practices require little explanation: the playing-off of one people or state against another; the cultivation of useful friends in foreign courts; the support of rebellious or dissident elements in a foreign power; the support or retention (or even detention) of a claimant to power from a foreign state; the adjudication of disputes among quarreling peoples, and even the appointment of a new ruler for them; the acquisition, by various means and for various ends, of client states. Above all, the lavish use of money as a diplomatic tool, as an alternative to military power or as a means of winning foreign favor. This Imperial "dollar diplomacy" might assume a variety of forms, from the liberal entertainment of ambassadors in order to impress them with the Empire's generosity towards friends and allies, to the giving of gifts and money payments to foreign powers whose cooperation the Empire desired, or to the payment of large subsidies — which were often in truth simply ill-disguised tribute — in order to persuade menacing neighbors to leave the Empire in peace.

On the whole, we might distinguish six principal (and often interrelated) spheres in which Justinian's diplomacy was active. One is his dealings with the barbarian kingdoms in the West, either those which he was determined to conquer or those which he hoped to use against his targets. These dealings might be characterized as a kind of "offensive diplomacy," and belong properly to our consideration of Justinian's Reconquest projects, which follows in the next chapter. A second sphere is Justinian's dealings with Persia. These deserve a place by themselves, since Persia was the only state with which he was able and indeed obliged to deal not as an inferior power but as an equal. Diplomatic relations with Persia, as an aspect of the military involvement already discussed, were usually for Justinian a matter of negotiating treaties of peace or truce, discussing points of dispute, and settling matters of mutual convenience, all with an end to preserving peace on the troublesome common frontiers — in other words, what we might call "defensive diplomacy." A third sphere of relations, again with defensive ends in mind, was that of his dealings with barbarian peoples of eastern Europe and the Balkans. Since the collapse of Attila's empire a century earlier, and the departure of Theodoric's Ostrogoths a generation after that, the area beyond the frontiers here was populated by a variety of Germanic and non-Germanic peoples, including the Gepids, the Lombards, the Heruls, the Rugians, and the Kotrigur Huns. They were constantly at odds with each other, and Justinian had some success in keeping them so, balancing them off against each other in shifting alliances, interfering in their internal affairs, when possible settling them on Imperial lands and drawing troops from them, and showering subsidies on them when they menaced Imperial territories.

The last three of the six diplomatic spheres are the most inter-related of all, and are often difficult to separate completely, though there are specific cases which can serve to represent each. One must appreciate Justinian's conscious sense of responsibility as the supreme Christian sovereign, whose duty it was to protect and increase the number of Christians abroad. Therefore, above and beyond questions of Church policy, Justinian was a zealous spon-sor of missionary activities, since he genuinely desired to advance the Faith, while he appreciated that its advancement would at the same time extend his Empire's political influence. Even here, however, the problem of sectarian rivalry could not be avoided, as in the case of Nubia. The Emperor sought to convert to Chris-tianity this area south of Egypt, using orthodox missionaries. We are told that they were, however, anticipated by the zeal of the Monophysites, supposedly with Theodora's encouragement. In point of fact, the Monophysites seem to have taken a particular interest in missionary work beyond the frontier, often with some degree of approval from Justinian.

Frequently related to the Emperor's Christian diplomatic re-sponsibilities was the fifth of these spheres, which involved his concerns with striking at the Persians by diplomatic means. We have already seen how Justinian courted the Lazians and Abas-gians in the Caucasus with the express object of frustrating Persian interests, while his cultivation of the Arab Ghassanids was sim-ilarly calculated to harry their particular rivals, the Lakhmid's own masters, the Persians. The Arabian peninsula occupied Jus-tinian's attentions further in these respects. Another focus came to be the area of the Sabaeans; that is, the southwest corner of the peninsula, present-day Yemen. It was at this time in its final phase of prosperity under the Himyarite rulers — or Homeritai, as the Greeks called them. This area had grown to be another center of Christian missionary penetration. It was also a center of Jewish tradition and proselytism among the Arabs. The last of the Himyarite Kings, dhu-Nuwas (or Dhu-Novas), was himself a Jew, and he chose to carry out a rigorous persecution of Christians in the land, culminating in a terrible massacre in October of 523. As theoretical protector of Christians everywhere, the Emperor could not long remain detached from these events. Through the appropriately Monophysite Patriarch of Alexandria, Justin I therefore entered into contact with the Monophysite African Christian state of Abyssinia, then known as Axum. This land was ruled by the latest of a long line of proud and tradition-conscious sovereigns, the *Negus* (or King) Kaleb Ela Asbeha (or Elesboas). He had been nourishing his own ambitions with regard to these lands across the Red Sea. As Christian powers both, regardless of sectarian differences, Abyssinia and the Empire naturally had mutual interests in the matter. So it was that Justin I and Justinian cordially supported an invasion of southwestern Arabia by the Abyssinian King in 525. The results were a triumph for the Christians, who defeated and uprooted the Jewish Himyarite power. The Abyssinians installed a puppet regime of their own and dominated the area for the next fifty years.

Together with their Christian Abyssinian allies, Justin and Justinian hoped that southwestern Arabia might serve as a new bastion of Christianity among the Arabs. Its capital, San'a', and its other great city Najran, were more than ever to be great commercial and ideological rivals to the Arab pagan center to the north, Makkah or Mecca. In addition this Christian outpost, as a toe-hold of Imperial influence, might serve to curtail Persian power in the peninsula. All this, however, was not to be. As the sixth century proceeded, this area declined. The next half-century would reveal that not Christian San'a', or Najran, but Mecca — turned from paganism to a vital new faith — would be the city of the future for the Arabs. Meanwhile, the natives of southwestern Arabia themselves, chafing under Abyssinian domination, were in 575 to call in Persian aid and overthrow their African masters, to become Sassanid subjects for half a century thereafter.

The relations of the Empire with Abyssinia had a further implication which constitutes our sixth sphere of Justinian's diplomatic interests. This is his concern for the trade of the Empire. Certainly commerce flourished in the Eastern Mediterranean under Justinian. Constantinople was a great center of exchange between the European, Asiatic, and Mediterranean worlds; and Syria in particular was a wealthy center of trade and industry. The Empire also had the benefit of a currency that remained wonderfully stable from Constantine to the eleventh century, and which was honored far and wide as an international medium of exchange. But, as noted previously, the Empire had an unfavorable balance of trade with the Far East. Trade with these parts meant a steady importation of luxury items, especially spices, gems, and silk, for which there was particular demand in the Roman world and in the West beyond. One of the cornerstones of Syrian prosperity was the finishing of silk goods, but though there may have been some native production there, the principal supply of raw silk was from abroad. Much of the trade in the Far Eastern luxury items, including silk, was in the hands of Persian middlemen. The Romans could hardly suffer the rival Persians to control the supply of commodities so important to the Empire.

Justinian was therefore eager to open alternative and direct routes to the Far East, to undercut the Persians, and also to strengthen the commercial position of the Empire. There was some hope for progress toward this end in Justinian's contacts with the Black Sea, Caucasus, and Caspian peoples. For this purpose, also, he did his best to strengthen the tenuous Roman position in the Crimea. In fact, little seems to have come of his hope for a practicable route through this area. Instead, it was a southern route, through the Red Sea, which soon seemed most promising. Hence Justinian's cultivation of Abyssinia and support of the latter's position across the Red Sea in Arabia. There appears to have been some lively competition in Ceylon and points east between Christian and Persian merchant interests in this period.[9]

The Abyssinians apparently did their best to cooperate with the

9. We find this situation reflected amid the clutter of the important and fascinating, but strange, work of this period, *The Christian Topography* by Cosmas Indicopleustes, or Cosmas "the Sailor-to-India." Useful general analysis of this material can be found in Vasiliev's *Justin the First*, pp. 367–371, and in Bury's *History of the Later Roman Empire* . . . (A.D. 395–565), II, 319–326.

Empire in this commercial goal, for a time, becoming useful middlemen for at least some of the luxury trade. For various reasons,
however, the Persians still managed to maintain their monopoly of
the silk trade. The hopes for the Red Sea route thus were not
realized in this regard. In the 532 treaty with Persia the latter was
once again acknowledged as the Empire's one source of raw silk.
The renewed hostilities beginning in 540 disrupted the trade again
and imposed great hardship on the Syrian silk-finishing industry.
The abortive attempts Justinian made at regulation of the silk
market only worsened matters. In 542 he took the suggestion of
Peter Barsymes, who was ever on the lookout for new sources of
revenue, and made silk production a state monopoly.

Justinian's ultimate success with the silk problem was the result, however, of his encouragement of a project to smuggle Asiatic
silkworm eggs into the Empire. According to a story which is
probably apocryphal, this feat was accomplished about 554 by
some missionaries who carried their precious cargo in a hollowed-
out staff.[10] However the break-through was achieved it became
possible at long last for the Empire to develop a large-scale native
production of raw silk to meet its needs. This great silk industry
was maintained for centuries thereafter as a vital part of the Byzantine economy and a state monopoly. Such success considerably
encouraged a renewal of prosperity under Justinian. Nevertheless,
in spite of all his efforts, the unfavorable balance of trade with the
Far East in other respects was still not entirely altered by the end
of his reign.

The questions of diplomacy, foreign relations, and trade which
occupied Justinian may serve as the best bridge between his attention to old and normal problems on the one hand and his devotion
to grand new projects on the other, since they are all closely related at many points through these channels. But we may observe
in passing that Justinian's diplomatic activity, though busy, elaborate, far-reaching, and connected with virtually all aspects of his
policies, was not, in spite of frequent successes, uniformly effective. Moreover, as we shall see, the expense it entailed would
combine with others aspects of his activities to produce complex
and gravely negative effects for his Empire.

10. Procopius, *Wars*, Book VIII, chap. xvii, secs. 1–7.

IV THE NEW PROJECTS

The Reconquest as a Policy

The most celebrated external aspect of Justinian's reign is his effort to recover the territories of the western Mediterranean which were in barbarian hands. This effort constituted one of the underlying themes in all that Justinian did, and affected every aspect of his reign. It also provided the setting for the greatest exploits of one of the outstanding personalities associated with him, the gifted general Belisarius.

We have already seen how four major states had been established by Germanic barbarian invaders in the fifth century amid the ruins of the Roman Empire's western provinces. The first was that of the Visigoths, initially in southern Gaul centering around Toulouse but gradually moving southward to encompass instead the Spanish peninsula. The indefatigable Gaiseric (428–477) had established the Vandals in North Africa, with his capital at the great maritime metropolis of Carthage. Then the Franks, united under Clovis (481–511), smashed the remnants of local Gallo-Roman authority in Gaul in 486, and began the absorption of that province, ultimately pushing the Visigoths south beyond the Pyrenees. Finally came the Ostrogothic occupation of Italy by Theodoric (493-526), who established his capital in Ravenna. A fifth, if less important, barbarian state may be added, that of the Burgundians, established before the middle of the fifth century in the area of modern Savoy, between Gaul and Italy. Britain, mean-

Italy and North Africa at the time of the Justinianic Reconquest. (Map courtesy of University of Wisconsin Cartographic Laboratory.)

while, had become the preserve of the pagan Saxons and their associates. These were the peoples who held the actual control of the former western portions of the old Roman world by the time Justinian came to power in Constantinople.

The relations between the Empire in the East and these barbarian kingdoms varied widely at different times. In general, most of the barbarian kings were willing to concede to some extent that the Emperor in Constantinople was the ultimate terrestrial sovereign, and even their overlord in some cases, however little they may have been under his actual control. In point of fact, while some of the kings eagerly sought the Emperor's favor, more often than not they tended to be hostile, overtly or otherwise, in their own policies. It is therefore not surprising that so powerful an Emperor as Justinian should have come to blows with some of these states. Yet, his wars with them were more than the results of mere ill will or conflicts of interest. Justinian's aim was to reconquer and annex as many of the barbarian realms as possible, regardless of the immediate grounds for war. Such an aggressive policy may seem unwarrantably bold to us, but the reasons for it were fully proper and logical in Justinian's eyes, as we must recognize in order to understand the nature of this aspect of the Emperor's reign.

In brief, there are two basic considerations which must be kept in mind with regard to Justinian's Reconquest efforts. First, there is the matter of the kind of state Justinian ruled and the outlook with which he ruled it. It is all too easy to think of Justinian's state as the *Eastern Empire*. With the western Mediterranean, the original seat of Roman power, lost to Imperial sovereignty, and with a group of local barbarian kings taking the place of the Emperor in the West, there is the temptation to suppose that the Roman Empire had ceased to exist, and that in the East there was now something different — something already on its way to becoming what we call the Byzantine Empire as distinct from the Roman. This supposition was certainly not shared by the people of the sixth century A.D., least of all by Justinian himself. For them and for the Emperor there was still a Roman Empire; the fact that Rome as a city and a geographical sphere had been lost was irrelevant, for the Imperial tradition was unbroken, even if it was now centered in the eastern Mediterranean, at the New Rome. In the eyes of all, the magic and misunderstood year of 476 had not ended the Roman Empire, but had merely reunited once again the sovereignty of the entire Roman — that is, the "ecumenical" or "inhabited" — world under the ruler in Constantine's city. As a result, the barbarian-held territories in the West were not those of a previous state that had ceased to exist. They belonged in quite meaningful theory to the Roman state which was still very much alive in the eastern Mediterranean. So, then, the Reconquest program was more than a matter of the "Eastern Empire" attempting to conquer the West. Justinian was less the successor of Arcadius than he was the heir of Constantine the Great and Augustus.

Finally, we must add to this picture Justinian's own perspective. It is true that the Eastern sphere of the Mediterranean world was largely Greek in outlook and was characterized by many aspects which marked it off naturally from the Western sphere, as already pointed out. Even so, the nature of this separation was still not fully visible to a man of his background. Unlike some of the Emperors who had preceded him in Constantinople in the previous century, Justinian came from European stock, and, more important, from a fully Latinized and Latin-speaking background. He would think of himself not merely as ruler of the eastern Mediterranean alone, but as the rightful sovereign of the entire Roman world of the past. In view of his fortunate circumstances and ambitious nature, he was in an unusually favored position for trying to convert this vision into fact. Under him the surviving Roman Empire would not just hold the line in the East: it would strike back against the presumptuous Germans and recover what was its own.

Secondly, to what we may call Justinian's Roman or all-Mediterranean perspective must be added another consideration, his Christian outlook. We have already seen that Justinian was much exercised in matters religious. As Emperor, God's ultimate deputy on earth, his responsibilities were not only secular, but were also bound up with the Christian Faith — that is, the Christian Faith as he understood it and was determined to enforce it. This outlook was no less a factor in his external preoccupations than in the internal ones, as has been noted, since Justinian stood forth as the ultimate champion of true Christians everywhere, even beyond the Empire's frontiers.

"True Christian" meant the orthodox Chalcedonian Catholic, as opposed to a heretic of whatever stripe. Now many of the barbarian powers were more than territorial usurpers in the Emperor's eyes. They were also enemies of the True Faith. For most of the barbarians had entered Imperial territories as Christians of the Arian sect, and it was among the barbarians that Arianism lingered on most strongly, after it had all but died out among the peoples of the Empire. The imposition of the Arian Germans over the orthodox provincials created much friction in these areas. It also made more difficult any really firm relationship between the barbarian kingdoms and the pious Emperor. Moreover, since the Arian rulers of the Vandal and Visigothic states, if not the Ostrogothic as well, often persecuted their orthodox subjects mercilessly, it became the Emperor's deep concern to champion the interests of these oppressed fellow-believers now in heretical bondage. Likewise, these orthodox provincials in the barbarian West looked to the Emperor as their one hope, especially when Justinian began his regime by ridding the court of Constantinople of its previous Monophysite tincture, restoring its orthodox Chalcedonian standing, and resuming cordial relations with the Bishop of Rome. Thus, Justinian's standing as the orthodox ruler par excellence in the eyes of the persecuted populations of the barbarian kingdoms served at once as an important motivation for his Reconquest plans and at the same time as a valuable asset in prosecuting them.

To be sure, there were exceptions to this religious situation. The Burgundians, for example, though Arian to begin with, had by the time of Justin I come under the rule of an orthodox King, who was particularly anxious to make his realm a dependency of the Empire. But the Burgundian state was to play a very limited role in these events, since it was soon overshadowed, curtailed, and ultimately absorbed by the Franks. More significant exceptions, however, are the barbarian peoples who did not enter Imperial territories as Christians of any cast whatsoever, but rather still as pagans. The most important of these were the Franks, who were thus open to orthodox blandishment. The conversion of Clovis and his people to orthodox Catholic Christianity — the traditional date for this is A.D. 496 — was an event of far-reaching importance in the development of the only Germanic people to found a durable major state in Western Europe. It enabled the Emperor Anastasius to recognize Frankish authority with a clear conscience; and the Frankish rulers would for centuries be noteworthy for their formal observance of the Emperor's nominal sovereignty over them, however ruthlessly they consulted their own interests in actual conduct. Their non-Arian stance, however, removed the religious incentive for any action against them, while their greater distance from East Roman reach also rendered them immune from any serious aggressive action by Justinian. He sought rather to cultivate them diplomatically in order to use them as allies against his other barbarian foes — unsuccessfully, as events were to prove. Another case of barbarians who entered the Empire as pagans was that of the Anglo-Saxon peoples who overran Britain and all but extinguished Christianity on that island. These savage warriors were to escape the allurements of orthodox conversion much longer than the Franks; for it was not until the end of the sixth century, when Pope Gregory I, "the Great," of Rome sent St. Augustine of Canterbury on his mission to Britain, that the island would be brought back into the Christian world. Meanwhile, for the purposes of Justinian, Britain was too distant for any reclamation by Roman arms, and it remained largely forgotten by the Roman world.

Thus, for reasons of religion and geography, Justinian's Reconquest program was limited in practical terms to the three major Arian Christian barbarian kingdoms of the western Mediterranean: Vandalic North Africa, Ostrogothic Italy, and Visigothic Spain. It is impossible to say precisely when Justinian conceived his plans. It seems likely, however, that they developed at an early stage, when he first had the prospects of power opened to him, and as he emerged to shape his uncle's government. Certainly he cultivated what were plainly opportunities in this direction from the very beginning.[1]

In setting his Reconquest plans in motion, Justinian had several undeniable advantages in his favor as against the barbarian kingdoms he opposed. First of all, of course, there was the fact that he could rely on the sympathies of the orthodox populations of the subjected provinces, who would welcome the Imperial forces as their liberators from an oppressive alien regime. Justinian had

1. Compare the comments of Bury, *History of the Later Roman Empire* . . . (A.D. 359–565), II, 124: "The idea of restoring the Empire to its ancient limits seems to have floated before the mind of Justinian, but it is difficult to say whether he conceived it from the beginning as a definite aim of policy. He seized so promptly the opportunities which chance presented to him of recovering lost provinces in the lands of the Mediterranean, that we suspect that he would have created pretexts if they had not occurred."

all the prestige of the ultimate Christian state, which was the legal owner of these areas. More practically, he had behind him the resources of a far more organized and sophisticated state than anything the barbarian kingdoms had developed. He had the elaborate bureaucratic and revenue machinery of his government to support his generals' operations in the field. He also had greater military resources. To be sure, the Roman military system was at the time rather precarious. It relied very heavily upon mercenary recruitment, which secured often valuable specialized skills, but also risked unruliness and undependability. Justinian's armies were polyglot congeries of barbarians of widely varied ethnic origins — Asiatic, Germanic, and whatever. As mercenaries they were also a continuously expensive drain on the Imperial treasury. In addition, the inconsistently organized or haphazardly maintained systems of pay and supplies often broke down, which undermined the always precarious loyalties both of the officers and of the men in the ranks, and thus made either the effective control or the effective use of such armies quite difficult.

Nevertheless, Justinian had at his disposal a number of highly competent generals, most notably Belisarius and Narses, who could surmount these obstacles and achieve miracles with desperately limited resources. Whatever the shortcomings of their troops, these were still generally superior to the forces which their barbarian opponents could muster. Moreover, despite the general deterioration of the Imperial military system, it had made at least one advance in this period in achieving a new mastery of cavalry tactics, an important factor added to the advantage of more effective command which these "Roman" armies of Justinian enjoyed. In many cases also the barbarians were not the formidable fighters they had once been, as a result of prolonged settlement and of semi-degeneration in climates often considerably more debilitating than those to which they and their ancestors had been accustomed. The barbarian lordship of the Western provinces was, after all, only a thin veneer spread over the provincial subject populations, and there was but limited intermingling or amalgamation of the two. Also, the rulers could very rarely count on the hostile provincials for any genuine support. It must, however, be emphasized that the Imperial armies employed in the Reconquest projects were surprisingly small, usually numbering between ten and twenty thousand men at a given time, and often less. The restricted size of these forces, and the eventually inadequate support which the Emperor chose or was able to give them, were usually the chief causes for the disastrous prolongation of operations (at least in the case of the Ostrogothic war), rather than the actual power of the barbarians themselves.

Of Justinian's efforts against his three barbarian targets, those against Visigothic Spain were the least substantial, significant, or productive. Indeed, they are almost ignored by the contemporary sources — Procopius says nothing of them, perhaps since Belisarius was not involved. It is true that Belisarius did, in the course of his African campaign in early 534, send a force to seize Septum on the Straits. But this was a purely tactical measure and an immediate precaution against Visigothic support of the Vandals, with no relation to any long-range plan of conquest in Spain.

It does seem likely that Justinian nourished some ambitions against this hostile Arian Christian power in Spain. He was for some time distracted from pursuing any such ambitions, as a result of the dogged and prolonged resistance of the Ostrogoths, and of other involvements which preoccupied him. Nevertheless, his interest was revealed quickly enough when an opportunity offered itself. The Visigothic royal house had become subject to disruption and strife. By the middle of the century two rival claimants, Agila and Athanagild, were locked in a struggle for the throne. Seeking to supplement his internal support, Athanagild seems to have appealed to the Emperor for help, apparently about the year 550. Though his forces were already deeply embroiled in Italy and elsewhere, Justinian dispatched a small expedition under the Patrician Liberius. In these circumstances the Imperial forces found it possible to capture a surprising amount of the southern coastal area around the Straits, including Gades (modern Cadiz) — thus enabling the panegyrists to claim that under Justinian the Empire once again extended to the Atlantic on both sides of the Straits of Gibraltar. Unfortunately, the precise extent of the Spanish conquests, and even the organization of them, are not fully known. At any rate, they were not to be extended any further. Athanagild soon realized that the Romans' progress was achieved for their own benefit rather than his. Once securely on the throne, in 554, the Visigothic leader turned on his erstwhile allies and restricted their advance, even recovering a little territory. The Imperial occupation continued in limited fashion where it could, but within some seventy years even this would be lost, the first of Justinian's reconquests to slip away again.

Justinian's Reconquest operations against the Visigoths can thus be dismissed easily here as a minor and obscure digression from his larger operations elsewhere. It is these other operations in the two remaining theaters, North Africa and Italy, which deserve consideration in their own turn as the principal aspects of the Emperor's ambitious Reconquest program.

The Vandalic War and the Recovery of North Africa

However plain it appears that Justinian cherished his Reconquest plans from his earliest days in power, it was some time before he could begin implementation of them. As we have seen, he was burdened from 524, in the reign of his uncle, with his first war with Persia, a war which gravely drained his finances and which tied down his best fighting forces and commanders. He was freed from this, however, by the "Perpetual Peace" in the spring of 532. Meanwhile, the shock of the Nika Riots had come and gone, leaving Justinian strengthened in power and in nerve, with deeper confidence in the loyal abilities of Belisarius. At last all was ripe for the projects he had in mind. No longer would the Emperor merely guard his present frontiers: he could now strike back boldly to restore the honor and territorial extent of the old Roman Empire.

As opportunities developed, North Africa became the first objective. The Vandal kingdom had changed much in its century of existence there. Under its founder, Gaiseric, it had become a formidable naval power, the only one among the various Germanic kingdoms. Not only did the Vandal squadrons ravage the western Mediterranean — their boldest stroke being the infamous sack of Rome in 455 — but they also extended their attentions to Greece and the Aegean islands. Gaiseric had beaten off Roman attempts to destroy his state, and in 476 he finally negotiated a treaty of peace with the Emperor Zeno. Thus he was able to die in the following year cloaked in unaccustomed peace and respectability. The peace was maintained, but the Vandal state was plainly independent and not the least bit friendly towards Imperial interests. Indeed, the successors of Gaiseric continued his policy of persecuting their non-Arian subjects and of obstructing any links of contact or sentiment between these subjects and the Emperor in Constantinople.

Time brought changes. The Vandal naval menace, still potentially strong, was in decline. In addition, the Vandals themselves, spread thinly over their realm, were beginning to deteriorate in character. Of the three barbarian kingdoms which Justinian attacked, all were in Mediterranean regions with relatively warm climates. In Africa, in particular, the Germanic conquerors were perhaps softened by the unaccustomed weather and the luxuries of the civilization they assumed. Nevertheless, it was to be developments in the Vandal royal regime itself which would seal the doom of this state.

In 523 a new King came to the throne, named Hilderic (or Ilderic). A grandson of the great Gaiseric, he had also had another interesting line of ancestry. Gaiseric's son and successor, Huneric (477–484), had been married to one of the choicest captives of the 455 raid on Rome, Eudocia, daughter of the late Western Emperor Valentinian III. As their son Hilderic was therefore half-Roman, and had in his veins the blood of the illustrious Theodosian house. He seems to have been acutely conscious and proud of this Roman background, exhibiting unusual sympathy for things Roman. The shrewd Justinian had assiduously cultivated Hilderic, winning his personal friendship. Hilderic even went so far as to become a convert to orthodox Catholicism, in defiance of his dynasty's Arian tradition. When Hilderic became King, therefore, a sharp change in Vandal policy was unavoidable.

Under Hilderic the Vandal kingdom became a close friend and ally of the Empire. Persecution of orthodox Christians was ended. The old Vandal policy of alignment with its natural friend, Ostrogothic Italy, was abandoned. Hilderic had his predecessor's widow, who was also Theodoric's daughter, cast into prison to die. Amid worsening relations between Constantinople and Ravenna at the time, the Vandals now cooperated uncharacteristically with the Empire against the Ostrogoths. Inevitably, this disrupting change of policy not only altered the balance of power in the western Mediterranean, but it also produced a strong reaction within the Vandal realm itself. A powerful faction arose which resented Hilderic's drastic pro-Roman innovations. The leader of the dissidents was the King's second cousin, Gelimer (or, more properly, Geilamir). This prince organized a coup which deposed and imprisoned Hilderic in 530 and established Gelimer on the throne in his place. Justinian's attempts to intervene on behalf of his fallen friend were bluntly rebuffed. Plainly, Gelimer was determined to renew the rugged old anti-Imperial, anti-orthodox, independent policies of the previous Vandal rulers.

The usurpation of Gelimer in Carthage quite changed Justinian's position. It had seemed that the Vandal kingdom under Hilderic could be used as a valuable collaborator against Ostrogothic Italy. Now it was the Vandal kingdom itself to which attention must be directed. Dispossessed African landowners pressed the Emperor anew for redress. But, besides his desire to recover Roman lands in the West and to liberate oppressed fellow-Christians, Justinian had the more immediate motive of protecting the interests of his fallen friend and ally. It is thus important to note that Justinian's operations in North Africa began as an avowed effort only to repress the tyrannical usurper and to restore Hilderic.

Justinian could not, of course, move immediately after Gelimer's coup. Though his hands were freed and his spirits were stirred after the Nika Riots had been crushed in 532, the Emperor found that other obstacles remained. The memories of Leo I's abortive expedition of 468 against the Vandals were still bitter. The Vandals might yet be expected to resist any invasion with fair chances of success. Nevertheless, Justinian would not be deterred by the prosaic realism of his counselors of caution. Under Belisarius an expedition was organized. It was a dangerously small one: its size is estimated at no more than 18,000 men. It departed by sea from Constantinople in June of 533, with prospects which were at best uncertain.

Fortunately for Justinian, and for Belisarius, circumstances played perfectly into their hands. A current phase of friendship between the Ostrogothic regime and the Emperor enabled the Imperial forces to land on Sicily and use it as the actual launching point for the attack. While in Sicily, the apprehensive Belisarius learned that, far from menacing his expedition, the Vandals were completely unprepared for it. The Romans' greatest advantage was Gelimer himself, an unstable and incompetent ruler. He had foolishly allowed a revolt to flourish unchecked in a part of his African realms, providing an area of safe landing for Belisarius; at the same time, he had likewise foolishly detached a vital part of his forces to put down another revolt, on the distant subject island of Sardinia. Totally unaware of the expedition approaching him, he never even tried to use his mighty fleet against Belisarius.

Learning of all this with surprised delight, Belisarius hastened to land his forces on the shores of Africa south of Hadrumentum. He decided to proceed along the coast, his army supported on its line of march by his fleet. He carefully announced his goal as the reversal of Gelimer's coup, not any design on the Vandal kingdom itself, while he did his best to protect the local population from the misconduct of his own unruly troops. Gelimer meanwhile roused himself to resistance. He rashly ordered the execution of the imprisoned Hilderic, which thus conveniently altered Belisarius' formal position; then he marched to meet the Imperial army. The two forces met in battle on September 13, 533, at a place ten miles from Carthage and hence designated as Ad Decimum, or "The Tenth Milestone." The fortunes of the fight wavered, and Gelimer might have won. Instead, he characteristically wasted his advantages, and the result was a victory for Belisarius. The wretched King lost heart. His army dissolved in flight after him. With his way cleared, Belisarius was able to enter Carthage unopposed on September 15, amid the jubilation of the orthodox populace.

Fearing possible Vandal counteraction, Belisarius set about entrenching himself in Carthage. The next action in fact occurred further west when another open battle was fought at Tricamaron, where Gelimer was rallying his forces for a second stand. When the fight was joined there in mid-December of 533, the Vandal army was broken. The Imperial soldiers fell into a wild orgy of enjoying their spoils. Gelimer again foolishly lost heart and, neglecting his chance to fall on them, instead fled to the mountains of Numidia. On Mount Papua the discredited monarch took refuge, holding out through the winter almost alone. His situation was hopeless, and he finally was coaxed into an honorable surrender in March of 534. Meanwhile, the Battle of Tricamaron had settled the fate of the Vandal kingdom. Had its ruler been a better man, its collapse might have been averted, or might at least have been less spectacular. As it happened, with all due credit to Belisarius, it was fundamentally the consistent blundering of Gelimer that destroyed it. The remnants of the Vandal nation surrendered. They were reduced to servility, were isolated from all political or social position, and were speedily absorbed by their conquerors. As a people, the Vandals soon ceased to exist. The Reconquest of Justinian simply wiped them from the face of Africa, as if they had been but crumbs on a table.

For the Empire this lightning success was a stunning triumph. Uneasy amid intriguing subordinates, Belisarius elected to return to Constantinople. With the captive Gelimer in his train, the general was awarded the unusual honor of an old-style Roman "triumph" — the ceremonial procession granted to a victorious general in pre-Imperial times — held in the Hippodrome in the autumn of 534.[2] The Vandal King was received courteously and allowed to settle for his remaining days on a suburban estate near the capital, staunchly persisting in his Arian faith. Belisarius, meanwhile, was prepared for his next assignment.

As for North Africa itself, Justinian proceeded to re-establish Roman rule, reorganizing the administration to confirm its incorporation into the Roman Empire once more. Nevertheless, if the Emperor imagined that the recovery of North Africa ended there, he was soon to be disabused of such illusions, for there was a second power to be reckoned with in this area: the Moors. The various Moorish tribes of the mountains had long been the scourge

2. For an interesting description of the triumph accorded Belisarius, see Downey, *Constantinople in the Age of Justinian*, pp. 87–91. It should be stressed that this was a remarkably generous gesture on Justinian's part, indicating the unusual nature of the occasion. For, since the days of Nero in the first century A.D., the jealous Emperors had ceased to grant triumphs to any general other than themselves.

of whoever ruled the territory. The Romans themselves had been obliged to cope with them in the earlier days of the Empire. The Moors had fought steadily against the Vandals, and their inroads upon them were another factor which had helped weaken the Vandals' strength down to the eve of Justinian's operations. The Moors had craftily stood aside in the struggle between Gelimer and Belisarius. Once the Vandal state was destroyed, they were eager to secure the fruits of victory for themselves. Their attacks on the recovered Roman territory began promptly, and they gravely retarded Justinian's re-establishment of his administration and defenses there. Development of a system of frontier outposts was begun, while efforts were made to subjugate these dangerous peoples. Had the Moors shown more unity by ending their regular quarrels amongst themselves, their joint efforts might have been disastrous for Imperial rule in North Africa. On the other hand, the limited numbers and the frequent unreliability of the Imperial troops, as well as the incompetence of some of the Emperor's commanders in Africa, prevented any consistent exploitation of Moorish weaknesses. The result was one that was to become depressingly familiar in the later decades of the Emperor's reign: semi-stalemate and an onerous struggle protracted long beyond expectation or expediency, which bore down severely on the restored Roman regime and the province under it.

At the outset operations proceeded well. Belisarius' successor in the supreme command of North Africa was the eunuch Prefect Solomon, who arrived in the fall of 534. His campaigns against the Moors began promptly and were attended with victory during 535. By 536 it seemed that the Moors had been firmly chastened. But this progress was soon undone when a mutiny broke out in Solomon's army. The troops were restless, underpaid, dissatisfied with their commander, and aroused by numerous grievances. A group of conspirators led by one Stotzas contrived to guide the mutiny so that they might seize North Africa for themselves. So grave was the situation that Solomon was obliged to flee to Sicily, where Belisarius was at the time. The great general returned with him and was able to frighten off the rebels from their siege of the loyal forces in Carthage. Belisarius could not remain, but in the ensuing shake-up in command Justinian replaced Solomon with the Emperor's own cousin, Germanus. The choice was a fortunate one, for Germanus was a commander of ability and tact who succeeded in restoring order in the Imperial forces. The remaining rebels under Stotzas were defeated in the spring of 537. Stotzas became a fugitive among the Moors and was finally slain in 545 while fighting on their side against the Imperial army.

Once Germanus had restored order, Solomon was reinstated in his command. He made some progress in building up the defenses in the African territories against the Moors. But the latter were needlessly provoked and in 544 Solomon was killed in battle against them. Justinian appointed Solomon's nephew Sergius as his replacement — a mistake, for this new general was quite incompetent. The confusion was then further compounded by the appointment of another unworthy as co-commander and then successor, one Areobindus, husband of the Emperor's niece. During an uprising in March of 546, Areobindus was assassinated by the ambitious commander Guntarith. This would-be usurper was himself assassinated within a month by a loyal officer, the Armenian Artabanes. The African provinces were by then in chaos.

This situation was finally remedied by the appointment, later in 546, of the ultimate hero of the Moorish wars, John Troglita. Within two years, by a combination of military energy and diplomatic skill, he was able to defeat or neutralize the restless tribes. The remaining Moorish chieftains were won over as dependents, and peace was restored, enabling a welcome repose and some order in North Africa at last. One final rising of the aggrieved tribesmen occurred in 563, and was put down. Otherwise, these recovered territories remained at peace for the balance of Justinian's reign.

The Ostrogothic War and the Recovery of Italy

The second major phase of Justinian's Reconquest program, and the one which was to prove the most arduous, may seem at first somewhat paradoxical. The Ostrogothic kingdom of Italy had, after all, been established with the full approval and encouragement of the Emperor in Constantinople, as a means of ridding Italy of the unpalatable Odovacar — while at the same time removing Theodoric from his menacing presence in the Balkans. Theodoric the Great ruled in Italy (493–526) as King of the Ostrogoths and as the Emperor's viceroy and commander for the area, an arrangement formally acknowledged by the Emperor Anastasius I in the year 497.

Certainly, too, Theodoric was one of the most remarkable of all the barbarian rulers. Though unlettered himself, he had a great respect for the Roman civilization which had become subject to him. He encouraged culture and endeavored to preserve this civilization in his realms, as far as was then possible. Such illustrious Roman men of letters as Cassiodorus and Boethius were drawn to his court. He was honest and just. He went out of his way to show deference to the position and claims of his nominal overlord in Constantinople. He retained the old Senate in the city of Rome and honored its empty functions and formalities. While preserving clear lines of distinction between his own people and his Roman subjects, Theodoric hoped that the Ostrogoths could elevate themselves to a level with the people they had subjugated.

There were, nevertheless, bases for unavoidable friction. The presence of a barbarian power in Italy could not but irritate the Emperor. However much that presence was glossed over in theory, it could never be fully accepted by the rightful lord of the Roman world. Suspicions flourished in both capitals, while Theodoric knew full well how questionable were his claims to the territory he held. Then, too, Theodoric and his Ostrogoths were Arian Christians. To be sure, his conduct in this regard was quite different from that of his Vandal contemporaries. The Ostrogothic King's religious policy was one of enlightened tolerance throughout most of his reign. Nevertheless, the orthodox population of Italy resented their alien and Arian masters. Italy was, as well, the seat of the Roman Papacy, which was only beginning to emerge in prestige as a citadel of Catholic orthodoxy. Theodoric's relationship with the Roman Pontificate was a delicate matter indeed.

Inevitably, the orthodox majority of Italy would be likely to look for an orthodox deliverer. Yet, they had been discouraged in any such hopes in so far as the Emperor in Constantinople was concerned, because of the Eastern court's growing preoccupation with Monophysitism. As long as a ruler so religiously tainted as Anastasius I was on the Imperial throne, the pious orthodox in Italy could have no sympathy with Constantinople. The situation was further complicated by the fact that Anastasius I, if no favorite of the orthodox, was also, as a crypto-Monophysite, on bad terms with the Arian Theodoric. This Emperor had grudgingly recognized the Ostrogothic King's official status as Imperial deputy in Italy in 497, but there was little love lost between them. Finally, Theodoric lacked a male heir. He had married his daughter Amalasuntha to a Gothic prince named Eutharic in 515. This, he hoped, would allow him to found an independent Gothic succession of kings in Italy, avoiding repossession or intervention by Constantinople in the actual exercise of authority there. Theodoric's position remained, however, theoretically dependent upon the will of the Emperor, and there was still some uncertainty about the viability of his succession plans. To bolster his position Theodoric became very much interested in building up a great chain of alliances through marriage among the various barbarian princes in the West. All of these projects could only feed anxieties in Constantinople.

Such was the complex situation when Justin I ascended the throne in 518. As we have seen, one of the immediate concerns of the new regime of Justin and his nephew was to restore the Eastern court to a proper stance of Chalcedonian orthodoxy and to renew good relations with the Roman Papacy. This change of religious atmosphere placed Theodoric in an ambiguous position. On the one hand it meant that the orthodox population of Italy could now look longingly to the East for some kind of relief, if not actual release, from the bondage to their Arian Ostrogothic masters; and, conversely, the Imperial government could be expected to interest itself more than ever in that population's affairs. On the other hand, the new regime's policies smoothed the way at the outset for more friendly relations between the Ostrogothic kingdom and the Empire on both ecclesiastical and political terms. Whatever his suspicions of Imperial intentions, Theodoric wished to secure his government and succession by continuing his accommodation with Constantinople if it were possible. He also wanted to retain the good will of the Papacy, which was obviously eager to renew good relations with the Emperor, if on its own terms. Theodoric therefore encouraged the process of Church reunion and renewed harmony, seeking thereby to improve his own standing with the new Imperial regime.

Justin and Justinian made several efforts to meet Theodoric halfway. In 519 the Emperor designated the King's son-in-law, Eutharic, as Consul. His celebration of assuming this venerable office in Rome in that year was an occasion of much rejoicing for the Goths. Eutharic himself seems to have been somewhat anti-Roman and anti-orthodox in his sentiments. Nevertheless, the role he might have played can only be conjectured, for in 522 he died unexpectedly, thereby disrupting the situation perhaps far more than he might have done had he lived. He left behind a four-year-old son by Amalasuntha, named Athalaric, and it was on this grandson of Theodoric that the mantle of Ostrogothic succession now fell. Justin made another gesture of good will in this same year of 522 by allowing Theodoric himself to name as the two new Consuls the distinguished Roman nobles Boethius and his father-in-law Symmachus, the leader of the Senate. The native Roman element was at a peak of favor with the King. It seemed as if Ravenna and Constantinople were in warm accord.

In 523 the tide changed. The Arian Ostrogoths became suspicious and resentful of the new Imperial government's persecution of heretics in the East, which included the few remaining Arians there. The reunion of the Churches was now beginning to bear bitter fruit, the more so as the Roman Pontificate was by late 523 occupied by John I, who was more identified with the pro-Imperial factions in Rome than his predecessor had been. The threat to Ostrogothic rule in Italy which Church reunion (and unified anti-Arianism) posed was becoming more apparent. Theodoric perhaps sensed already the dreams of Imperial reconquest which were taking shape in Justinian's mind. Then, too, the accession of Hilderic to the Vandalic throne in 523 began a phase of cordial cooperation between Carthage and Constantinople, decidedly anti-Ostrogothic in both its implications and its externals. That entente deprived Theodoric of his most natural ally among the barbarian states, isolating him in the western Mediterranean. An old man by this time, Theodoric seems to have entered a period of heightened suspicions and ultra-sensitivity in his closing years. By the winter of 523–524 he began to cast away the caution which had marked his long reign and to become a ruthless tyrant.

The first sign of the change came in the famous episode of Boethius' fall. The eminent scholar-philosopher was unpopular at court and was accused, rightly or wrongly, of treasonable communication with the Imperial government. Now deeply mistrustful of the Senate and the nativist faction in Rome, Theodoric reacted with uncharacteristic and intemperate arbitrariness. He ignored the normal procedures of judicial inquiry and had Boethius summarily imprisoned. It was during this period of confinement that Boethius wrote his celebrated *Consolation of Philosophy*. Shortly afterwards, late in 524, the King had Boethius brutally executed, and the same fate was meted out to Symmachus, as an example to the Senate. Fearing attack, Theodoric began to build a fleet to defend himself against any possible Imperial aggression. It was under these circumstances of anger and suspicion that Theodoric, his anxieties further stirred by the mounting anti-Arian measures of the Imperial government in the East, attempted to use the visit of Pope John I to Constantinople in 526 for the purpose of winning a relaxation of the Emperor's policies against the Arians. John did his best, but Theodoric was dissatisfied with the results. The King's ill-treatment of the Pope on his return in May of 526 hastened the ailing Pontiff's death. Theodoric could take satisfaction in the election of Felix IV as the new Pope, for he promised to be a more pro-Gothic Pontiff. But Theodoric's health began to deteriorate, and on August 30, 526, he died, leaving Imperial-Ostrogothic relations at a low ebb.

The death of the King actually eased the ill will between Ravenna and Constantinople for the moment. Nevertheless, it left the Ostrogothic kingdom in a precarious position. The throne was now occupied by the eight-year-old Athalaric, with his mother Amalasuntha as regent. Amalasuntha (or Amalaswintha) was a woman of great perception, ability, beauty, and charm. She had received a Roman education herself and had lofty plans for her son. Her control over him, however, was seriously challenged by dissatisfied and nationalistic elements among the Gothic nobility.

The boy himself soon proved to be devoid of either ability or stability. Surrounded by hostile intrigue at her court, Amalasuntha found her kingdom increasingly cut off from any friends or supporters in the barbarian world around her. She therefore opened communications with Justinian, with possible flight in mind. Now Emperor in his own right, Justinian would plainly welcome opportunities for intervention in Ostrogothic affairs. The Emperor, once his war against the Vandal kingdom was launched in 533, also welcomed her cooperation in allowing him to use Sicily as a base of operations for his army.

It began to appear that Justinian would profit further from the difficulties of the Ostrogothic kingdom. Amalasuntha's position was becoming even more untenable. Her son, weakened by premature intemperance, was all but dying, and, with him gone, she would have no hope of remaining in power. Her only kinsman and possible rival or successor was a selfish noble named Theodahad, who was at that time negotiating with Justinian for permission to retire to a life of ease in Constantinople. Under these circumstances, Amalasuntha seems to have entered into secret negotiations for the transference of the Ostrogothic realms to the direct authority of the Emperor. It is unlikely that such an arrangement could have been carried out without resistance by the Goths themselves. Justinian took the plan seriously, however, and dispatched the Patrician Peter of Thessalonica as his commissioner to Italy to pursue the matter.

Unfortunately for everyone concerned, the Gothic Queen changed her mind when the crisis came. Athalaric had died on October 2, 534, and Amalasuntha chose not to resign but to prolong her days in power. She invited Theodahad to marry her and take the royal title, while supposedly leaving actual authority to her. Nothing loath, Theodahad agreed. But the new King was as treacherous as he was worthless. Harboring various grudges against Amalasuntha, he quickly marshalled her enemies, had her supporters butchered, and ordered her seized and imprisoned. Amid these new developments the Imperial commissioner Peter arrived with instructions from Justinian to support the deposed Queen. Whatever efforts were made on her behalf, however, Amalasuntha was soon murdered, possibly with the secret connivance of none other than the Empress Theodora.[3] Theodahad glibly protested personal innocence, but Peter informed him that the Queen's execution was a declaration of war.

The murder of Amalasuntha, which apparently occurred in April of 535, did indeed mean war. Peter returned to Constantinople with messages of peace and good will from Theodahad. By this time, however, Justinian was determined to have Ostrogothic Italy in his own hands. The pose of avenging a fallen ally was one of his favorite justifications for foreign intervention, and the present opportunity was too tempting to be missed. The Vandal kingdom had been destroyed. The Emperor's confident ambition hastened the next step. Belisarius awaited his orders, ready for new triumphs, and military preparations were set in motion. Justinian's only reply to Theodahad was the message Peter carried back to Italy, bidding him to abdicate and to yield the Ostrogothic kingdom to its rightful overlord, the Emperor. There was nothing anyone could do now to bar Justinian from his recovery of Italy.

The actual preparations for the war were made with great secrecy. Justinian and Belisarius had learned the value of surprise in the Vandalic war and were determined to make even further use of it now. The expeditionary force which was organized for the great general was barely half the size of the one he had led against North Africa. While a second force under Mundus advanced by land in the late summer of 535 to occupy Ostrogothic territory in Dalmatia, on the eastern shore of the Adriatic, Belisarius set out by sea. His destination was publicized as Imperial North Africa. His real and secret purpose was to test the strength of Ostrogothic Sicily. As it happened, fortune again smiled with remarkable be-

3. Procopius, in his *Anékdota*, chap. xvi, secs. 1–5, charges that Theodora was jealous of the Gothic Queen and feared that the energetic and beautiful Amalasuntha might be a serious rival to her should she ever come to the capital and win the favor of the Emperor. Therefore, says Procopius, Theodora secretly instructed Peter to persuade Theodahad to have the Queen murdered. The story is often dismissed as one of the crowning instances of the bitter historian's slander of Theodora. But Bury, *History of the Later Roman Empire* . . . (A.D. 395–565), II, 165–167, examines it seriously as perhaps containing some elements of truth; cf. Ure, *Justinian and his Age*, pp. 215 ff.

nevolence upon Imperial ambitions. The Gothic garrisons were small, unprepared, and inadequate, while the Sicilian populace was only too eager to welcome its liberators. A quick landing was followed by rapid progress throughout the fall of 535. Only in Syracuse was there any serious resistance, and this was soon put down. On December 31 Belisarius entered that city, and the rest of Sicily was at his mercy.

Once again, the Emperor's forces had seemed spectacularly irresistible. To complete his preparations against the Ostrogothic kingdom, meanwhile, Justinian was in diplomatic contact with the three Merovingian kings among whom Frankish Gaul was now divided. As fellow orthodox Catholics, the Franks were invited to cooperate against the common Arian foe, though it was more the Emperor's liberal gifts which secured their agreement than the interests of their common religion.

The outlook for Theodahad was now black indeed. Realizing that he was caught between two fires, he hastened to negotiate. To the Franks Theodahad promised a large sum of money and an extensive cession of territory, in exchange for the perfidious promises of neutrality which they gave. Desperate to soften the Emperor's aggressive impulses, the King persuaded Pope Agapetus to journey to Constantinople as his emissary to Justinian. This was the impetus behind the Pontiff's visit to the Eastern capital in early 536. As we have seen, the main preoccupation of his stay in Constantinople was ecclesiastical, and his death there in April of that year left Theodahad further isolated. Meanwhile, during the winter of 535–536, Belisarius was completing the conquest of Sicily. The ubiquitous diplomat Peter returned to Italy on Justinian's business. In negotiations with the frightened King, Peter secured a virtual promise of abdication from Theodahad. When, in late winter, steps were taken to implement this arrangement, the vacillating Theodahad changed his mind. The death of Mundus in Dalmatia and the turn of the tide there in Gothic favor encouraged the King to stand fast, and his Gothic people were more than ready to support him in this. The skirmishing and maneuvering were ended: both sides were fully committed to war in Italy.

A further Imperial effort was made in Dalmatia, with renewed success. It was now Belisarius' task to invade Italy itself. He was distracted briefly in late March of 536 by having to hasten to Carthage to help put down the mutiny which had broken out there. Returning to his assignment, he opened his spring campaign by crossing the Straits of Messina to the mainland. The Gothic forces offered no serious resistance, and by autumn the Imperial army stood before Naples. The city chose to resist, and was placed under siege. The investment went badly and was nearly abandoned when an unexpected point of entry was found in an abandoned aqueduct leading into the city. By such means Naples was taken and was subjected to some pillaging. Its fall, with no effort on Theodahad's part to relieve it, was an intolerable blow to the King's reputation. In anger and contempt, the more warlike of his people decided to depose him. If they were going to resist the Imperial invasion they would fight under a real leader.

In November of 536 a concourse of Gothic warriors declared Theodahad dethroned and, lacking any further member of the royal house, elected a man of obscure birth but of some military experience named Wittigis. In retrospect, the choice was not the best they might have made, but it provided an improvement over Theodahad, who was captured in flight and executed. The new King attempted to secure his title by marrying Matasuntha, a daughter of Amalasuntha. He then turned to face the Imperial menace. Instead of hastening into battle, Wittigis himself began negotiating. He undertook to carry out his predecessor's promise to the Franks, seemingly winning their assurances of neutrality for the moment. Some contact with Justinian was also attempted, fruitlessly. Nevertheless, such efforts were of little value. From newly-won Naples, Belisarius was quickly moving on Rome itself. With the Neapolitan example before it, the people of Rome chose to abandon any bonds of allegiance to the Goths and opened their city to Belisarius. Entering the former capital on December 9, 536, the Imperial general passed in through one gate while the Gothic garrison left by another.

Rome at this time was still something of the great city it had been in past centuries, though signs of depopulation and decay were already visible. With a few repairs, the old third-century Walls of Aurelian were still usable. Nevertheless, though it was

expected that Wittigis might try to recover Rome, no one foresaw
the ordeal which lay in store for the old seat of the Empire.
Belisarius confidently sent out advance troops to seize further
fortresses to the north. He very soon found that he was to face
a new kind of test. Wittigis' forces had been badly beaten thus
far, especially in efforts to recover Dalmatia. The Goths needed
some major success. When it was realized how pitifully small a
force Belisarius had to hold Rome, it seemed plain to the King
that the logical step was to exert every effort against that city.
The troops which proceeded to muster for this purpose have been
reckoned to number as high as 15,000 men, which would have
been about three times the size of Belisarius' force. Plainly, whatever his shortcomings, Wittigis was no Gelimer, and the Imperial
general was faced with a different kind of barbarian war from that
which he had seen previously. The Gothic King cleared away the
Imperial outposts northward of Rome, while Belisarius' attempts
to delay the King's march on Rome were unsuccessful. By late
winter of 537 the Ostrogothic siege of Rome began.

Although Belisarius was perhaps the greatest field commander
of his day, most at home in the open pitched battle of which he
was the master, the siege of Rome was surely one of his finest
hours. With boundless energy and unflagging spirits he managed
to overcome all odds during a harrowing beleaguerment of more
than a year. The Goths concentrated their attacks at only specific
points along the walls, but there were some fierce assaults which
had to be withstood repeatedly. Desperate for more men, Belisarius secured some reinforcements from the Emperor by the spring.
Nevertheless, the siege brought new shortages of supplies in the
beleaguered city, while disease was increasing. The populace of
Rome had submitted to Belisarius in the first place to avoid a
siege at his hands, and were hardly disposed to endure one patiently under him. It was in this atmosphere of suspicion and
uncertain loyalties that Belisarius participated, if unwillingly, in
the deposition of Theodahad's Pope Silverius, in favor of Theodora's candidate Vigilius, in March of 537.

The Goths, however, were also suffering from hunger and disease, and their advantages were beginning to melt away. In
November a new body of Imperial reinforcements, which would

double Belisarius' forces, arrived under the command of the general John, together with extensive provisions. The Goths tried in vain to block their arrival, and this failure cast grave doubts on Wittigis' chances of success before Rome. The Emperor's fleet commanded the waterways, a crucial advantage. The Goths began to negotiate, and a three-month truce was granted. Belisarius used it to strengthen his position and to make some moves to the north. When the truce was broken by Gothic attempts to force a secret entry into Rome, Belisarius retaliated by sending the general John out to ravage behind Wittigis' lines, seizing the fortress of Ariminum among other places. Now in despair, Wittigis abandoned the siege of Rome. As the Gothic army withdrew in March of 538, Belisarius inflicted heavy losses upon it.

The badly discredited Wittigis next endeavored to salvage what was left in northern Italy. In April 538 he turned his attentions to Ariminum, which the Imperial army had just taken. Belisarius had ordered John to withdraw from it, but, in a fashion which was to become depressingly characteristic of Belisarius' troubles thereafter, John refused to obey his orders. Since this John was, as it happened, a nephew of the former rebel Vitalian, such insubordination may have come naturally. For his pains he was now closely invested by the Goths. Belisarius had hoped to advance cautiously northward in a systematic manner, and this development raised the problem of whether he should abandon his plan to relieve John in Ariminum. At this point further reinforcements arrived, accompanied by the Grand Chamberlain and trusted minister, the eunuch Narses, who was a personal friend of John. Inevitably, Narses persuaded Belisarius to concentrate on breaking Wittigis' siege of Ariminum. Once he committed himself to this course, Belisarius succeeded brilliantly, but the incident left a heritage of dissension in the Imperial command. Narses had successfully challenged Belisarius' will as commander, and he became a rival for the supreme authority which he believed should not belong to Belisarius alone. These differences poisoned successive operations through northern Italy.

Nevertheless, events were marching in Belisarius' favor. In the spring of 538 the general had sent a force to the Ligurian coast, and it had managed to penetrate to Milan and to occupy that important city with the cooperation of its population. Seeking to recover it, Wittigis made overtures to the Franks. King Theudebert I of Austrasia (533–548), a grandson of Clovis, ignoring his supposed obligations to help the Emperor, dispatched some of his subject Burgundians to help the Goths besiege Milan. Belisarius attempted to relieve it, but his efforts were hamstrung by the shameful disloyalty and backbiting among his subordinates, who now supported Narses against him. As a result, the Imperial garrison in Milan was starved and beaten into capitulation in March of 539. The population of Milan was subjected to a frightful massacre by the German soldiers as a punishment for their disloyalty. The only positive result of this disaster, in which 300,000 were reported to have perished, was that it persuaded Justinian to recall Narses, leaving Belisarius in uncontested command.

In spite of some success in Milan and Liguria, Wittigis was now desperate. Time was on Belisarius' side. In vain the King appealed for further help from neighboring barbarian peoples. It was also at this time, by the spring of 539, that he sent his message to the court of Persia to urge King Khusru to attack Justinian in the East, as already noted. The Eastern situation was beginning to concern Justinian, and in the wake of such mounting distractions he considered the possibility of a negotiated settlement with the Goths. Belisarius would soon be needed to fight the Persians. Meanwhile, the great general was busily moving towards the final reckoning. The remaining fortresses south of the Po River were being reduced, and Auximum, the key to the royal capital of Ravenna itself, was placed under siege. Amid the last agonies of Wittigis' reign an ominous intervention suddenly emerged from Frankish Gaul. The treacherous Theudebert thought he saw a good opportunity to profit himself, unhampered by loyalties to either side. Under him a great host of Franks crossed the Po and fell upon Gothic forces, who were amazed to find supposed allies transformed into greedy enemies. As fate would have it, however, it was only the Goths who bore this onslaught. Before the Franks could make any impact on the Imperial lines, they fell victims to the terrible pestilence and famine now spreading through the ravaged peninsula and were soon obliged to withdraw in disorder.

Meanwhile, Wittigis lost his chance to relieve the all-important outpost of Auximum, which was forced to capitulate in the autumn of 539. It remained only to take Ravenna, Wittigis' capital. This last step was not to be achieved by force. With the threat of a new intervention by Theudebert and the Franks in the offing, Belisarius persuaded Wittigis to avoid throwing in his lot with such an untrustworthy ally and to agree rather to negotiations with the Emperor. Justinian, meanwhile, definitely confronted with new hostilities with Persia, authorized remarkably liberal terms of peace by which the Ostrogoths would be allowed to retain Italy north of the Po River.

Belisarius' staff welcomed this solution, but to the general himself it was a disappointment of his hopes of full victory over the Ostrogoths, which he thought he might yet achieve. Wittigis was most willing to accept these terms, but he became antagonized by Belisarius' delays in implementing them. The deadlock was unexpectedly broken when some of the Gothic leaders, tired of the ineffectual Wittigis, proposed a daring plan. The Ostrogoths would, they said, abandon Wittigis and submit themselves not to Justinian but to Belisarius, if he would assume the title of Emperor of the West himself. The offer was a tribute to the respect which Belisarius inspired in his opponents. But it reckoned neither with his unshakable loyalty to Justinian, nor with his unsuspected capacities for deceit, almost uniquely revealed in this instance. Belisarius pretended to accept the Gothic plan; Wittigis agreed to it, and everything appeared to be settled. Belisarius entered Ravenna in May of 540 to accept the Ostrogothic submission; only then did he reveal that he had no intention of seizing any throne or abandoning his devotion to his Emperor. He then made provisions for securing the remnants of the Ostrogothic kingdom, taking Wittigis and his Queen as his captives and possessing himself of the royal treasures of Ravenna.

In late spring of 540 Belisarius returned to Constantinople. Justinian needed him on the Persian front. In addition, the Emperor had no desire to let Belisarius remain long in Ravenna after such imperial temptations. Whatever suspicions Justinian may have harbored of his general's loyalty, he could only resent the high-handed fashion in which Belisarius had resolved the peace settlement in his own way — a way that must have made an autocrat like Justinian shudder for a number of reasons. The commander was received coldly, was not allowed another triumph, and was kept waiting in the capital before being sent on to his new post. Wittigis was given much the same generous treatment that Gelimer had received, surviving for some two years thereafter.

As irritating to Justinian as Belisarius' settlement in Italy had been, it seemed to end the war there. Ostrogothic Italy had been added to Vandalic North Africa on the tally-sheet of the Reconquest. To be sure, this second achievement was considerably less dazzling than the first. Thanks to circumstances and the nature of his Vandalic opponent, the war in North Africa had taken Belisarius only a year, and as a result of only two major battles it had wiped the Vandal power off the face of the earth. By contrast, the Ostrogothic war had taken five years: his opponent in it, if undistinguished, had at least held his people together in determined resistance; and the principal actions were not open battles but prolonged and bitter sieges, which had borne heavily on all concerned, especially the local populace.[4]

Worst of all, however, the war was not truly ended. The peace which Belisarius established was an impossible one. Justinian might think that he was justified in recalling Belisarius; the captivity of the Ostrogothic King and his treasury might delude him into presuming that this barbarian nation was subdued; but these suppositions were in fact incorrect, for Italy was not yet genuinely won.

At the time of Belisarius' crafty settlement and departure, leading Goths had been outraged and frustrated by the general's trickery. In the light of this they saw no reason why they should abide by their submission, and so they sought a new king to lead them in renewed defiance of the Empire. Their choice fell on a noble named Ildebad. The situation was certainly ripe for resistance. The hasty recall of Belisarius had been unwise from a

---

4. Cf. Bury, *History of the Later Roman Empire* . . . (A.D. 395–565), II, 194: "It had been, and was to be, a war of sieges; if the enemy had met him in the open field, after the arrival of reinforcements [Bury is speaking specifically of 538, after the first Ostrogothic siege of Rome], it is possible that he would have won a decisive victory, and the conquest of Italy might have been achieved almost as rapidly as the conquest of Africa."

I. Justinianic Medallion. See Notes on the Illustrations, pages 286–287. (Courtesy of the British Museum.)

II. Justinian's Cistern in Constantinople, Now Called Yere-Batan Serai. See Notes on the Illustrations, page 287. (Courtesy of Hirmer Verlag München.)

III. Interior of Justinian's Church of Haghía Eirénē (St. Irene) in Constantinople. See Notes on the Illustrations, pages 287–288. (Courtesy of the Byzantine Institute, Inc.)

IV. Apse Mosaic Panel Representing the Emperor Justinian with Attendants, Church of San Vitale, Ravenna. See Notes on the Illustrations, page 288. (Courtesy of Hirmer Verlag München.)

V. Apse Mosaic Panel Representing the Empress Theodora with Attendants, Church of San Vitale, Ravenna. See Notes on the Illustrations, page 288. (Courtesy of Hirmer Verlag München.)

VI. Mosaic Supposedly Representing Justinian (Originally Theodoric?), in Church of San Apollinare Nuovo, Ravenna. See Notes on the Illustrations, page 288–289. (Courtesy of Thompson Webb, Jr.)

VII. Exterior of Justinian's Church of Haghía Sophía (St. Sophia) in Constantinople. See Notes on the Illustrations, page 289. (Courtesy of the Byzantine Institute, Inc.)

VIII. Interior of Justinian's Church of Haghía Sophía (St. Sophia) in Constantinople. See Notes on the Illustrations, page 289. (Courtesy of the Byzantine Institute, Inc.)

IX. Mosaic Representing Justinian and Constantine with the Virgin and Child, in Haghía Sophía, Constantinople. See Notes on the Illustrations, pages 289–290. (Courtesy of the Byzantine Institute, Inc.)

X. Sketch of the Equestrian Statue Supposedly of Justinian. See Notes on the Illustrations, pages 290–292. (Courtesy of the Budapest University Library and G. Moravcsik.)

XI. A. Justinianic Gold Coin of Constantinople
    B. Justinianic Gold Coin of Constantinople
    C. Justinianic Silver Coin of Constantinople
    D. Justinianic Bronze Coin of Constantinople
    E. Justinianic Bronze Coin of Nicomedia
    F. Justinianic Bronze Coin of Antioch
    G. Justinianic Bronze Coin of Antioch. See Notes on
       the Illustrations, pages 292–293. (Courtesy of the
       Dumbarton Oaks Collection.)

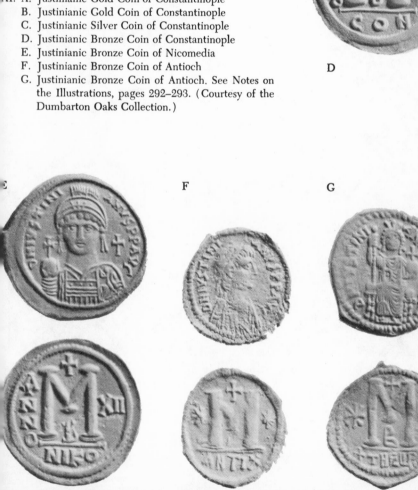

military point of view, especially since he was not replaced with anyone of reasonable competence. The blunderings of the disunited subordinates whom he left behind were aggravated by the abuses of the Imperial administrators who were proceeding to organize the recovered province in a fashion typical of Justinian's regime elsewhere. The position which Imperial arms had so stubbornly won now degenerated rapidly. The population which had once welcomed the Romans was so alienated that it gave the Goths themselves sufficient encouragement to renew the struggle for all of another dozen years.

Ildebad's reign was short-lived: he was assassinated in the spring of 541 after barely a year on the throne. The Gothic position was muddled further by the discreditable reign of the usurper Eraric. He was soon assassinated in his turn and was replaced by a more worthy candidate, Ildebad's nephew, Totila (also known as Baduila), in the autumn of 541. Totila was all that the Ostrogoths could have wanted as a leader — all that the Vandal Gelimer had never been, all that the Ostrogoths had hoped Wittigis would be, and all that the Romans must have dreaded in an opponent.

Before the disorganized Imperial commanders took any effective action against the Gothic power remaining beyond the Po, Totila was able to win a handsome victory against them. The Gothic King then opened a new offensive, sweeping southward as the Imperial lines crumbled before him. Only Ravenna remained untouched. By-passing Rome, Totila proceeded to lay siege to Naples. Justinian's commanders were incapable of either opposing him or relieving Naples. By spring of 543 this city was compelled to surrender, and Totila treated it with shrewd leniency. Rome, under the general John, was the next objective. As 544 dawned it appeared as if everything that Belisarius had achieved was on the brink of total collapse.

The one hope for saving it was to recall the man who had achieved what was at stake. In the spring of 544, therefore, Belisarius was withdrawn from the Persian front and placed in supreme command once again in Italy. He arrived in the summer of that year, doing his best to raise new forces and with them to relieve the fortresses then beleaguered by the Goths — most notably the coastal base of Otranto on the heel of the peninsula. By the following year he realized how hopeless the Imperial position was in Italy unless substantial reinforcements and financial support were sent. He so informed the Emperor. It was only in late 545 that any such help finally arrived, but by then Totila was completing his mopping-up of remaining Imperial fortresses. By the winter of 545–546 Totila was ready to press in person a new Gothic siege of Rome.

Once again the old Imperial city was submitted to severe hardship. Bessus, the Imperial commander in the city, only took advantage of the peoples' plight by engaging in shameful peculation. Attempts to send food and supplies were blocked by the vigorous Totila, who would allow no leniency in his terms for the city's release. Plainly, Belisarius himself was needed in Rome. He succeeded in making his way to Portus, one of the two old ports of Rome at the mouth of the Tiber River. Here he awaited John, who marched leisurely northward, clearing out some Gothic opposition in the south, but deliberately delaying the necessary rendezvous. With insufficient forces to relieve Rome directly, Belisarius made an attempt to get some provisions through to it. In this move he was, however, frustrated at the point of success by the unreliability of his subordinates. In the wake of failure he fell ill. Rome's position was now hopeless. Thanks to the incompetence of Bessus, Totila was able to storm and enter it on December 17, 546, and the miserable remnant of the city's ravaged and starving population was given over to massacre and pillage.

If the first siege of Rome had drawn from Belisarius one of his finest performances, the second was virtually his Waterloo. Confident after this success, Totila sent word to Justinian that he would grant peace on terms of a renewal of the *status quo ante bellum*, that is, the continuation of the Ostrogothic kingdom of Italy under him, as the Emperor's nominal viceroy. Justinian rejected this offer, and the King's threats, with the reply that Belisarius was in supreme command in Italy and any proposals for peace should be addressed to him — a remarkable reply in view of the 540 peace debacle. In reality, there was not much Belisarius could do, especially as John lingered in the south avoiding a union of their forces. Justinian was determined to continue the war, but its effective prosecution was dependent on how much support he gave his forces.

In early 547 Totila decided to abandon Rome. He was barely dissuaded from demolishing it and contented himself with pulling down some of its fortifications, after which he marched southward. Belisarius himself then entered Rome boldly in the spring of 547. After the second siege and the Ostrogothic ravages it was a ruined and all but uninhabited wreck. Nevertheless, with remarkable determination he rebuilt its defenses as best he could. Totila turned back on it and was amazed to find his army successfully held off. As both Goths and Romans learned for the first time, Totila was not completely invincible.

During the ensuing year Totila was again occupied in the south. After suffering a few reverses at the hands of the Imperial commander John, the King was able to defeat him. Hostilities continued in the southern part of Italy while Belisarius, starved until now for reinforcements, received at long last some new troops. With them he achieved a few limited successes. Nevertheless, Belisarius was unable to loosen Totila's hold on the bulk of the mainland. The Imperial fleet still commanded the sea, but Belisarius could only flit from one port to another, his access limited to coastal areas. It was clear that he could accomplish nothing substantial without a far greater commitment of men and supplies than Justinian had thus far been willing to provide. In Totila he had met his apparent match. It is difficult to say who would have won had Belisarius had the resources for an open battle on reasonable terms. As it was, the great general knew that all his past achievements were eclipsed by his present stalemate. In despair he sent his wife, Antonina, to use her influence at court to secure new forces. When she reached the capital she found that her friend, the Empress Theodora, was dead and that Belisarius' enemies had the Emperor's ear. There was nothing to do but ask for recall. At the beginning of 549 the dispirited Belisarius left Italy and his last real command to return home to neglect and retirement.

With Belisarius gone, his subordinates could do no more than he had done. Totila besieged Rome once again in the summer of 549. The city held out surprisingly well under the circumstances, but it was taken by surprise on January 16, 550. The Gothic King now did his best to rebuild the frightfully battered old city. Stronger than ever, he renewed overtures of peace to Justinian.

The Emperor stubbornly refused to abandon the struggle in which he had already expended so much effort.

By this time (549) the Imperial holdings in Italy had been reduced to Sicily, some crucial coastal fortresses in the south of the peninsula, a few outposts further inland and northward, and of course Ravenna. A serious expenditure of men and money was necessary to recover control of the situation. A capable commander was also required. Justinian decided that he had such a commander in his cousin, Germanus. The latter had proven himself an able general. In view of his qualities and his popularity, Germanus had long been regarded with suspicion and hatred by the Empress Theodora as a dangerous aspirant to the throne. As a result, she had done her best to oppose his and his family's interests, and had prevented any clear designation of him as a successor. Only with Theodora's death in 548 did Germanus' prospects flourish unhindered, and he emerged as the most likely heir to the childless Emperor. For his own part, Germanus welcomed the chance to distinguish himself with great military achievements in Italy. His prospects there were enhanced by the degree of support, much greater than that available to Belisarius, which he could expect from his Imperial kinsman.

Germanus prepared diligently for what promised to be a formidable new Imperial effort. He further strengthened his position by shrewdly marrying Matasuntha, the widow of Wittigis and the daughter of Amalasuntha. His union with the illustrious princess of the house of Theodoric was a magnificent propaganda stroke which had great effect in loosening the loyalty of thoughtful Goths to Totila. Germanus' arrival in Italy would therefore have been a well-nigh decisive step in Justinian's Ostrogothic wars. But it never came. Germanus fell ill in the autumn of 550, on the eve of his departure, and soon died.

In the continued absence of a new supreme commander, Justinian's generals carried on against Totila as best they could. John — who had for some years also been the son-in-law of Germanus [5] — comported himself with some limited success, but the

5. This fact may provide at least a partial explanation for some of John's insubordination during Belisarius' second Gothic campaign. In 545, when back in the capital to appeal on his superior's behalf for more men and

Gothic King far excelled him in ability and strength. Taking the opportunity now to attack Sicily, whose initial defection to the Empire the Goths had never forgiven, Totila briefly besieged Syracuse and then raided other points on the island.

The fortunes of war, however, were about to change. Totila had already been forced to compromise himself in the north when the Frankish King Theudebert once again took advantage of the struggle in Italy to seize territory. Throwing off any semblance of loyalty to the Empire, Theudebert proceeded to annex extensive portions of northern Italy. Totila had no choice but to recognize these conquests, which were retained after Theudebert's death in 548 by his son and successor. Plainly, whoever won the war in Italy would eventually have to deal with the greedy Franks. Nor was Totila long to prevail in Italy. He had reduced the remaining Imperial fortresses on the mainland to a mere handful by 551. In this year, however, a new personality was at hand. Though he was not new to Italy, he would unexpectedly prove to be the last great hero of Justinian's wars, a worthy successor to Belisarius, and the fatal nemesis of Totila. In the latter part of 550 Justinian decided to appoint as supreme commander the eunuch Grand Chamberlain, Narses. Pious, popular, easygoing personally, he was without much genuine military experience. Nevertheless, he had Justinian's confidence and full support, and his friendship with John would guarantee dependable advice in the field, also sparing him the conflicts within his staff which he himself had helped inflict on Belisarius. Finally, as events proved, Narses was a commander of true genius.

---

support, John arranged to marry Justina, the daughter of Germanus. Theodora, the enemy of her husband's cousin, realized that this alliance gave Germanus a useful ally. She therefore made it clear that she would let John feel her ill will, and supposedly charged her friend Antonina with the task of murdering John. John's fear of Belisarius' wife was therefore the reason why he lingered in the south of Italy while Belisarius needed him at Rome during the second Ostrogothic siege of the city and later, when John also consistently avoided joining his commander. At least such is the story told by Procopius (*Anékdota*, chap. v, secs. 8-17). It seems to tally with our other information on Theodora's machinations against Germanus, and it is generally accepted as more or less true. If so, it indicates how complex was the web of intrigue spun by the Empress, and how wide were its effects upon current events.

Narses' progress to Italy was delayed by preparations. Totila used the time to establish his position as securely as possible and to destroy remaining Imperial strongholds. While his fleet ravaged as far as the coasts of Greece, Totila concentrated his efforts on a joint land and sea investment of Ancona in the autumn of 551. In their attempts to relieve it, the Imperial naval forces fell in with a Gothic squadron off Sena Gallica, to the north of Ancona on the Adriatic coast, and won a handsome victory, thus freeing this besieged city from its investment. Imperial progress elsewhere made the Goths realize that they were increasingly on the defensive. Overtures of peace were again sent to the Emperor. Justinian would hear nothing of peace now. Totila made one last aggressive move in the fall of 551, winning the dubious prizes of Sardinia and Corsica. But early the following year his siege of Croton in the south was also broken by Imperial relief. All that was needed to tip the balance decisively was Narses' offensive.

In the spring of 552 that offensive began. Narses marched his large army around the head of the Adriatic to Ravenna. The decision of three decades of war was now to be reached in an open battle at last. Narses moved south and Totila northward. They met at a place called Busta Gallorum (also Teginae) in Umbria. Narses laid his plans with consummate skill, while Totila revealed at last his relative lack of tactical ability. The result was a crushing defeat for the Goths. Their King himself escaped, but in the confusion after the battle he was killed and hastily buried. Such was the Romans' fear of this barbarian foe that they had to dig up his body to convince themselves that he was really dead after all. With Totila perished the hope of the Ostrogothic nation.

This is not to say that the Gothic resistance was ended. The remnants of the Gothic forces regrouped and chose as their new King one of Totila's commanders, Teïas (or Theias). Narses moved to recover strategic points. Overwhelming the Gothic garrison in ravaged Rome, he retook that city in the summer and proceeded to clear out various points in the Campania. In their last stands the Goths behaved with great savagery, but their end was at hand. Seeking to relieve Cumae, which Narses was besieging, Teïas marched his army around all obstacles and appeared near Naples in the hills around Mount Vesuvius. After a series of maneuvers the two armies finally confronted each other on a spur of the old volcano called Mons Lactarius. With little room for formal tactics, the fight was simply a pitched battle centering around the person of the Gothic King. Teïas was at last mortally wounded and dispatched. The remaining Goths fought on in desperation for another full day, until those who survived finally submitted. They were granted the right to depart from Imperial territory and settle somewhere on their own. Thus the Ostrogothic nation passed out of Roman history, and out of practical existence.

In the year which followed the decisive victories of Busta Gallorum and Mons Lactarius in 552, Narses had two remaining tasks to accomplish. First, he had to complete the reduction of Cumae and the various other pockets of scattered Gothic resistance still continuing here and there in the peninsula. But this was not easily done, particularly in view of the second problem, that of renewed foreign intervention. Though he had ignored all the last Ostrogothic King's pleas for help, the son and successor of Theudebert as King of Austrasia, Theudebald (548–555), chose this opportunity to seek Frankish advantage in Italy once again. With Theudebald's active encouragement, some Franks and a large force of his subject people, the Alemannians, invaded Italy in the spring of 553. They ravaged freely, and their successes encouraged some of the remaining Gothic garrisons to hold out. Narses chose to conserve his forces through the winter of 553–554, distributing them through the major cities and leaving the open countryside to the mercy of the savage Franks and Alemannians. These barbarians pillaged their way southward without check, but, in the spring, as they were moving northward to leave Italy, Narses finally regathered his forces for the kill. The barbarians were led into an open battle near Capua, where they were all but annihilated.

Fortunately, this Frankish attack was not repeated. With his hands freed, Narses spent the next eight years gradually reducing the final patches of Gothic resistance. At the same time, as military governor of Italy, Narses set about reorganizing the administration of the recovered territory and rebuilding its shattered life. The peninsula had been terribly battered by the long struggle, its prosperity ruined and its population decimated. Nevertheless, in the final years before his death Justinian could congratulate himself that at long, long last, Italy was again a part of the Roman Empire, as he had intended, together with North Africa and at least a little of Spain.

Justinian the Lawgiver

The Reconquest program represents the external part of Justinian's new projects. Whatever character the Reconquest may assume for us in retrospect, it was of course for him a natural and necessary part of his policies. The same is true of the new internal projects. They were undeniably his most constructive ventures, however, leaving behind him his most enduring monuments. It is with the two categories of the new internal activities that the remainder of this chapter will be concerned.

Just as the Reconquest program was an inevitable expression of Justinian's lofty conception of his responsibilities as a Roman Emperor, so too was his work in the field of law. The legal system developed by Roman civilization is one of its grandest contributions to human history. For the peoples who lived under it in the days of the later Roman Empire it was a particular symbol of high and venerable civilization which was theirs, on a level which could be matched by none of the lesser peoples known to them beyond the pale of the Roman state. It was also a living and continuous link with the heritage of their past, which they looked upon as far from dead or remote. As Emperor, Justinian was the conscientious custodian of these legal traditions. Once again, however, he was far from content simply to maintain things as they were: his reign must make its mark in this sphere as well. There can be no doubt that he succeeded. What ruler could hope to leave a more significant monument than the *Corpus juris civilis*?

The evolution of Roman Law involved a long process of growth. From a body of institutions developing under the Republic, from the Twelve Tables through the enactments of the popular assemblies and the Senate, law had during the Empire come to acquire a connotation which was to be of considerable importance in centuries to follow. For Roman Law was becoming an elaborate system no longer derived from popular will but rather from the exalted embodiment of all power and justice in the civilized world, that is, the ruler. The legislation of the Roman Empire actually existed in the form of the Edicts and *Constitutiones* of the Emperors themselves. Developing early in the Principate, the concept of the Emperor as the sole source of law was further expanded by the enhanced status of the Imperial office in Christian thought. As God's earthly deputy, the Emperor had both the prerogatives and the responsibilities to put the Divine Will into action through his capacities as a lawgiver. His subjects must be disciplined, guided, protected, and nurtured by his application of Christian principles to the regulation of their lives and action. Ironically, a kind of paradox was involved. For Justinian, as a conservative, was dealing with a legal system which was largely pagan in its origins. Yet, his new obligations as a Christian actually harmonized quite well with old Roman conservatism in this case, since the Emperors, even the most pagan and Christian-persecuting ones, had in spite of themselves had a divine responsibility as lawgivers, and their conscientious discharge of this role entitled their enactments to due respect. Indeed, the very man who was the chief agent of Justinian in his legal work, Tribonian, was himself still a pagan.

The practical exercise of Roman Law had come to be based upon the application of the Imperial legislation. This legislation was traditionally made available in collections for the use of judicial authorities and legal experts. Several such collections had been made over the course of the centuries before Justinian. The two most important ones dated from the period of Diocletian and Constantine. One had been made by Gregorius, embodying the enactments of the Emperors from Hadrian to Diocletian, that is roughly A.D. 117–294. The second had been compiled by Hermogenianus, covering the period from 296 to 324. As already noted, a subsequent codification of the law was carried out under the Emperor Theodosius II, covering the acts of the Emperors from Constantine the Great to his own reign. This *Codex Theodosianus*, issued in 438, became a most important legal corpus, not only for the Empire itself, but also for the barbarian states in the West, whose main knowledge of Roman Law was for centuries derived from it. Nevertheless, by the early sixth century the existing legal collections, particularly that of Theodosius, were out of date. Law is, it must be appreciated, a living thing, always subject to change and new needs. Much of the old legal system was obsolescent or inadequate. Such a situation could not have found a more appropriate man to resolve it than the grand-thinking Justinian. Any Emperor of his period would have had to do something about it. What Justinian did was far more than any other ruler might have been expected to do.

It is generally agreed that Justinian had developed the idea of a major revision of the legal system some time before his personal assumption of power.[6] Once on the throne in his own name he acted with an alacrity that indicates both his immediate concern for the situation and an advanced background of thought and preparation. On February 13, 528, slightly over six months after his accession, he issued a decree by which a commission of ten legal scholars was appointed to prepare an entirely new edition of the laws, an edition which would be up to date and clarified. Among the ten were the learned jurist and official Tribonian, and Theophilus, a professor of law at the Higher School (University) of Constantinople. This commission worked diligently, collating texts, removing needless repetitions or contradictions, bringing passages up to date, and working out an orderly arrangement. Such was their dispatch that after barely a year the Emperor could announce and authorize the issuance of the *Codex Justinianus* in a constitution of April 7, 529.

This initial version of the *Codex*, or Code, was not, however, to remain unchanged. Indeed, its very text is lost to us. The further activities of Justinian's legal advisers soon made it necessary to revise it. A new edition was therefore prepared, and was formally issued on November 16, 534. In it the original format of ten books, in which the 529 edition had been cast, was expanded to the final form of twelve, containing a total of 4,562 laws. The first book is prefaced by the Emperor's successive decrees which had called forth and heralded the Code, and then continues with the body of ecclesiastical law — significantly given a pre-eminent place — fol-

6. For Justinian's role in the legal activities of his uncle, see Vasiliev, *Justin the First*, pp. 389–413, especially 391.

lowed by material on the theory and administration of law. The next seven books deal with private law, while Book Nine covers criminal law, and the final three books involve administrative measures. Here and there some softening influence of Christian principles may be traced, but on the whole the compilation of the Code was concerned primarily with preserving and setting forth the old statements of the law in a clear and systematic form. The compilation covers the full range of recognized Imperial enactments, from Hadrian to Justinian in 534. The various Imperial enactments are quoted in their appropriate topical place, each book being subdivided into *tituli*, or "titles," on each specific point of law; where more than one enactment is given they are placed in chronological order, and all with precise citation by Emperor and date.

Roman Law, however, is more than simply a matter of the bare enactments. From the early second through the fourth centuries there had grown up a large body of recognized literature on the interpretation and elucidation of the law — what is called Jurisprudence. The writings of the interpreters, the famous jurisconsults, became important guides for those who had to use and apply the law in actual practice, and their work was fully authorized by Imperial authority as well as tradition. Among the most eminent of these jurisconsults were Pomponius, the great Gaius, Papinian, Paulus, Modestinus, and Ulpian, all of whom lived mainly during the second and early third centuries A.D. As important as were their writings, however, these were numerous, scattered, and not always fully available. Often, also, there were contradictions or confusions among their interpretations. Justinian and his legal staff therefore decided characteristically to go one step beyond the formal codification of the law to prepare a systematic synthesis of this wide but indispensable literature.

As a preliminary move in this direction, the Emperor and his staff prepared the document known as the Fifty Decisions, issued during the winter of 530–531. This was a definitive statement of rulings on a number of common cases on which the old authorities disagreed, now settled once and for all to spare judges the chore of having to go over the literature themselves each time to choose between contradictions. Once this step was taken, it was possible to attend to the full scope of the work. On December 15, 530, the Emperor issued his formal order for the new compilation. Another commission was appointed, of which Tribonian was now the recognized president. Under him were sixteen assistants, several of them veterans of the work on the Code, including Theophilus of the University of Constantinople. Another great law school, and one of the centers of legal studies in Antiquity, Berytus (or Beirut), was represented by Dorotheus, and the rest of the commission included a high official and eleven professional lawyers.

Again the work proceeded briskly. Tribonian was a man of vast legal learning, whatever his personal failings, and he could place at the commission's disposal his invaluable and matchless library of law books. He had his commission subdivided into three committees so that the literature could be distributed among them. The commission once again had full discretionary authority to delete, abridge, harmonize, collate, update, and clarify these texts, drawn from some 2,000 books written by some thirty-nine different authorities. All this was reduced to a text divided into fifty books, again subdivided into *tituli* on the respective points of law. For this staggering task of digestion and regurgitation ten years had been assigned. Yet, it was accomplished within three years and in December of 533 the Digest, or Pandects, was completed.

Adding to the magnitude of this accomplishment, Tribonian had also, with the help of Theophilus of Constantinople and Dorotheus of Berytus, prepared the *Institutiones*, or Institutes, a newly revised and updated edition of Gaius' old Commentaries, which could serve as a handbook for students. It was in the light of all this work that Tribonian, with Dorotheus and three others of his commission, was given the task of preparing the revised edition of the Code.

Such, then, are the first three components of the *Corpus juris civilis*, the "Body of Civil Law," which, as the title implies, was intended by Justinian to fill the entire legal needs of his state and age, serving at the same time as the fundamental summation of Roman legal development through the centuries. The Code provided the raw material of the law, the enactments of the Emperors; the Digest or Pandects assembled definitively the literature of

Roman jurisprudence, the accumulated experience of the learned legal authorities in interpreting and explaining the law; and the Institutes provided the official manual for students of law. Each of these components was authoritative, all previous or other such works on law being declared superseded and invalid, since these three parts contained all that was necessary in a self-sufficient whole.[7]

Except, that is, for one final component. The rulers of the Later, Christian, Empire continued to be proudly aware that Roman Law was a living and ever-unfolding tradition, and that they were its continuing source. The capacity to modify or extend the Law also served the purpose of bringing the great Roman legal system of the pagan past into more consistent alignment with Christian concepts and needs.[8] So it is that the fourth part of Justinian's *Corpus* is the collection of his *Novéllai*, the "Novels" or New Laws, which were issued by him during the remainder of his reign after the second edition of the Code in 534. Here we find one significant change, however. The previous portions of the *Corpus* had all been issued in Latin, the traditional language of the Roman state and, of course, the language of the old texts involved. When Justinian issued his New Laws, however, they were written in the Greek language, so that they could be more easily understood by

7. There has been one attempt at an English rendering of Justinian's legal compilations: *The Civil Law*, trans. S. P. Scott (17 vols., Cincinnati, 1932); but this is gravely flawed by incompleteness and inaccuracy. Otherwise, unfortunately, there is no integral translation of the entire *Corpus juris civilis* into a modern language, and the Code itself is still unavailable in an English rendering.

8. Note the perceptive observations of Downey: "The new legislation [i.e., of Justinian himself] both maintained the essential character of classical Roman law and adapted it where necessary to the changing needs of the society it had to serve. It was possible to preserve Roman law as a single system in the new Christian state because Constantine the Great had offered the Christians full membership in the state on terms of Roman law. While a few modifications had to be made, it was possible to keep the body of the law unchanged in its main features. If Constantine had not taken the opportunity to incorporate the Christians in the state in this way, and if the action had not come solely from the side of the state, the character of the legal system would have been altered." — *Constantinople in the Age of Justinian* (Copyright, 1960, University of Oklahoma Press), p. 77.

everyone, as he frankly admitted. It is true that the use of Latin had never really taken firm root in the East, where Greek was the normal medium of expression. What is significant is that by this time even many of the Imperial officials knew no Latin and that the very bureaucracy which had to run the Roman Empire was becoming unable to use its traditional language. Conservative and Latin-minded though he was, Justinian could only bow to necessity. The very fact that he had to do so, not only because of popular usage but because of official necessity as well, gives some indication of the changes taking place in his world, whether or not he liked them or even understood them.

These "Novels," 160 in number, are most valuable for our understanding of Justinian's aim as a ruler.[9] They reveal him as vitally concerned with the minutiae of his society. Many of them involve problems of official procedure and administration. A large body of them deal with the regulation of the conduct, morality, prosperity, and general well-being of his subjects as individuals. Of course, the state religion is much in evidence, not only in terms of the introduction of Christian principles into the legal system, but in the emphasis on proper belief, as well as proper conduct, as a necessity for good citizenship. It is above all in evidence in the extensive legislation by the Emperor to regulate the affairs of the Church, its administration, its properties and privileges, and the details of clerical and monastic life. Here indeed in these New Laws is Justinian "the Emperor who never sleeps," benevolent, implaca-

9. Unfortunately, the Novels have been neglected in relation to the rest of the *Corpus juris civilis*. This is so partly because they represent the section of it which is distinctly Justinian's, in contrast to the other three parts which represent the broader background of Roman Law and as such are of cardinal importance to all scholars of legal history as a whole. But it is to the Novels one must turn for an understanding of the more specifically Justinianic legal efforts on an everyday plane. Also unfortunately, the Novels are not available in translation, at least in English. There is, however, a most useful and unusually extensive general analysis of Justinian's Novels by Ure in *Justinian and his Age*, pp. 146–167, complete with quotations from or synopses of specific Novels. There is also a good perspective on the Novels as a part of the Emperor's legislative outlook by Bury, *History of the Later Roman Empire . . .* (A.D. 395–565), II, 400–416, and 334 ff. In addition, note the comments of Downey, *Constantinople in the Age of Justinian*, pp. 77–79.

ble, paternalistic, authoritarian, watching carefully over every detail of his subjects' lives.

To complete our appreciation of Justinian as a legislator we must be aware of a perspective beyond that of the *Corpus juris civilis* alone. The Emperor was more than the divinely placed capstone on a great pyramid of legal authority: he also had to govern and administer a great Empire. As a result, he was involved in considerable extra-judicial legislation, most notably as set forth in his Edicts.

Many of these Edicts deal with strictly administrative concerns, such as the organization of the newly conquered provinces or the reorganization of old ones. In this respect Justinian's reign was an important stage in the modification of a part of the Imperial system established by Diocletian, in terms that would set crucial precedents for the reorganization of the Empire in the century to follow Justinian's age. Again ironically, the conservative Emperor becomes, unwittingly or not, an actual innovator in coping with practical realities, a fact which is itself a symptom of inevitably changing times. The circumstances which had elicited many of Diocletian's administrative reforms were no longer operative by the sixth century. As a result, Justinian could dispense with some of the "checks and balances" in the provincial system, eliminating intermediate functions on the intermediary diocesan level and reuniting small provinces as larger units.

More crucially, he began the process of discarding Diocletian's old principle of strict separation between civil and military authority. One can see this principle flouted most vividly in the case of such extraordinary commanders as Belisarius and Narses in their campaigns in North Africa and Italy. The former was in fact given a new and almost unprecedented rank, roughly corresponding to the old Roman title of *Imperator*: in the actual Greek, *strategòs autokrátor*, a style that combines the word for "general" with the formal Greek equivalent of the Latin designation of *imperator*, which had become the Emperor's military title. In effect, this commander was made the Emperor's alter ego in the field, responsible for all civil and judicial functions as well as military in the area of his assignment, as if representing the Emperor's own person. The establishment of this extraordinary authority in North Africa and Italy anticipates developments there later in the sixth century. Such drastic breaches of Diocletian's former separation of civil and military authority were not limited simply to the conquerors of these restored provinces and their successors. Justinian also thoroughly reorganized the government of Egypt, and there, too, the Diocletianic principle was abandoned. The same was true in the vital area of Thrace, the very environs of the capital, in many parts of Asia Minor, and elsewhere. It should be emphasized that these steps were often taken as ad hoc measures. By themselves they constituted no sweeping revision of the Empire's administrative system, such as was to come in later periods. Such steps did, however, establish important foundations for subsequent changes. Further, they indicated that Justinian, despite his zeal in preserving the institutions and achievements of the past, was quite willing to discard them when the interests of his times required that he do so.

In this connection, too, we might note that it was also ironically in the period of this conservative-minded sovereign that the most venerable office of the old Roman state finally disappeared. The consulship had been, since the establishment of the Augustan Principate, an empty formality, devoid of the actual power by which its annual pair of occupants had once governed the Roman Republic. It had instead become an honor which the Emperor could bestow upon private individuals of merit or ambition, and it came to involve in particular the offering of lavish entertainments to the populace of the capital. Much as the common people enjoyed this, the expenses were becoming so exorbitant that no private individual could afford the office; the state had to underwrite it, which was an increasing drain on the treasury. It was therefore not unnatural that, after efforts to alleviate the situation, and in spite of popular discontent, Justinian was forced first to curtail the expenditures and finally to allow the office to lapse after the year 542. Thereafter the title served only as one which each Emperor assumed meaninglessly during the first year of his reign.

One of the principal concerns of Justinian's Edicts was the fiscal administration. As already indicated, Justinian was caught in something of a self-made trap, common to many rulers who had maintained the existing Imperial machinery, but intensified in his case. His ambitious projects demanded vast amounts of money and compelled him to preside over a government which was oppressive and extortionate in the extreme. His chief administrators, such as Peter Barsymes and the notorious John of Cappadocia, were chosen specifically because of their ruthless and ingenious talents for squeezing money out of the people of the Empire. Yet, at the same time, Justinian never abandoned the desire to make his government honest as well as efficient. He tried repeatedly to reduce the abuses of his officials and to protect his subjects against unjust agents of the revenue and governmental system. He was particularly anxious to eliminate or curtail the sale of public office, an abuse which itself only bred further misconduct on the part of the new office-holders. The repeated emphasis upon such themes throughout his legislation indicate that Justinian found it difficult to achieve the goal of honest government. Moreover, so compromised was he by using the corrupt but revenue-producing officials whom his financial requirements demanded, that his protection of his subjects inevitably became merely a matter of preserving the goose which laid the much-needed golden eggs. For all his good intentions, Justinian's government was not an easy one to live under. In all justice, it should perhaps be stressed that Justinian's fiscal dilemmas were not unusual. They were the result of the basic nature of a system little changed for more than two centuries. The least that can be said for Justinian is that he had little success in overcoming or substantially revising it.

In the final analysis, Justinian's achievement as a legislator was a mixed one. He sought an up-to-date, efficient, and honest government. Yet, his own great financial needs vitiated his efforts in this regard. He sought to preserve a great and venerable legal system by modifying it to existing needs and by revitalizing it with Christian concepts. Without doubt his legislation revealed a genuine sense of humanity and a concern for the oppressed and the underprivileged. At the same time, however, his legislation was baldly conservative in that it attempted frankly to preserve the privileges and possessions of the propertied classes; in that it tried to regulate ruthlessly the details of men's conduct in all spheres, even their religious beliefs; and in that it imposed pen-

alties that were sharply graduated by class and were often in-
humanly severe. These factors have often won scorn for the Later
Roman state, especially in connection with the use of mutilation
as a punishment — one which became sickeningly common in later
centuries. Of course it should be remembered that class distinctions in punishment derive from the earliest stages of law in pre-
Roman Antiquity, were also common among the barbarians as
well as the Romans and Byzantines, and existed in European nations down to modern times. As for judicial mutilation, it was
neither invented by the Byzantines, nor did its use cease with
them, by many centuries; moveover, it was often regarded by the
Later Romans as a humane substitute for the greater extreme of
capital punishment. Whatever these mitigations, the legislative
activity of Justinian was undoubtedly of a kind that reflects all
the repugnant aspects of a state which was politically authoritative, socially highly stratified, and ideologically intolerant. For
all this, however, it was not without genuine positive features, and
its historical importance is enormous. It further reveals Justinian
as earnestly dedicated to governing his realm in the best and most
thorough way he knew. In the *Corpus juris civilis* he produced
a monument such as few sovereigns anywhere or at any time
have been able to leave behind them.[10]

10. For another evaluation of Justinian's legislative work, especially as
embodied in the Novels, note Ure in *Justinian and his Age*, pp. 166–167:
"The problem of combining conservatism with progress is fundamental to all
good statesmanship in any civilized society. But those who hold that conservatism of the best kind is the opposite of mummification must admit that
the past weighed far too heavily on Justinian in almost everything he undertook. If his whole conception of the world was not wrong, Christianity had
brought into it something new and vivifying, but it is hard to see the effect
of any really new and vitalizing influence in the well-intentioned tinkering
with the traditional law of Rome which is what his efforts actually amounted
to. The last great attempt to make a new world by the union of the Graeco-
Roman and the Christian traditions failed not only because external conditions were against it, but also and still more because the men who made it
knew not what manner of spirit they were of. Heresy hunting and the savage suppression of deviationists are sure signs of something radically wrong
either with the gospel on whose behalf they are invoked or with those who
use such methods to propagate it. Justinian's legislation to enforce orthodoxy
makes depressing reading. All the same it would be wrong to end . . . on

Justinian the Builder

Of all Justinian's new projects, his Reconquest program was probably the most ambitious and expensive. His legislative activity could come nowhere near it in terms of cost, and, of course, some of it was actually a function of his Reconquest achievements. Nevertheless, there was another drain on the Emperor's resources, one which he considered every bit as essential: this was the third of his new projects, his building program. For Justinian was determined to leave his mark on the Empire in this way as well as in others. In this regard he was following the example of his predecessors, both pagan and Christian. Their building activities were symbols of their prestige and their power as rulers. Nevertheless, few sovereigns, Roman or otherwise, ever undertook quite so ambitious an architectural program as did Justinian. One may even wonder if modern times contain anything its equal in scope or in artistic fruitfulness.

As has been noted, one of the writings of the contemporary historian Procopius is his treatise *On the Buildings*, sometimes also called the *Book of Edifices*. Written about 559 or 560, this is a systematic survey of Justinian's building activity throughout his Empire to the time of its composition. It is a panegyric, and its tone is frankly adulatory. This fact, together with its format, limits its interest as literature. Nevertheless, it is of necessity the all-important source for our knowledge of that activity, and it contains invaluable information on more than the architectural state of the Empire. Its arrangement, in six books, is geographical. The first book is devoted to the capital, and the remainder to the provinces: Book Two to Mesopotamia and Syria; Book Three to Armenia, the far-flung outposts of the Crimea, and the western area of the Black Sea coast; Book Four covers the Balkan peninsula

---

a note of unqualified condemnation. Perhaps the most attractive thing about the *Novels* is the way that admissions of fallibility are constantly breaking through. Those who find their inspiration in the prophets, sacred or secular, will not discover in the legislation of Justinian any fresh source of the divine fire, but they may be helped to a more sympathetic understanding of an age that knew not the prophets and sought salvation in the law."

including Illyricum, Thrace, and Greece; Book Five deals with Asia Minor and Palestine; and Book Six with Egypt and Africa.[11]

The nature and purpose of Justinian's building activities might be divided roughly into two aspects, the practical and the ornamental, though the distinction between them should be kept very fluid. Numerically the first category was dominated by military fortifications and other defensive structures. It is revealing for us to learn from Procopius' descriptions how terribly exposed were many parts of the Empire, often even those far from the frontiers. Justinian's goal was to strengthen the more dangerous frontiers with elaborate chains of border outposts and defensive systems, while at the same time securing the immediate safety of specific sites and areas deeper within Imperial territory.

The practical category included such other structures as bridges, aqueducts, reservoirs, roads, storehouses, asylums, and various buildings for normal public use. Some of them, such as cisterns, had a defensive value also, but most were built as a result of local needs, often aggravated by the ravages of time or of enemy attacks, or perhaps by neglect in the reign of the economy-minded Anastasius I. Sometimes the Emperor's buildings combined the functional and the ornamental, as in the cases of baths, law courts, and other places of public gathering. Perhaps the best single synthesis of both aspects is represented by the great fortress-monastery of St. Catherine of Mount Sinai, which still stands, despite later accretions, as a vivid architectural survival of the age of Justinian and a matchless repository of early Christian and Byzantine art.

It is generally the monasteries, and especially the churches, which constitute the chief of Justinian's ornamental buildings. These, of course, reflected also the Emperor's piety as a zealous Christian sovereign. Many of his churches still stand, giving us a picture of his activities at their best, far beyond anything the

11. This work is, of course, available in the excellent English translation by H. B. Dewing, with G. Downey, as Vol. VII (1940) of the Loeb series' complete edition of Procopius; a revised and corrected edition has been prepared, for publication at a future date still uncertain. Note also the useful synopsis of the work provided by Ure in the course of his stimulating chapter on Justinian's building in *Justinian and his Age*, pp. 218–244.

scattered if impressive remains of many of his other and more practical structures could provide.

His churches were built with a wide variety of decorations and forms — from the traditional and simple rectangular basilica style, to octagonal or other more complex patterns. Three sites in particular benefited richly from his church-building. His great church in honor of the Virgin Mary in Jerusalem no longer stands; perhaps the best substitute we can still enjoy in its place is his church at Mount Sinai, which might suggest on a smaller scale some of Jerusalem's splendors. A second important site was Ravenna, an Imperial capital under the later Western Emperors, and then the Ostrogothic capital of Italy. Justinian chose to leave his own imprint upon it, partly as a symbol of his recovery of it and of the rest of Italy. The still-surviving monuments are particularly noteworthy here. One is the octagonal Church of San Vitale (St. Vitalis), begun by the Goths but completed in 547 after Justinian's reoccupation of the city. Here may be found the famous pair of mosaic panels showing Justinian and Theodora with their respective retinues (see Plates IV and V). Outside the actual limits of the city, in the adjacent port of Classis, is the basilican Church of San Apollinare in Classe (to St. Apollinaris), completed in 549, though with some of its internal decoration from a later period. Curiously enough, neither of these eminent monuments is described by Procopius, who, it may be noted, omits Italy from his architectural survey of the Empire — perhaps because its final reduction was not completed at the time of his writing, but also because he apparently did not finish the book as planned.

The third and most important site of the Emperor's building activity was of course the Imperial capital, Constantinople itself. Justinian probably had conceived great building plans for the city even before he ascended the throne on his own in 527. Such plans were then given particular point by the episode which provided so much impetus to his activities in general, the Nika Riots. As a result of that terrible upheaval in January of 532 the capital was left a shambles, with large areas of its most important regions reduced to smoldering ruins. Such circumstances were tailor-made for the ambitious builder-Emperor, who saw this as an almost God-given opportunity to rebuild the city on a more glorious

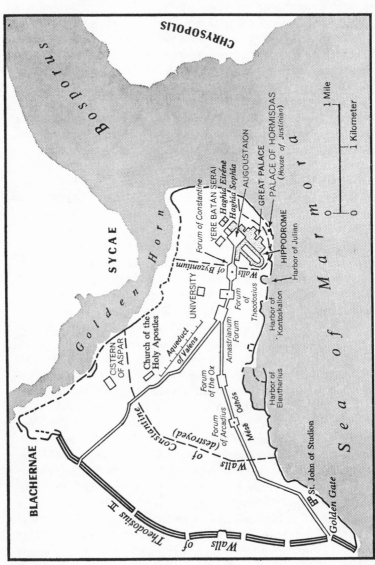

Byzantine Constantinople, including the important monuments of the Justinianic era. (Courtesy of

scale than ever. It is not an exaggeration to say that it was as much to Justinian as to any one else that the city of Constantine owed its beginning as the most splendid city in medieval Christendom.

Justinian's building activities in Constantinople were widely varied, as could be expected. He provided for the first really systematic conservation of its water supply by building great cisterns, of which two still survive in the city to this day (see Plate II). In the wake of the Nika Riots' destruction he built or rebuilt baths, colonnades, and other places of public gathering, adding also charitable institutions, including a hospital and asylums for the poor or unfortunate — institutions which Theodora particularly supported. In the great forum, the *Augoustaîon*, a large equestrian statue of Justinian himself, with the attributes of Achilles, was set atop a column as if to set a seal upon his rebuilding of the city. (See Plate X.) For his own purposes he enlarged the Grand Palace of the Emperors, extending it to enclose the old Palace of Hormisdas on the Marmora shore that he had previously rebuilt for his own use during his uncle's reign. The shores and the suburbs around the city were also developed and beautified.

The Emperor's greatest passion as a builder was to increase the city's churches and monasteries, which he undertook to do on a lavish scale. He was particularly interested, even before his accession to the throne, in building churches in honor of the early martyrs associated with old Byzantium and its environs. During his reign proper, large numbers of churches were built or rebuilt. This gave his architects an opportunity to work with a wide range of designs and decorations. Particularly interesting among these is the handsome little domed octagonal Church of Saints Sergius and Bacchus, which still stands today near the shore of the Sea of Marmora. Far more monumental was Justinian's Church of the Holy Apostles. The original structure, one of Constantine the Great's churches, had fallen into decay by the early sixth century, and, in typical fashion, Justinian chose to rebuild it entirely, on a more splendid scale than ever. Through much of the Empire's history this edifice was noteworthy as the regular site of Imperial burials, and, though it no longer stands in modern times, its design is reputed to be reflected in such imitations as the Church of San Marco, the famous basilica of the Doges in Venice. But Justinian's name is most firmly linked with two particular churches which survive in the city. Both were Justinian's reconstructions of old Constantinian churches destroyed in the Nika conflagrations. They were intended as a pair, symbolizing two aspects of God's blessings upon mankind. One was dedicated to the Holy Peace (*Haghía Eiréné*), the other to the Holy Wisdom (*Haghía Sophía*) — not, be it emphasized, to individual saints named Irene and Sophia. Haghía Eiréné (or "St. Irene," in the common usage) has been altered somewhat since Justinian's day (see Plate III), has suffered through hard times, and has never attained its sister's prestige. It is rather with Haghía Sophía (or "Sancta Sophia," in preference to "St. Sophia") that Justinian the builder comes most to life for us. This became the Great Church of the Empire, enduring and being embellished through the centuries as one of the great focal points 'of Byzantine history and art, and as one of the supreme buildings of Christian worship until the Turks made it a mosque in 1453. In 1935 Mustafa Kemal Atatürk converted it into a museum. Thus it now stands for us, one of the most fabulous pieces of architecture and living history preserved in our time (see Plates VII and VIII).

Much has been written of this magnificent monument, and there is much that yet remains to be written about it in the light of new study. For our purposes here, however, the most cursory comments may suffice.

As the smoke settled on the ruins of the gutted original, in 532, Justinian put in motion his scheme to build a replacement of his own for it. He assigned to the task the outstanding architect, engineer, and mathematician of the day, Anthemius of Tralles, associating with him another distinguished mathematician from Asia Minor, Isidore of Miletus. According to our information, the plans were completed within forty days, suggesting that there had been considerable prior preparation even before the Nika Riots had actually made necessary the rebuilding of the church. The work on the new edifice proceeded at a frantic pace under the Emperor's impatient supervision. He is represented as having frequently given divinely inspired guidance to his architects, often solving crucial problems for them. Money for the construction and the decoration was lavished without stinting. After the almost unbelievably short time of five years, the church was finished. On December 26, 537, accompanied by the Patriarch and a vast throng, the Emperor formally consecrated it. According to one account, Justinian was so overwhelmed by his achievement that he exclaimed, "Glory be to God Who considered me worthy of this task! O Solomon, I have outdone thee!" [12]

But the building failed. The design had been too radical, the architects' knowledge of their materials too uncertain, and, above all, the haste of construction too intense. Excessive weight had been placed prematurely upon the masonry as it was built, before it had been allowed to settle sufficiently. As a result, the structure was subjected to impossible stresses and strains, causing a degree of deformation that brought the great dome crashing to the ground in May of 558. The work of redressing the damage was given to the son of one of the original architects, Isidore the Younger. Realizing that the original dome had been too low and too daring, and appreciating the deformation that had occasioned the failure of the original design, he built a new dome, higher and less precarious, compensating for the structural failings. This second dome has since been damaged and replaced several times in its long history, but the building survives now largely as it was when Isidore the Younger repaired it. In its revised form Justinian himself re-inaugurated it on Christmas Eve of 562.

The basic features of Haghía Sophía represent a dramatic and almost revolutionary new design in church-building, one of great size and stunning esthetic effect, and one virtually unique even in

12. This exclamation is, however, quite probably apocryphal. It appears only in a source of a much later period, the Greek title of which translates as *On the Structure of the Temple of the Holy Wisdom*, known also by the Latin title of *Narratio de aedificatione templi Sanctae Sophiae*, formerly ascribed to the fourteenth-century Byzantine writer Georgios Kodinos, but now held to be an earlier work of perhaps the eleventh or twelfth century. The passage in question may be found in its standard publications, ed. I. Bekker in the *Bonn Corpus* collection of Pseudo-Codinus (Bonn, 1843), p. 143, or in the collection, *Scriptores originum Constantinopolitanarum*, ed. T. Preger for the Teubner Series (Leipzig, 1901), I, 105. Note also the comments of P. Maas, in an article on Romanos the Melode in *Byzantinische Zeitschrift*, 15 (1906), 5–6, who discusses the passage in relation to relevant texts by Romanos and the poet Corippus, both actual sixth-century contemporaries of Justinian.

Byzantine architecture as it was to develop. Its focal element is the inner square of the nave, somewhat over 100 feet on each side, its corners marked by the four great masonry piers' which support the four arches that rise from them. These arches bear the church's ultimate feature, its central dome, symbolic of the Dome of Heaven itself. The accomplishment of successfully setting this circular crown on a square base was achieved by the epoch-making use of what are called pendentives. These are curved triangular surfaces between the arches which begin at the point where the arches spring from the piers, and then rise upwards to provide the dome's circular base that is thus tangential on the four sides to the crowns of the arches. On this circular base the dome rests, in its second form some 180 feet from the floor. The base of the dome itself is pierced with windows so that light pours in, giving the illusion, as Procopius says, that the dome is suspended from on high as if it did not touch the rest of the building. The nave is extended on either end to a length of 250 feet by a pair of semi-domes, and at the four corners by semi-cylindrical exedras with their own smaller half-domes, all increasing the spatial effects. Colonnades and galleries flank the nave on the sides in great complexity. With the rich ornamentation and trappings of worship added to its architectural splendor, the initial aspect of this church must have been every bit as overwhelming to its contemporaries as Procopius' fulsome description portrays it.

Such then, was the pinnacle of Justinian's accomplishment as a builder. Certainly in architectural brilliance and innovation alone his age deserves to be rated as a great one.[13] Haghía Sophía, one of the greatest achievements of Christian, or human, architecture, and the *Corpus juris civilis*, a supreme landmark of Roman, and European, Law, stand forth as Justinian's most enviable monuments. What ruler could hope to leave finer ones?

13. Compare the comments of Ure, *Justinian and his Age*, pp. 243–244, on the significance of the fact that the epoch of Justinian should allow such genius as that of Anthemius of Tralles and his colleagues to flourish so creatively, even if it did stifle the human spirit in other spheres. For some stimulating comments on the artistic spirit of the age of Justinian, see G. Mathew's new book, *Byzantine Aesthetics* (London, 1963), especially pp. 62–93.

V   THE LAST YEARS

Justinian Without Theodora

In tracing the various spheres of activity of the whole of Justinian's reign, we have seen much of the positive and constructive side of it, especially in its earlier phase of greatest accomplishment.[1] We have now to consider more of the negative aspects of the reign, especially in the last period, when the flavor of the great Emperor's age seems to have turned more sour. There is no single date at which we can say that such a period specifically began, but something of a point of reference may be found in an event which affected Justinian personally as few others could: the loss of the person who had been closer to him than any other human being.

Theodora died on June 28, 548, of an illness now identifiable as cancer. Inevitably, her death very much altered the political atmosphere of the court and of the entire Empire, relieving her enemies of her hatred and depriving her friends of her support. Factions realigned and new voices began to win the Emperor's ear. It was Justinian himself who would have to suffer most. To

---

1. Compare Bury, *History of the Later Roman Empire* . . . (A.D. 395–565), II, 55: "The nine or ten years following the suppression of the Nika revolt were the most glorious period of Justinian's reign. He was at peace with Persia; Africa and Italy were restored to his dominion. The great legal works which he had undertaken were brought to a successful conclusion; and Constantinople . . . arose from its ashes more magnificent than ever."

be sure, the death of his wife removed a person who had worked secretly against his wishes in some instances, and who had terribly complicated the intrigue-ridden atmosphere of the court. But Theodora had been a devoted and faithful — in all senses of that word — partner to her husband. She had often supplied crucial support, as at the time of the Nika Riots, and she had further served him as a stabilizing influence.

It would be a mistake to see everything that happened after 548 as representing a drastic change solely because of her departure from the scene. Justinian was too deeply rooted in his outlook, and too deeply committed to it, to do anything but carry on. Yet, one can note subtle changes of direction or emphasis which may reflect the absence of her influence. Of course, Justinian the widower was also Justinian the older man, and as he aged he changed. Nevertheless, the loneliness to which the Emperor was now condemned by Theodora's death, in combination with increasing difficulties during the latter part of his reign, bore down the more heavily upon him as the years passed, accelerating the advance of his senility. Justinian was, then, for various reasons, an increasingly different man and Emperor from what he had been before his wife's death.

The effects of her passing can be traced most clearly in the years which immediately followed it. Among the areas of Theodora's highhanded interference was that of Justinian's family. She and her husband had no children, and in their lack of a direct heir much attention was naturally directed towards those among the Emperor's kinsmen who might succeed him. As we have seen, Theodora chose sides in this dispute, turning her enmity against Justinian's cousin, Germanus, and his family, whom she chose to regard as actual rivals to herself and even to her husband. This enmity helped arouse considerable ill will amongst Justinian's relatives. In this way Theodora left a heritage of animosities after her death, whatever the change that event variously meant for those relatives. Such animosities came to a head in the year 548 itself, during the months after her death, when a conspiracy against the Emperor was formed.

The commander Artabanes, an Armenian in origin and an individual whom we encountered briefly in the confused North African scene during 546, became the leader of the plot. In his service in North Africa he had met Praejecta, the daughter of the Emperor's sister Vigilantia, who at the time was the wife of the ill-fated commander there, Areobindus. Artabanes had become enamored of her, and when Praejecta returned as a widow to Constantinople, he followed her. He was given to understand that his hopes of marrying her were vain, however, and as a result he nourished a grievance against the Emperor. Encouraged by others with grudges of their own, Artabanes began to identify his quest for vengeance with the interests of Germanus and his family, on whose behalf he was inspired to develop his conspiracy. His plan was to assassinate Justinian, together with Belisarius, at the time of the general's second return from Italy and then to declare Germanus Emperor. The plot was revealed, however, and easily squelched. Artabanes himself was even returned soon to favor and command. But, trifling as it was in its consequences, the incident suggests the mounting unrest unleashed by Theodora's death.

An even more specific indication of the changes attending her passing was the very recall of Belisarius in 548. Whatever may have been Theodora's appreciation of Belisarius' military genius, she supported him with virtual consistency to the end of her life because of her friendship with his wife, Antonina. As has been noted, it was Antonina's mission in 548 to try to win more support for her husband from Justinian through her influence with the Empress. When she arrived in the capital for this purpose, she found Theodora dead and her own situation changed. With the Emperor's support for him withdrawn, Belisarius' enemies could now poison Justinian's mind further against him. The result was Belisarius' own request to be recalled. This time, however, it was recall not to another post but to retirement, while others strove to capture his laurels. Germanus' death alone prevented him from doing just this, and the role of Belisarius' successor fell instead to Narses. That Germanus might have succeeded, and that Narses did succeed, where Belisarius had failed in Italy does not necessarily indicate their superiority in ability over Belisarius. The veteran commander had failed for lack of the full resources of men and money which were, however, made available to these two men, and with which Narses was able to win the final triumph. Yet, these facts could provide little consolation to Belisarius, and they reflect ingloriously upon the Emperor, who allowed his best general's talents to go to waste after 548. At that time, after all, Belisarius was probably not yet fifty years old and was by no means past his prime.

One might assume also that the loss of Theodora would have affected Justinian's religious policies. With her predisposition to Monophysitism she had complicated the Emperor's handling of the terribly difficult problem of Church dissent. Her removal from this sphere could have been crucial. The actual situation was somewhat less dramatic than might have been expected, however. Justinian was, after all, deeply involved in a course of policy at the time of her death, and one can trace no immediate break thereafter. Her absence must be traced here in more subtle ways.

The episode of the Three Chapters was already in progress as her end approached. She had witnessed with satisfaction before she died the first stages of the humiliation of her old enemy, Pope Vigilius. Her spirit certainly lived on in the further phases of his abasement as Justinian imposed his program on the Fifth Ecumenical Council in the spring of 553, completing the Pope's humiliation in the months thereafter.

Nor did Justinian's policies with regard to the Monophysites change substantially after 553 any more than after 548, at least in kind. Indeed, they could not. The question of reconciling the Monophysites was bound up both in fundamental theological issues vital to the people of that age and in the political situation of crucial provinces in the Empire, where local sentiments were deeply committed in the controversy. Justinian refused to abandon his hopes that some formula of reconciliation could be found to solve the far-reaching disputes.

The Fifth Council had not provided the desired formula after all. For all the efforts and involvements it comprised, the condemnation of the three disputed theologians by the Council was a forlorn hope. It left still untouched the basic issue of the controversy, the Christological question of the one or the two Natures of the Son. Did Christ comprise two Natures, the Human and the Divine, distinct yet somehow united, as the Council of Chalcedon had set forth in the orthodox position? Or was He of one single all-embracing Divine Nature which submerged any distinct aspects of humanity, as the Monophysites persistently maintained? Only when this dispute was resolved could there be any reconciliation between Chalcedonians and Monophysites. Since the equation "one equals two" is not an easy one to prove convincingly, especially when fraught with so many theological implications, reconciliation was perhaps really impossible. Mutual tolerance, on the other hand, was simply out of the question in that day and age. Correct belief, *orthodoxía*, had to be settled one way or another.

The Fifth Council had brought Justinian to the pinnacle of his caesaropapism. No other Emperor before him — and, indeed, few after him — ever made his will so supreme in matters of faith. By fiat he had imposed one after another of the theological formulas by which he proposed to establish peace in the Church. At the risk of alienating his own orthodox supporters, he had succeeded formally in effecting his impositions, although the impositions themselves had done no good. He could not decree belief and allegiance. For all the effort he had expended, the Monophysites resisted as stubbornly as ever any compromise of their beliefs. The consuming religious problem of Justinian's life was no closer to solution.

Justinian had long steeped himself in theology. In the isolation into which he was plunged by his wife's death he seems to have sought refuge by pursuing this study even more deeply. His waking hours were increasingly spent in the examination of religious texts and in disputation among a corporal's guard of theologians with which he surrounded himself. Other affairs of state were neglected, or at least so we are told. Certainly vital decision-making seems frequently to have been deferred while the Emperor himself became more detached from normal routine. In the deepening theological preoccupation of his closing years, Justinian embarked upon one last project of dogmatic innovation. This was more than merely a matter of senile surrender to his theological absorption, however, for the project was also intended as another attempt to meet the never-ending challenge of appeasing the Monophysites.

Among the Monophysites themselves there had developed,

earlier in the sixth century, a divisive faction whose point of view was expounded by the theologian Julian of Halicarnassus. Built on the earlier doctrine of Docetism, the theory that Christ's Humanity was only an insubstantial appearance (*dókēsis*), Julian's concept involved a compromise system of gradation, a distinction between normal human flesh and the flesh of the Saviour. Christ thus indeed possessed human characteristics, but they were different from those of ordinary mortals as a result of the entrance of the Logos into His earthly form. Christ therefore did have a certain human aspect, He was of the flesh; but His flesh was of a non-human variety, incorruptible, and itself partaking of Divinity. The Greek adjective for "incorruptible" (*áphthartos*) gave the name to this new theory, Aphthartodocetism.

In it Justinian thought he had found a new prospect for bridging the gap between the Chalcedonians and the Monophysites, between the believers in Christ's Humanity and Divinity conjoined, and the advocates of His Divinity alone. Unfortunately, he ignored the fact that many of the Monophysites themselves bitterly opposed this approach as gravely incompatible with their beliefs. Also, he had still not learned that compromise measures between these two extremes never worked in any event. Once again, therefore, his efforts were doomed from the beginning as a reconciliation measure of any genuine practicability.

Of course, the staunchly orthodox Chalcedonians would have none of the Emperor's latest theological foible. Even Patriarch Eutychius of Constantinople (522–565), who had supported Justinian in the Emperor's baldly caesaropapistic use of the Fifth Council, could not give his acquiescence. Nevertheless, Justinian ignored the obstacles with even more blindness than ever. Perhaps his very arbitrariness here demonstrates the deterioration of his sense of perspective after Theodora's death, though she would probably have approved at least of his intentions in this instance. In the last year of his life Justinian imposed the Aphthartodocetist position on the Church by edict. When Eutychius refused to approve it, the Emperor had him arrested, on January 22, 565, and hustled off into exile. Opposition continued to mount on all sides. All factions could at least unite in rejecting the Emperor's latest ecclesiastical policy. Embittered and infuriated, Justinian prepared to retaliate against all opponents in whatever camp. Persecution was in the air, and more religious strife than ever seemed imminent, when Justinian's death relieved the situation by ending the Aphthartodocetist episode.

This last and most futile of all of his religious policies ends Justinian's activities in this sphere on an ironic note. He had begun his long period in power by establishing himself and his government as a champion of Chalcedonian orthodoxy and as a restorer of the central government to a pure position in that camp. For the length of his entire reign, he had been absorbed in the problem of finding a basis for reconciliation between the Chalcedonian position he represented and the dissident Monophysites. To his credit, he realized the vital importance of reaching some solution to this problem, to preserve the unity of both the Church and the Empire. It was the means for doing so which he could never discover. In pursuit of his goal he had gone to all sorts of extremes of compromise and arbitrary Imperial high-handedness. He had only managed to antagonize his own orthodox fellows while still failing to assuage the Monophysites. His final attempt was devoted to the most potentially disruptive of all his schemes. He died on the brink of bringing even worse conflict to the Church in a fit of senile exasperation. His death left the Monophysite problem unsolved and still a perilous issue for his successors.

The death of Theodora can hardly, then, be blamed for all that happened in the years during which Justinian survived her. Yet, her death serves as a symbolic landmark, in personal terms, of the deterioration which those years brought. The worsening of Justinian's era after her death was something less than coincidental. Of course the times had been darkening long before her death. There had been great discontent as a result of his government's fiscal policies almost from the beginning. Little was changed in this respect after the fall from power of John of Cappadocia in 541, an event which Theodora herself helped bring about. The woes of Justinian's subjects were then increased by a terrible plague, the like of which would not be seen again in Christendom until the Black Death in the fourteenth century. It began in the summer of 542 in Egypt, apparently brought from the East — an unexpected bonus, perhaps, of Justinian's southern trade route to the Far East. It soon spread to Constantinople and then throughout most of the Empire, even in the West. The Emperor himself was not immune, though his case was not fatal. The plague ran its course into the following year, leaving in its wake a staggering number of victims.[2] Its ravages imposed terrible hardships upon the common people, hardships renewed, if on a smaller scale, in a later attack of the plague in 558.

It was in the years following Theodora's death that popular resentments seem to have reached ominous intensity. The determined glories of Justinian's reign had borne heavily on the Empire. His building program, and above all the Reconquest, had imposed fearsome burdens on its finances. Indeed, he had gone too far. Not only were his ambitions more than the Empire as it had come to be could really afford, but the oppressions they required were extended as a result of the unexpected prolongation of the wars in Italy and elsewhere, and their cost thus multiplied. Commercial prosperity had been increased in some respects through the Emperor's efforts, but only to be ruthlessly exploited for the government's own ends. The promise of the regime's recharged orthodoxy had been tarnished fruitlessly by bitter ecclesiastical conflict. The brilliance of Justinian's earlier days began to give way to ruin and exhaustion as his years advanced.

Amid oppression and popular discontent, one incident in particular served to bring irritation out into the open. In a lapse of the truce during the second Persian war, the Great King, in 551, sent to Constantinople his ambassador Izedh-Gushnasp, or Isdigounas as Procopius calls him, to negotiate a renewal. The Emperor's subjects were furious in the first place that Justinian felt obliged to purchase peace from the Persians at the cost of great sums of money — money which had been extorted from them, of course. There was further indignation that the Emperor should at the same time receive the arrogant Persian ambassador with exaggerated cordiality, lavish gifts, and excessively deferential ceremony. (As a person particularly sensitive to questions of cere-

2. Following the example of his model, Thucydides, Procopius gives a vivid description of this plague, *Wars*, Book II, chaps. xxii–xxiii. Bury, *History of the Later Roman Empire* . . . (A.D. 395–565), II, 62–86, includes a translation of part of this passage, with valuable comments.

monial, Theodora might have helped Justinian to be more moderate on at least that point.) Further, he allowed the insolent Persian and his retinue the complete freedom of Constantinople and its markets during his stay in the city. Even Justinian's official historian makes no attempt to conceal the expression of dissatisfaction by the populace.[3]

The incident was indeed symptomatic. It was becoming apparent that Justinian's ambitions had overshot their mark. Just how dire were the ill effects of his regime on his Empire can be seen as we turn to the blackest aspect of Justinian's closing years.

Thunder in the Balkans

The expenditures required by Justinian's bold projects had made a sufficiently serious impact on the internal life of the Empire in terms of financial exhaustion and ruin. There were, however, external implications even graver still.

At least part of the expensive building efforts of the reign had gone into elaborate frontier fortification to protect the Empire's borders. Frontiers, however, are guarded by more than masonry. In order to fight his wars Justinian was obliged to reduce the numbers of his soldiers stationed on various frontiers. After 540 the second Persian war forced Justinian to fight on two broad fronts — if one can consider the numerous theaters of the struggle with the Persians, from Lazica to Syria, as constituting a single front. The disastrous prolongation of war in Italy, not to mention the hard task of curbing the Moors in North Africa, made the strain on the Empire's military capacity ever more burdensome. The results were twofold. First, there was simply a progressive deterioration in the actual defenses on many frontiers. Secondly, there was an increasing reliance on other means of protecting the Empire from attack.

The other means have already been indicated in our brief consideration of Justinian's diplomacy. They involved the elaborate use of subsidies and gifts of money to foreign peoples to buy their friendship, and usually to induce their peaceful respect for the

3. Procopius, *Wars*, Book VIII, chap. xv, secs. 1–20.

Emperor's borders. Since the Imperial army was largely mercenary in composition, an arrangement which was expensive in itself, this lavish use of "foreign aid" — in a somewhat inverted sense of the phrase — as an adjunct to military power only added to the heavy financial burdens of the state. As the military resources of the Empire were consumed or engaged on distant fronts, these subsidies tended to become an *alternative* to military strength in the absence of genuinely adequate and practical defenses. The perils of such a situation are self-evident. Procopius does not hesitate to charge that these policies only encouraged the enemies of the Empire.[4] The barbarians realized that they stood to gain more as the Emperor's foes than as his friends, since they could actually plunder at will within Roman territory and then expect his subsidies thereafter to buy peace.[5]

The true effects of these policies were most dramatically revealed in the Balkan peninsula. It is true that Justinian continued to be able to control, exploit, and play off such familiar barbarians as the Lombards and the Gepids, as he had all through his reign. Emerging to prominence in this area, however, were two peoples who would become important new factors: the Slavs and the Avars.

The origins of the Slavs have been much debated. For our purposes we may say that they came from somewhere in the wilds of north central Europe beyond the Elbe River. We have only very limited scraps of information about their early development and movements. They were extensively affected by the turmoil of migrations and invasions in late Antiquity, being jostled and often dominated by the major peoples of the *Völkerwanderung*, most notably the Huns. With the breaking up of the Hun Empire after Attila's death in 453, the Slavs were freed, and they were gradually able to expand southward, especially as the remaining Germanic peoples in central Europe withdrew to the west and

4. Specifically, Procopius charges (*Anékdota*, chap. xix, secs. 13–16) that the Emperor's extravagance merely attracted more and more money-hungry barbarians, seeking gifts, so that soon they owned all the wealth of the Empire; and (*Anékdota*, chap. viii, secs. 4–6) that such exposure to the prosperity of the Empire, instead of curbing barbarians, only tempted them to plunder it.

5. Procopius, *Anékdota*, chap. xi, secs. 5–10.

left a vacuum in these and the Balkan areas. One branch of the Slavs, identified as the Antae or Antes, came into active contact with the Roman world and even furnished men for the Roman army.

More frequently, however, the disposition of the Slavonic Antae was hostile. Having settled in the Danubian area, in some places perhaps for a considerable time, they began to direct their eyes to the wealth of Roman territories beyond. Unfortunately for the Empire, the Balkan provinces seem to have been badly defended in the late fifth and early sixth centuries, while their administrative and military establishments became very disorganized. The situation naturally attracted Slavonic raids. It is possible that some Slavs may have been involved in the revolt of Vitalian, who is himself credited with the possibility of some Slavonic ancestry. Certainly that upheaval in the early years of the sixth century revealed to many of the barbarian peoples in the area how easily Roman lands could be attacked. It was in 517 that the first major recorded Slavonic raid across the Danube occurred. At that time large groups of Slavs and other peoples penetrated deeply into Imperial territory, aiming for Greece, and ravaged their way as far as Thermopylae. It was the menace which their depredations posed in Thrace that prompted the Emperor Anastasius I to build his "Long Wall" across the Thracian peninsula about forty miles from Constantinople to protect the frightened capital. But the Imperial defensive measures proved insufficient. Assisted by the destruction wrought by recent earthquakes, the barbarian inroads continued on a serious scale.

These attacks, including those by the Slavs, increased during the reign of Justin I.[6] In this period their penetration became so determined that the government attempted its first major counter-offensive. At some time during Justin I's reign, his nephew Germanus, Justinian's cousin, was given the command of Thrace and sent to oppose a Slavonic force which had crossed the Danube into the Empire. Germanus succeeded in defeating and slaughtering them, thus laying the basis for his own great military reputation. This one victory, however, could not stem the growing

6. For useful general background on these developments in this period, see Vasiliev's *Justin the First*, pp. 302–312, especially 309 ff.

tide, and the incursions continued in the early years of Justinian's own reign. When in 529 Slavs and other barbarians defeated Roman forces, they raided their way through western Balkan territory. In 530 another incursion was checked with difficulty by the Imperial general Mundus. During the early 530's some progress was made in halting their attacks, but it was short-lived. Though Justinian could claim to have conquered the Antae, the menace which they, other Slavs, and still other barbarians posed to the European provinces was far from ended.

By about the year 540 the Slavonic peoples began directing their pressures westward, through Illyricum and towards the Adriatic Sea, raiding in Dalmatia, and even as far south as Dyrrachium (Durazzo, modern Dures in Albania) on the Adriatic coast in 548. Their attacks on Illyricum continued steadily through the 540's and the 550's. Meanwhile, the Slavs were probably involved in a motley barbarian attack which in 540 dangerously threatened Constantinople and which then turned to ravage mainland Greece. For a while thereafter, at least some of the Slavonic tribes seemed to have been won over as allies of the Empire, though others remained hostile and were occasionally defeated by Roman forces. The Emperor pressed his fortification-building to bolster the Balkan defenses. During Justinian's later years it almost seemed as if the Emperor could successfully hold off the attacks to some degree. Nevertheless, amid their continued attacks on Illyricum, the menace of the Slavs began to move southwards, threatening the great city of Thessalonica on the northern Aegean coast of Greece. In this move they were brought up short in 550 by Germanus. Preparing to take command in Italy, and just a few months before his untimely death, this respected veteran of previous Balkan fighting was able to frighten off the attacking Slavs. Nonetheless, the invaders turned northwards again and continued their ravages in Dalmatia. In the very year 550 itself Slavonic hordes again advanced into Thrace, defeated a Roman army at Adrianople, and were stopped only after they had broken through the Long Walls of Anastasius.

Thus, all through Justinian's reign, the increasing depredations by the Slavonic peoples continued and grew worse, in spite of some Imperial success in opposing them. Given time and no complicating circumstances, the Empire might have been able to cope with them. Two factors, however, prevented it from either reducing or assimilating this grave border menace. One was the weakening of the defensive system by the withdrawal of the already limited troops in the Balkan provinces to serve on other fronts. Thus denuded, the frontier fortifications, however elaborate, could not be adequately maintained. To be sure, many of Justinian's fortifications farther within Imperial territory might at times provide places of refuge, if nothing more, for the local populations, thereby reducing the number of casualties. But the government lacked sufficient resources to control these barbarians on the border by force. Without such force, subsidies and bribes had little durable effect.

The second factor was the arrival of another people on the scene, disrupting the already precarious situation there. These were the Avars, an Asiatic, Altaic, people related to the Huns and the Turks. They had built up a great empire in central Asia, but this fell apart about the middle of the sixth century as a result of the revolt of the Turks who had been previously subject to them. Remnants and former dependents of these Avar peoples began to move westward, and by the end of Justinian's reign they had reached the fringes of the Roman world. They began subjecting various other barbarian peoples, and emerged as a formidable new power. Among the peoples whom they came to dominate were large numbers of the Slavs. Meanwhile, their Chagan (chieftain), named Baian, entered into diplomatic contact with Justinian, in about the last year of the Emperor's life. A flimsy alliance was planned, but it soon broke down amid growing hostility. It is true, however, that the full impact of the Avar emergence was to come only after Justinian's death. Thus discussion of the drastic shifting of the balance which they brought about in the Balkans must be deferred to the next chapter. Yet, it was even before his reign ended that this new cloud was drawing over the Balkan peninsula, a cloud which would soon bring more terrible storms upon this area. Thus it was the age of Justinian, and the early sixth century in general, which experienced the first pressures of Slavonic peoples on the Balkan area they would soon overrun.

The final crisis in the Balkans during Justinian's reign involved still other peoples. The breaking up of Attila's empire had left the Hunnic tribes disorganized and scattered. Many of them provided important sources of recruits for the Imperial armies. There were still several major groups of them active in eastern Europe, such as the Unogundurs, the Utigurs, and the Kotrigurs, all related, and generally to be found in the steppes of what is now modern Russia and the Crimean area. The last of these three tribes seems to have been the most threatening. Justinian had endeavored steadily to keep them away from Imperial lands, through various subsidies and treaties granted to them or to their neighbors. Even so, about the year 551, a force of Kotrigurs crossed the eastern reaches of the Danube and plundered Roman territory. Justinian was by this time unable to muster any of his own troops against them. Nevertheless, on this occasion he succeeded in diverting the Kotrigurs by inducing their neighbors, the Utigurs, to attack their home territory and thus draw them back there.

The Kotrigur Huns soon revived their aggressions, and this time more significantly. Their chieftain, named Zabergan, began a vast new expedition against the Empire in late 558. He boldly divided his host into three units, each with a definite sphere of attention: one assigned to Greece, one to the western area of Thrace, and the third, under his personal command, to eastern Thrace against Constantinople itself. His audacity was justified by the circumstances of the Balkan provinces at this late period in Justinian's reign. The Emperor's military resources were squandered or exhausted in his wars elsewhere. His treasury was drained by decades of expenditures. His fortifications were useful mainly as places of refuge alone. Justinian's government could do nothing to keep out the barbarians. They ravaged at will, inflicting frightful devastation and outrage on the wretched populations of Greece and Thrace. Worst of all, the Kotrigurs could even in 559 pose a grave menace to the capital. The dilapidated Long Walls of Anastasius were of little value, and what soldiers Justinian had on hand in the city were almost useless. Panic spread throughout Constantinople. To such had the glorious era of Justinian come.

In this moment of humiliation and impending disaster, Justinian swallowed his pride and turned for help to a ghost of the past. Belisarius had been living in retirement in Constantinople since his return from Italy in 548. By 559 he could not have been much older than sixty, if that old, but he had long ceased active service as his years advanced. He did not hesitate, however, to heed his sovereign's call. He gathered together what troops were available. Most of them were untrustworthy, though he had a core of some three hundred men who were veterans of his campaigns in Italy, many of whom had presumably remained with him as his personal body of retainers. With these pitifully limited forces he marched out to defend the city and what was left of Thrace. His actions promptly showed that his old genius had not been dulled by inactivity. Through a masterly use of ruses and skillful positioning, he tricked Zabergan's Huns into thinking that they were about to be defeated by a great army. In terror they turned and fled, abandoning their attack on Constantinople and withdrawing from Thrace. Meanwhile, the two remaining portions of the Kotrigur attack were foiled in their turn. The central column was halted before the defenses of western Thrace and the able commander there managed to beat them off at last. The third force plundered its way into Greece. An Imperial stand at the fortifications in the historic pass of Thermopylae checked them and they turned back. The Kotrigurs' advance was finally stalled. Laden with their booty they straggled home, leaving Macedonia, Thessaly, and Thrace terribly devastated. Justinian was in no position to strike them on their way out of Imperial territory, but he was able once again through diplomatic means to incite the Utigur Huns against the Kotrigurs. The two tribes thereafter wasted themselves in conflicts with each other until they were absorbed shortly by the Avars and others.

The heroic defense of Constantinople by the retired Belisarius had, however, an ironic and tragic sequel. The aging general settled once more into obscurity after his feat of 559. He was not allowed to rest long. In 562 a new conspiracy was organized to assassinate the Emperor. It was discovered in November of that year, and the plotters were arrested. Their frenetic confessions implicated Belisarius, who was hailed before a high tribunal with little regard for his past service or for the unlikelihood of his guilt. Without protest he submitted to being stripped of his force of armed retainers and was placed under house arrest. He endured

this unjust disgrace until the Emperor was persuaded to rein-
state him in July of the following year. Belisarius did not long
survive this latest suspicion of his loyalty, however, for he died
in March of 565, only a matter of months before his master followed him to the grave. Belisarius' wife, Antonina, though older
than her husband, survived him by several years in the serenity
of a convent. On his death, however, the general's properties had
been confiscated by the state.

The disgrace of Belisarius gave rise to fantastic legends in later
times, which had him blinded and made a beggar in the highways
of Constantinople. Such stories are certainly false, but they reflect the romantic reaction to the Emperor's abuse of his old
commander. Justinian may have had occasional justification for
resentment against Belisarius, most notably after the latter's
unauthorized settlement in Italy in 540. Autocrats are also
bound to be naturally suspicious of able and popular subordinates. Yet Belisarius' loyalty was proven beyond all doubt. The
irascible Emperor's poor support of him during the second Italian
campaign, his indifferent mustering-out of Belisarius into retirement, and then his final humiliation of him after the eleventh-hour
service in 559, reflect badly on Justinian as a ruler, as a judge of
men, and as a person.

It is on such a sour note that Justinian's disastrous record in the
Balkan peninsula must end. The policies which brought glory
also brought ruin, and this ruin was nowhere felt so severely in
the Empire as in the Balkan provinces. Procopius bitterly pictures
their helpless exposure to almost annual raids by unopposed
hordes of Slavs and Huns, who ravaged the land, committed outrages, and slaughtered Imperial citizens by the hundreds of
thousands, leaving a veritable wilderness in their wake.[7] While
this picture may be overdrawn, there can be no doubt that the
situation in the Balkans at the end of Justinian's reign was a bleak
one, and one which would become worse in ways that few could
foresee. It was this portion of the Empire which suffered the first
and the most ominous consequences of the age of Justinian.

7. *Anékdota*, chap. xviii, secs. 20–21. Compare Bury, *History of the Later
Roman Empire* . . . (A.D. 395–565), II, 308–310.

Death and Assessment

Justinian's last years were, as just described, marked by misfortunes and disappointments. The Italian wars were finally brought to a successful termination by Narses, but only after a dishearteningly long struggle which left once-prosperous Italy a devastated ruin in most of its areas. Moreover, though it could not be foreseen at the time, there would be only a brief respite for some work of restoration there before Italy would face the new ordeal that fate had in store for it. Peace with Persia was achieved for the moment, but on humiliating and costly terms of tribute. Even North Africa, scene of the initial and most brilliant phase of the Reconquest, had struggled through many long years of conflict with the Moors, who were only lately pacified. In the Balkans, as we have seen, the breakdown of the Imperial defensive system — or, rather, the failure of Justinian to establish a really viable defensive system — was disastrously evident from the devastations of these territories by Slavs, Huns, and others. The finances and the economy of the Empire were overworked and exhausted by the strains of Justinian's endless building and military expenditures. The terrible Monophysite controversy raged unabated after a reign full of religious strife, while the dangers of the local unrest and opposition to the central government that were related to the theological issues menaced the Empire's unity. In the Emperor's last years even the circus factions would not leave him in peace: a new generation of demesmen who had not experienced personally the Nika bloodshed revived the old factional unrest and violence.

Wherever Justinian might look he could see the miseries as well as the glories which his reign had brought to the realm. His government was hated by his subjects. All through the provinces there were people who had ample reason to curse the Emperor: the oppressed, the ruined, the religiously dissident or the religiously orthodox, the refugees battered or dispossessed in the wake of barbarian inroads. The peoples of the recovered provinces in the West, who had welcomed his armies as fellow-catholic and fellow-Roman liberators, had soon been given ample cause to change their minds. Often, especially in Italy, they found war prolonged about them, to their ruin or worse. Then had come the Imperial administrators, to reorganize the area into provinces of the Empire once again. We are told that the "liberated" provincials came to fear the Emperor's army of tax-gatherers more than they had feared the barbarian hordes from which they had been rescued. The benefits and blessings of "liberation" were not unmixed.

By many, then, the Emperor was looked upon as a tyrant. Even his own supporters and propagandists had inwardly turned against him. The vile diatribes of the *Anékdota*, the *Secret History* of Procopius, constituted more than the twisted revenge of an embittered historian. They symbolized the disillusionment with an age of gold that had turned to dross. Justinian might well, then, have looked about him in his closing days and wondered what had happened, where he had failed.

Unfortunately, we do not know the Emperor's thoughts in his last years — even less, indeed, than we know them for the earlier period. Considering his personality and his behavior to the end, he was probably incapable of admitting defeat or failure, or even of recognizing them fully. His perspectives doubtless remained unaltered, and his understanding of contemporary events had probably changed or deepened little since he had ascended the throne, so inflexibly had his entire political orientation been shaped from the beginning by his background and personality. Perhaps his closest parallel in this respect was Philip II of Spain, self-effacingly dedicated to his duty as he understood it, despite all setbacks. All we know of Justinian's personal life after Theodora's death is that he immersed himself increasingly in theology and surrounded himself more completely with its supposed experts. His last, dogged, unrealistic measure to deal with the Monophysite problem, his adoption of Aphthartodocetism, was a partial result of this preoccupation, as we have seen.

By 562, the year of the last assassination plot against him, Justinian was eighty years old. His age, and the wear from his long reign, made it likely that the end of his days could not be much longer deferred. Conspiracies made him only the more conscious of the need for a clear-cut succession. Yet, the outlook was still not certain in this matter. Theodora had not given the Emperor an heir of their own. The choice must be made amongst Justinian's kinsmen. As already noted, the most logical choice, the Emperor's cousin Germanus, was feared and hated by Theodora, who did her best to hinder his prospects. When Theodora died in 548 Germanus was briefly left as the favorite for the succession; but within little more than two years, in 550, he was dead himself. He left behind him two sons, Justin and Justinian, both of whom became loyal and capable commanders in their own right. The elder, Justin, was in service in the Caucasus against the Persians and was popular. His choice as successor would not have been unnatural.

Even from the grave Theodora's influence would be felt. In her hatred of Germanus and his children she had turned her favor to a different branch of her husband's family. The Emperor's sister, Vigilantia, had a son, also named Justin. Theodora sought to advance him, and, as a mark of her personal approval, had him marry one of her own nieces, named Sophia. After Germanus' death in 550 Justinian was thus faced with a decision between Justin the nephew and Justin the second cousin. Vacillating for various reasons, and surrounded by factional intrigue, he made no open choice between them, so that no formal heir to the throne was designated. The only suggestion of preference was that Justin the nephew was given some slight preferments, and that he had the advantage of being at court while his rival was still abroad in service.

Such was the situation in the year 565. On November 14 of that year the aged Emperor died. He was eighty-three, and he had reigned in his own name for more than thirty-eight years. Strongly entrenched in the capital, his nephew, Vigilantia's son, had the support of the aristocracy and the cooperation of Tiberius, the commander of the Excubitors. In carefully staged scenes, almost reminiscent of those attending Justin I's rise, Justin II was called to assume the purple. He ascended the throne with promises of reforming abuses, payment of debts, and a new, brighter regime. The mortal remains of his deceased predecessor were conveyed to the Church of the Holy Apostles, which Justinian had so gloriously rebuilt, and which had become the chief place of Imperial interment. There, in a tomb which he had had prepared for himself, Justinian was laid to rest. The atmosphere attending the elevation of Justinian's successor seems as ironic to us as it would have been outrageous to the late sovereign. The new Emperor Justin's accession was greeted by populace and panegyrist alike not as the ending of a great past era, but as the beginning of a great new one. To them a long-lived tyrant was at last gone. A successor was at hand, full of promise and with his destiny — the terrible meanness of which could not yet be seen — still ahead of him.[8]

Nevertheless, an era *had* ended, an era which was as misunderstood by those who had had to endure it and who had hailed its end, as it had been by the Emperor who had presided over it. To a degree this paradox can be appreciated only in the light of what happened after him, as will be related in the final chapter. Meanwhile, we must come to terms with this Emperor himself. Justinian was a man of many complexities, and if we are to make some final assessment of him we must understand him on several levels, as a person and as a ruler.

Justinian the man poses perhaps the least difficulty. It is of course very difficult to describe accurately the personality of a man long dead, particularly when our information about him is relatively restricted, and above all when we lack truly personal statements in his own words as a key to his attitudes. We can, of course, cautiously analyze his actual thoughts to some extent, but only as reconstructed in his formal statements of his official enactments and from the record of his conduct, as it can be established from the reports of others. Moreover, his private convictions and his official positions may not have always been the same.

In considering Justinian the ruler, however, we are perhaps more fortunate than we might expect to be, and certainly more than we are in the case of most Later Roman Emperors. We have extensive source material for Justinian and his age, including vivid portraits of him in art works such as the celebrated Ravenna mosaic (see Plate IV). Above all, there is Procopius. Despite the fierce bias of the *Anékdota*, or *Secret History*, we find in it a remarkable amount of convincingly reliable personal informa-

---

8. The joyously welcomed accession of Justin II was celebrated by the African poet Corippus in his Latin panegyric, *De laudibus Justini Augusti minoris* (*In praise of the Augustus Justin the Younger*), a hexameter poem in four books. Corippus was also, incidentally, the author of a quasi-epic poem, the *Johannis*, in celebration of the victories of Justinian's general John Troglita over the Moors in the poet's homeland.

tion about the Emperor. It is true that the historian represents him as malicious, tyrannical, mischievous, malevolent, gullible, fatuous, flattery-prone, greedy, hypocritical, and of actually demonic nature. At the same time, Procopius cannot conceal some positive information which reveals not unappealing qualities, as may be seen in the following passages:

But I do not consider it to be out of place to indicate the appearance of this man. In form he was neither tall nor short, but of moderate stature, yet not thin but somewhat plump, while his face was rounded and not unattractive; for it retained its ruddiness even when he had fasted for two days.[9]

.   .   .   .

And for the most part he did without sleep; while he never took an excess of food or drink, but usually, after he had tasted it on his finger tips, he left off. For such concerns seemed to him as if they were something incidental, imposed on him by Nature, since he often went without food for two days and nights, particularly when the period before the feast called Easter required such a course. Then he frequently went without food for two days, as has been said, and he chose to subsist on a little water and some wild plants; and sleeping for, it might be a single hour, he would then spend the remaining time constantly moving about.[10]

.   .   .   .

But while Justinian was of such [i.e., evil] general character as has been recounted, he was yet quite accessible and gentle to those who came into his presence, and no one at all ever found himself excluded from approaching him; yet, not even with someone who appeared or spoke improperly before him did he ever behave at all harshly.[11]

.   .   .   .

Thus it was possible for Justinian to attend to everything easily, not only because of his good-natured personality, but also because he usually

9. *Anékdota*, chap. viii, sec. 12; in the ensuing passage Procopius archly discusses the resemblance of Justinian's features to those of Domitian, the hated Roman Emperor of the first century A.D.

10. *Anékdota*, chap. xiii, secs. 28–30; Procopius then sullenly adds that such admirable conservation of the Emperor's time and constitution was applied destructively instead of constructively.

11. *Anékdota*, chap. xiii, sec. 1; Procopius adds that Justinian could maintain his pose of lamb-like mildness even when plotting or ordering the most maliciously evil acts.

dispensed with sleeping, as has been said, and was every bit the most approachable of all men. . . .[12]

To his qualities of mild disposition Justinian could often add a dutiful and genuine sense of charity and leniency, as many recorded occasions testify. However difficult he may have been in private, we have no evidence of any friction between him and the one person closest to him, Theodora. Their aims often differed, but we may conclude that there was general concord and understanding between them personally. Even the worst detractors make no serious suggestion of any unfaithfulness on the part of either of them, and it would seem that Justinian never once indicated any regrets in his choice of a spouse, or any feeling for her other than deep affection and respect.

As he grew older, Justinian apparently avoided all self-indulgence, to the point of asceticism, as Procopius' testimony suggests. This Emperor was, above all, a man of duty, one who had dedicated himself utterly to his enormous tasks. Autocratic he might be, but his was an utterly unselfish tyranny, with no thought of his own aggrandizement or pleasure. All his energies were directed towards the good of his realm and of his subjects, as he understood it. He busied himself to a fault in all aspects of his government and its operations. This rigorous attitude with regard to himself was naturally carried over into his treatment of others. His was an age — as most others have been also — when the individual mattered for little as such. The interests of others concerned Justinian only in relation to the service which those around him gave in fulfillment of the callings imposed upon them by the needs of the state, and, by implication, by God's will. Our recognition of this attitude may not justify all of this Emperor's behavior, but it may help to explain it.

The same can also be said of his attitude towards his state. To Justinian, whatever changes he saw about him were mere incidentals, of importance relative only to the immutable realities which he took for granted. Among the truths which he held to

12. *Anékdota*, chap. xv, sec. 11; Procopius gives this description to contrast Justinian's openness and accessibility with Theodora's elaborate and ceremonious detachment and her self-indulgence.

be self-evident were: the unassailable position and rights of the Roman Empire as the only legal order in the Mediterranean world; the instrumentality of that Empire in the Christian understanding of life and the universe; and his divinely instituted function as Emperor to employ that instrument in accordance with God's wishes — which he presumed he understood more fully than any other human being. That the old pagan world-state of Rome and the Christian Faith were now one in their existence and their interests was a reality which had been established by Constantine the Great. In token of that union stood the capital, from which Justinian ruled and which he rarely left: New Rome, Constantine's City, one of the most cosmopolitan cities of history, and one which existed as a symbol of its political and religious mission. All that Justinian did as Emperor was derived from these Romano-Christian "self-evident" truths. Added to them, as part of his Latin-minded conservatism, was his veneration for the works of Antiquity as detached from their pagan connotations. What he labored to restore and revitalize throughout all aspects of his state and society was the world of Antiquity. His efforts were those of a man who seeks to revive the past not because he fears the future but because the past obviously represented in all ways the best that civilized humanity had achieved. It is perhaps appropriate that the great statue of Justinian which the Emperor had placed atop the central column of the Augoustaîon or Forum near the palace depicted him in the garb and attributes of a personality who represented so much of ancient character and achievement — Achilles. Nor was there the least element of inconsistency in Justinian's quest, within the scope of his role as the ultimate Christian sovereign, for a *renovatio* of the Classical past.

Within his own frames of reference Justinian's outlook was both consistent and correct. That he was wrong, in the light of our subsequent perspective, is perhaps not entirely his fault. His errors were mainly a result of the perennial difficulty of knowing what one's own time is really all about. In any age, the present cannot truly be understood in proper perspective until it is past. Such is the nature of the historian's one advantage over the people of whom he writes: hindsight. In not completely perceiving what his age was witnessing, Justinian was wholly consistent with himself and with his background, and probably at one also with his contemporaries. Justinian's actual failure was twofold: first, that he could not fulfill his intentions to the satisfaction of his contemporaries, for reasons which were, again, not completely within his control; and secondly, that he acted on his natural misinterpretations of his time with a zeal and determination that only made the consequences, negative as well as positive, more pronounced.

The self-evident truths by which Justinian lived were not after all immutable. Justinian was not unaware of or averse to change. But he could understand only changes which were immediate or superficial, not the ones that were fundamental and that were actually altering the truths he thought immutable. The Mediterranean world was in fact undergoing vital transformations, of a kind in which the old Roman order would no longer have a place. The cleavage between the Western and Eastern halves of the world was too real to be bridged, even by force of arms. New peoples were changing the make-up of Europe. Out of centuries of ferment to come there would later emerge a new and quite different civilization, one whose debt to Rome and to Antiquity would be an indirect and redefined one.

Yet, the Imperial tradition refused to die. The remaining elements of ancient Mediterranean civilization and of the Classical and Hellenistic Greek tradition, identified now with Christian Roman sovereignty, had not lost all their vitality or their will to survive. Survive they would, but in an Eastern Mediterranean scene, quite devoid of any immediate national identity, representing rather the persistence of actual civilization as it had been known and understood in the past. If this survival was to be secured, however, its essentially Eastern Mediterranean orientation had to be recognized. It was precisely this fact which Justinian would not recognize. His background made him look Westward and think in terms of the entire Mediterranean world, the Latin sphere as well as the Greek. In his eyes the Reconquest was a good and proper and necessary thing, and all other external preoccupations were but distractions from his goal of restoring the Roman Empire as it had been. Such was reality in his old Roman Imperial perspective. Yet, that perspective was no longer valid. What the

Empire now had to be concerned with was not restoration but retrenchment, transformation, and survival. What should have been his chief concerns as essential to viable Eastern survival of the Empire were indeed the very external distractions which he underestimated. They were also the ones to become the predominant concerns of his successors: the challenges of Persia, and of the power which succeeded her on the southeastern frontiers; and the challenge of new invaders in the Balkans. Justinian's reign was in effect a splendid final flowering of an all-Mediterranean conception of the old Roman state, a conception fully understandable, but nonetheless by then obsolete. In this respect, this Emperor was a kind of brilliant actor badly miscast in his role.

It is common to think of the Roman Empire as dead by 565, if not by 476. The world of the late fifth century and of Justinian is from this viewpoint but a shadowy bridge into a long stage of decline. Thus, the remnant of the ancient world refused to die as it should have done. Instead it insisted on lingering on, almost a fossilized "relic state" in the Toynbeean sense. To be sure, the state which was evolving into what we call the Byzantine Empire was indeed a relic, a survival of the ancient world and the Roman state. But it was more than that. For it did also develop into something on its own terms, a vital and individual society for all its older origins and identities. To develop an analogy, we might compare it to the caterpillar which becomes a butterfly. Each appears at its end of the process as a strikingly different being, but both are ultimately the same organism which has gone through an elaborate process of evolutionary development. For the Roman Empire, the period from Constantine the Great to Justinian the Great — or perhaps even more properly, to Leo III in the early eighth century — is, if you will, the cocoon.

Justinian himself would surely have resented any portrayal of himself as merely the lord of a maturing cocoon — the more ironic for his development of a native silk industry! Indeed, he might have been somewhat justified. By whatever standards we view him, whether ours or his own, there is no escaping Justinian's stature and significance as a ruler. There can be some exoneration for the unintentional damage he caused as a result of his misunderstanding of his time — the exhaustion and exposure of the surviving East by his efforts to recover the West — if only in view of the genuinely positive works he left behind. His Western Re-conquest fixation, if ruinous, was the product of a rationale both natural to and persistent in his world, and a product which his contemporaries approved and perhaps even expected. Moreover, he gave the Empire, in its process of transformation, an age not without its very tangible glories. Above all, for all his reign's futil-ity as a nearly disastrous climax of the old Roman tradition, Justinian gave the Empire an unforgettable reminder of its Roman past and of its very meaningful (if misunderstood) link with that past. In the metamorphosis from the Roman to Byzantine, this Emperior's era was indeed crucial. For all his faults, he presided over it in a manner which makes it at once exciting, tragic, ad-mirable, and memorable.[13]

13. One of the best concise estimates of Justinian's character was written by an outstanding modern historian of his reign, Charles Diehl, and is found not in his major book on the man and his time but rather in his brief résumé in the first of his two chapters on Justinian in *The Cambridge Medieval History*, II, 2–5. Though there are some questionable details in it, and some parallelism of themes stressed here, the reader is strongly referred to Diehl's estimate, from which at least the following extract might be quoted here: "Thus, in spite of his undoubted good qualities, his badly-balanced mind, his nature full of contrasts, his weak will, childish vanity, jealous disposition and fussy activity, make up a character of only mediocre quality. But, if his character was mediocre, Justinian's soul did not lack greatness. This Mace-donian peasant, seated on the throne of the Caesars, was the successor and heir of the Roman Emperors. He was, to the world of the sixth century, the living representative of two great ideas, that of the Empire, and that of Christianity. This position he was determined to fill; and because he filled it, he was a great sovereign" (p. 3).

VI   THE AFTERMATH: THE ROMAN WORLD AFTER JUSTINIAN

The Collapse of the Justinianic Empire

Justin II (565–578) established himself on his late uncle's throne amid scenes of great public rejoicing and anticipation. To secure his position, he soon had his rival, Justin the son of Germanus, seized and put to death. A few other executions followed, to satisfy Justin of his safety on the throne. Thus appeased, the new Emperor set about demolishing the precariously balanced system by which Justinian had ruled the Empire.

Justin II promised fiscal reform and an end to abuses in the government. He made some honest efforts in this direction. Like his uncle, however, he soon found that needs quickly overcame principles. Thus, some abuses, if ended, were merely replaced by others. The government continued to be corrupt and oppressive. In some ways the situation was even worse, because of the resurgence of power of the aristocrats and the officeholders, who were becoming increasingly independent of the sovereign's control. Even in the provinces the government was forced to make administrative concessions to separatist tendencies.

Indeed, Justin II was hardly the man to cope with the difficulties of the period. He was shallow and not particularly perceptive, for all his good intentions: not an evil man, but merely a worthless one. Moody and petulant, he exhibited an instability which was symptomatic of the mental deterioration soon to overtake him. For the moment he was highly susceptible to the strong-willed

211

people around him, such as the important commander Tiberius. Chief among the court personalities, however, was Justin's wife, the Empress Sophia. Inspired by the grand example of her aunt, Theodora, Sophia was determined to be a powerful Empress of the same cast. As a result, she played a lively, if not always constructive, role in events to come.

Sophia's role, indeed, raises an interesting point. We may observe that from the early fifth century through the late sixth century there was an almost unbroken line of women who dominated or played a vital part in the history of the Empire: Eudoxia, Pulcheria, Eudocia, Verina, Ariadne, Theodora, and Sophia; also Heraclius' Empress, Martina, a generation later in the seventh century. Moreover, the early fifth-century West witnessed the corresponding career of Galla Placidia. Perhaps we may see as the prototype for such feminine dynastic influence no less a person than St. Helena, the mother of the first Christian Emperor, Constantine the Great. We may also note that the later centuries were to produce many other individual Empresses of great influence, a particular characteristic of Byzantine Christian society as it matured. If it is true, as someone has suggested, that a civilization may be judged by the way it treats its women, the Byzantine must rank high.

Among the unsolved problems left by Justinian was that of the Monophysite dissent. Both Justin and Sophia had in earlier years inclined to the Monophysitic belief themselves, doubtless under Theodora's influence. Subsequently, they had chosen to convert to Chalcedonian orthodoxy to further their rise to power. With their accession the Empire again had an Imperial couple united in their orthodox devotion. For all the disruption and intrigue it had brought about, at least the division in sectarian loyalty between Justinian and Theodora had given the Monophysites the feeling that they could find some sympathy in the capital. This advantage was not to be revived now, and so one more link was lost in the overstrained chain of Monophysite loyalty to the central government. At least at the outset Justin II did make an earnest effort to extend his predecessor's policies of conciliation to the Monophysites. Among his gestures was an invitation to the venerable Jacob Baradaeus to come to the capital. The invitation was refused, and many other overtures were likewise rebuffed by the militant believers in the One Nature. Justin became increasingly irritated. Under the influence of his Patriarch, John Scholasticus (565–577), by the year 572 he turned to violent measures of persecution. They were applied with great rigor, with the inevitable result that the smoldering Monophysite problem was only further aggravated.

It was in the sphere of foreign affairs that Justin II's abandonment of Justinian's methods was most pronounced and its results most disastrous. It is perhaps an indication of the difficulties which Justinian had faced that, wrong as his policies often were, the alternatives were often worse. This argument might serve to some extent to condone some of the things Justinian had done. In some respects, however, the alternatives to Justinian's policies had become more dangerous simply *as a result* of those policies' effects. Justin seems to have had some awareness of the fallacies of his predecessor's system, but his own problem was that he could indeed offer no really practical substitute. In essence, his regime was based on three principles. The first was a lofty conception of the Roman tradition, which called for a return to the stern virtues of the past in order to maintain the glories and strength of the Empire. He looked to the aristocracy, his chief supporters, as the main pillars of such spiritual regeneration. Here he could only be disappointed, especially by their performance in governmental functions. His two other principles were that lavish expenditure and wasteful drains on the Imperial finances must be ended, and that the Empire must present a bolder, more determined front to its hostile neighbors. Both principles were praiseworthy in themselves, of course, but they were also extremely difficult to implement. To such a pass had Justinian's misunderstanding of his problems brought the Empire that even a reversal of his policies was now perilous. It is the measure of the impracticality of Justin II's puerilely idealistic principles that it was in precisely the spheres of foreign affairs, where Justinian had enjoyed least success, that Justin failed most deplorably.

On the other hand, there was the Avar situation. As we have seen, these newcomers to the Balkans had already begun to cause difficulties for Justinian in the last years of his life. He had subsidized them with minimal success, and they had occupied them-selves with attacking the Antae and other Slavonic peoples in their path. On his accession Justin II was confronted with Avar demands for a renewal of subsidies. Determined to end these wasteful expenditures, he refused. The move was bold and popular. It might also have been reckless, but at least in this case it proved immediately justifiable. For the moment the Avars were not in a position to avenge the rebuff. Nevertheless, circumstances soon drew the Avars into a dangerous maelstrom of change.

The long hostility between the two major Germanic peoples remaining in the Balkan regions, the Lombards and the Gepids, was now reaching its climax. Imperial support had alternated between them, and in general Justinian's diplomacy had succeeded in keeping them balanced against each other. He had at times drawn upon the Lombards for soldiers; a large detachment of them had served under Narses at the Battle of Busta Gallorum. Within two years after Justinian's death, however, events moved to a crisis. In a new war between the traditional rivals, the Gepids had managed to win an alliance with the Empire. The Lombards moved to offset that alliance by taking advantage of the appear-ance of the Avars. The Lombard King, Alboin, offered to Baian, the ambitious Avar Chagan, an alliance against the Gepids. The Avars accepted, on most advantageous terms. Recognizing the dangers of the combination, the Empire gave some aid to the Gep-ids, but when the clash came in 567 the allied Lombards and Avars all but annihilated the Gepid nation.

As agreed, the Avars occupied former Gepid lands, and con-sequently assumed a position of much greater power. The Pan-nonian plain (modern Hungary) became the center of their growing realms. They began to emerge as the true successors to the Huns. The Slavs had been themselves spreading in all direc-tions, but now they — including most of those in the Balkans — came under Avar domination. These Slavonic peoples now found themselves the auxiliaries and spearheads of Avar attacks south-ward. At last the Avars could repay the haughty insults of Justin.

The Imperial government had hoped to profit from the fall of the Gepids. On its own initiative it had occupied some of their former territories before the Avars could take them, especially the essential fortress of Sirmium (Sremska Mitrovica) on the Danube. The Avars, already ill-disposed to the Empire, angrily demanded these areas as their rightful spoils of war. When they were again rebuffed, war ensued. As Avar subjects and allies, the Slavs were accordingly let loose on Roman territory in Macedonia and Greece. The general Tiberius was sent against them and was soundly defeated. Thus were the doctrinaire policies of Justin revealed in their emptiness: a bold and haughty front against the barbarians would not succeed because it could not be backed up by sufficient force of arms. By about 570, when defeat had dictated its necessity, a peace was negotiated with the Avars on the initiative of the more realistic Tiberius. By its terms, Sirmium was retained by the Empire, but a tribute of 80,000 pieces of gold was paid the Avars. They were placated for the moment only, and the menace of Slavonic penetration southward was likewise far from ended.

There were further consequences of the rise of the Avars after 567. Having won their victory over the Gepids with Avar help, the Lombards began to realize that in place of their old foes their Avar allies had become a new threat which they themselves had helped to create. Finding their situation no longer comfortable as a result of Avar growth, the Lombards decided to move on. Among those who had done service in Narses' Italian campaign the memories of the peninsula were strong. It was also a natural step in their path; indeed, Italy had attracted their interest previously. The regimes of Narses and of his new successor had been struggling to heal the wounds of the Ostrogothic wars and their aftermath, a task still far from completed. Under the circumstances the Imperial government in Italy could offer little effective resistance to attack. In 568 the Lombards proceeded to fall upon Italy. With this step began the last episode of the barbarian migrations.

The Lombards swarmed into the Po River Valley and beyond, occupying the land with little difficulty. Imperial forces managed to hold Ravenna and a few coastal areas, but Alboin moved as far south as Tuscany, while other groups under ambitious Lombard nobles penetrated as far as Beneventum in the center of the peninsula. Then the Lombard advance began to stall, and in 573 Alboin was assassinated. Strangely enough, the Lombards made no effort to establish a strong line of kings after him. The majority of them were content to accept for some time thereafter a rather ramshackle form of government which allowed them to enjoy what they had already won, if not adding more to it. In 574 the Franks began to challenge them in the north. Meanwhile, the Roman forces, from Ravenna and Rome, blocked further progress southward, and attempted occasional if ineffectual counteroffensives. Thus the situation in Italy became one of burdensome stalemate, with the peninsula in effect divided between the Lombards and the Empire.

The disastrous deterioration of conditions in the Balkans and in Italy after Justin II's high-sounding rejection of Justinian's policies was not completely his fault. It resulted in part from the combination of unforeseen circumstances with the ill effects of his predecessor's reign. Much more distinctly Justin's fault was his terrible blunder in the East. The peace of 562 between Justinian and Khusru I had left some issues still unsettled, especially with regard to conflicting claims in the Caucasus and in the Syrian territories of the Empire's Ghassanid allies. Haggling over these issues was still in progress at the time of Justin II's accession in 565, and helped to poison the new government's relations with Persia. From the outset the new Emperor adopted an excessively truculent attitude. Only a few sparks were needed to produce an explosion.

The sparks were soon struck. In 568 the new Emperor received an embassy of Turks. The first groups of these great peoples were moving westward and were coming into direct contact with the Black Sea and Mediterranean world. As the foes of the Emperor's Avar enemies, the Turks offered Justin an alliance against them. As an additional part of the proposed alliance, they offered Justin the dazzling prospect of something which Justinian had dreamed of but had never achieved: a viable trade route to the Far East northward, around the borders of the Persians, with whom the Turks were also on bad terms. Such an arrangement would thus be magnificently beneficial to the Emperor's commerce, and would at the same time work against Persia. Justin listened with interest, and negotiations were pressed. Naturally, the Persians resented and feared such a potential combination against them. They managed by various means to hinder negotiations between Constantinople and the Turks for some time. The episode, which petered out inconsequentially after beginning with such dazzling prospects, helped to add new antagonisms to Imperial-Persian relations. A further spark was struck when Persarmenia revolted in 571. Oppressed and persecuted by their Zoroastrian masters, the Armenians appealed to the supreme Christian sovereign in Constantinople for assistance. The prospect of Imperial intervention could hardly, of course, be tolerated by the Great King. Conversely, the Empire was concerned about Persian intervention in the affairs of the Christian Himyarites (or Homeritai) of southwestern Arabia (modern Yemen); although the actual overthrow by the Persians of the Abyssinian regime there, and the consequent Christian appeal to Constantinople, seem not to have come until about 575. Meanwhile, events were rapidly moving towards the breaking point when Justin decided to abandon all efforts at preserving the peace and chose instead to precipitate a conflict. In 572 a new installment of tribute to Persia was due in accordance with the treaty of ten years before. With lofty disdain for the expensive humiliation which his predecessor's policies had imposed on the Empire by such a concession, Justin refused to pay and prepared for war.

It was a foolish move. "Millions for defense, but not one cent for tribute!" is a stirring cry; but one must have both the millions and the means of defense. The Empire was exposing itself to the dangers of war on two fronts. True, this had happened under Justinian, though the Emperor had not sought the predicament, had recognized its undesirability, and had done his best to escape it. In this case, however, the other front was not an aggressive one in far-off Italy. It was right in the Empire's back yard, in the Balkan peninsula. For, although momentary peace with the Avars prevailed there, the dangers posed by them and by their Slavonic subjects could develop into grave fighting at any moment. Also, the Empire was even less prepared for dual hostilities than it had been under Justinian. It would have been far more suitable for Justin to have tried to maintain peace with the Persians, humiliating and costly as it might have been. On that point Justinian had been wise.

To make matters worse, Justin's war with Persia was miserably unsuccessful. In the summer of 572 he ordered hostilities to begin, and in the following spring, after some success, an attack was mounted on Persian Nisibis. Through the Emperor's ill-advised interference, the effort failed just short of success. Then, in a fit of pique, he needlessly antagonized al-Mundhir, al-Harith's successor as the Ghassanid Phylarch. The Persians took the initiative, devastating Syria, and next besieging Imperial Daras. After a long siege the latter fortress, supposedly impregnable, fell on November 15, 573.

This was a great success for the Persians and gave them a vast new strategic advantage in Mesopotamia. Correspondingly, for Justin it was a dreadful disaster. Not only for his policies but also for his personal condition it seems to have been the last straw. He had long shown signs of emotional instability, and this shock now snapped his mind. He became almost hopelessly insane. We are told that in his mental lapses his conduct was violent and unpredictable: in fits of frenzy he would fall upon his courtiers and bite them. Small things amused or soothed him, such as being wheeled about the palace in a cart while music was played to calm him. When his fits became too severe, all that would control them was the whispered warning that al-Harith was coming: such was Justin's awe of the late Ghassanid prince, who had made such an impression on his last visit to Constantinople, that the Arab Phylarch could be used as a bogeyman to frighten the poor Imperial lunatic into silence.

The actual exercise of authority now fell to the Empress Sophia. Realizing the need for help, she relied increasingly on Tiberius, the Thracian-born commander of the Excubitors, the ranking general, and Justin's principal prop from the time of his elevation. Together they ran the Empire as well as the situation allowed, but they had to agree to a humiliating one-year truce with Khusru on terms of a large money payment to Persia. Justin's mental incapacity became such that a more formal arrangement was necessary to continue the government. On Sophia's initiative Justin was persuaded to make Tiberius his heir, with the title of Caesar. In one of his sane moments Justin presided over the ceremonies of investment, on December 7, 574, making a pathetic if noble speech in which he acknowledged his own failure. Justin remained as Augustus, the actual Emperor, however, and Sophia jealously maintained her position as Augusta. The old Emperor, lapsing again into insanity, lingered on for almost four more years. In September of 578 he briefly regained his faculties once more and on the 26th of the month crowned Tiberius as full Augustus. On October 4 next, death ended Justin's miseries. To this pitiful deterioration had come the man who was expected to eclipse the era of Justinian with a new golden age of his own. With him the Macedonian peasant dynasty of Justin I came to an end.

Tiberius II Constantine (578–582) soon threw off the Empress Sophia's unrealistic pretenses of continued importance and took over the palace in his own right. The embittered widow of Justin attempted a plot against him, which failed; her reward was seclusion and the end of her power. Supreme in authority, Tiberius returned to his responsibilities, with which he had already been occupied actively since 574. He comes down to us with the contemporary reputation of a savior who died too soon. He has been criticized for some unwise policies, especially his excessive extravagance, and the free rein he gave to the popular factions of the capital — though the latter were encouraged perhaps as a counterweight to the powerful aristocracy. Nevertheless, Tiberius took important steps towards reorganizing the army. He was often wise in the choice of commanders, most notably the Cappadocian general Maurice. Some have even maintained that Tiberius was the first Emperor to understand the realities and needs of the specifically Eastern survival of the Empire.

Tiberius' most pressing concern was the Persian war. Under the command of Justinian, the younger son of Germanus, the Imperial forces had done well in 576, and in spite of dissension among the commanders they drove Khusru into a shameful flight before them. There was talk of peace, but a Persian victory in 577 roused the Great King's hopes. The year 578 witnessed the rise of Tiberius' new general Maurice, who proved to be one of the outstanding officers of his time; to such an extent that he was reputed to be author of the first great Byzantine treatise on military strategy. Under his command the war went well. Changes on the respective thrones, however, inclined both states to peace. Supreme in his own name in 578, Tiberius pressed for terms, and Khusru was on the verge of agreeing when the King himself died in the spring of 579. His successor, Hormizd IV (579–590), dallied in negotiation, finally refusing Tiberius' terms, which included the Persian surrender of Daras. Hostilities continued during the ensuing years.

Meanwhile, the Balkan front was again drawing the new ruler's attentions. After the treaty of 570 a brief period of uneasy peace had settled on the area. Nevertheless, disorders had mounted in these provinces, and the Emperor's forces had taken the field again. In 574 the Avars had made another full-scale attack. Once more Tiberius, soon to be made Caesar, was defeated by them. Choosing to free his forces for the struggle with Persia, he had made a new treaty with the Avars which promised them an annual tribute of 80,000 gold pieces. This seems to have quieted the Avars themselves for the time being. The Slavs, however, only loosely under Avar control, were not so firmly bound. Within a few years they had begun to swarm over Illyricum and Thrace, leaving desolation in their wake. All that the government could do was to attempt Justinian's old trick of playing off one barbarian people against another, spurring on the Avars against recalcitrant Slavonic subjects whenever possible.

The Avars were not content merely with extracting tribute payments from the Empire. Baian had never abandoned his demands for the contested stronghold of Sirmium. By ruse and stratagems the Chagan built up his advantages against this increasingly isolated outpost. Tiberius had no forces with which to relieve it, but he stubbornly refused to surrender the town, since he recognized its focal importance in the upper Danubian area. The Avars and their Slavonic subjects brazenly laid siege to it. By 582 the Emperor was forced to agree to its surrender. In accordance with the new peace terms, further tribute payments were also promised the Avars.

As Justin II had his Daras, so Tiberius II had his Sirmium. Though still relatively young, his health had given way, perhaps as a reaction to this new disaster on the Danube. Lacking any male issue, Tiberius summoned his protégé Maurice from the Persian front and made him his heir. On August 5, 582, Maurice was crowned Caesar by the dying Emperor. Tiberius elevated him to the rank of full Augustus on August 13, and having thus secured the succession, died on the following day. Wrote an annalist of the next century: "It was owing to the sins of men that his days were so few; for they were not worthy of such a Godloving emperor, and so they lost this gracious and good man."[1] To his successor, Tiberius left the still unsolved problems of guaranteeing the Empire's continued survival in the East.

Maurice hastily carried out one of his predecessor's wishes by marrying Tiberius' daughter, Constantina, and then took up his burdens. He was confronted with grave challenges, but it was fortunate for the Empire that he was worthy of them. Maurice (582–602) was in some ways the most able Emperor in Constantinople since at least Justinian. Indeed, in certain respects he was able to appreciate his situation and to cope with it far better than Justinian had done.

Nevertheless, the problems at the outset of his reign might well have seemed insuperable. The freedom with which Tiberius spent the Imperial monies during his short reign had left the treasury almost empty. Maurice was obliged to introduce drastic economies. Thorough reorganization was required in the army and in the provinces. Attacks were mounting on all sides, and the Empire faced an intensive struggle on two major fronts, in the East and in the Balkans, supplemented by the Lombard stalemate in Italy.

As his predecessor had done, Maurice chose to concentrate attention first on the Persian war. Now Emperor, Maurice followed tradition by ruling in the capital and appointing his generals to do the actual commanding in the field. Hostilities dragged on, and the sovereign was unfortunate in his choice of generals. Under his brother-in-law, Philippicus, some progress was made in 586 until illness curbed his effectiveness. Under these circumstances Maurice made a bad miscalculation: he decided to replace Philippicus with a new general, Priscus, and, in the interests of economy, to impose a large cut in the soldiers' pay. Priscus arrived in the camp in early 588 to carry out these orders, unpopular in their

1. This is the comment of the seventh-century Egyptian historian, John of Nikiou, chap. xciv, sec. 25, quoted in the English rendering of R. H. Charles, *The Chronicle of John, Bishop of Nikiu, Translated from Zotenberg's Ethiopic Text* (London, 1916), p. 151.

own right, and handled himself so badly that the exasperated troops broke into mutiny. For a while they even attempted to set up their own Emperor, and at the least refused to recognize Maurice. It was only by 590 that order could be restored under Philippicus, who had returned to his command. In these circumstances, the Imperial front against the Persians was reduced to chaos. The opportunity was not wasted on the enemy. When the Persians took the important Armenian city of Martyropolis, about 590, Philippicus was replaced by Comentiolus. He proved one of the Emperor's poorer choices of generals, and it was really another commander, Heraclius, father of the future Emperor, who helped regain some success for Roman arms.

Actually, however, the Persians had not taken so much advantage as they might have of the 588–590 mutiny, as a result of important internal distractions of their own. The Persian general Vahram Choben had succeeded in putting down a revolt in Persian territories to the east and in curbing the menace of the Turks, but he had then been worsted by the Imperial forces in Armenia. When the angry King Hormizd disgraced him, this general rose in revolt. Hormizd was dethroned and slain in 590, and his son Khusru was installed in his place. Vahram, however, had his own designs on the crown. He drove the rightful heir from Ctesiphon and ascended the throne as Vahram VI. In desperation the fugitive Khusru took the only step remaining to him: he threw himself on the mercy of the Emperor Maurice. The Persian prince begged Imperial assistance in securing his rightful throne, in return for which he promised restoration of Daras, Martyropolis, and certain Armenian territories, as well as an honorable peace and friendship. Maurice's advisers and the Senate were skeptical and counseled against acceptance. Maurice acted on his own initiative, however, with a bold agreement. The Imperial army was now placed in Khusru's service, and during 591 it succeeded in defeating the usurper's forces. With Vahram dethroned, Khusru II Parviz ("Victorius," his later surname) began his reign (591–628). The new King kept his promises. The stipulated territories were surrendered, while amity and peace were established. He even surrounded himself with a Roman bodyguard. Most important of all, the novel bond between Maurice and Khusru assured a stable peace in the East at last.

Before we turn from Persian affairs, however, we should note in passing one subordinate development which was to have later consequences. We have already referred to the Empire's Arab allies, the Ghassanids, whose antagonism was aroused by Justin II in 573. After the death of al-Harith II (569), his son and successor, al-Mundhir (another "Alamoundaros" to the Byzantines), continued the tradition of zealous service to the Empire in the struggle against the Persians and the rival Lakhmid Saracens. The Ghassanids, however, also remained loyal to Monophysitism. This fact had won al-Mundhir Justin II's disfavor. Difficulties were eased under Tiberius, since that Emperor attempted a more conciliatory attitude towards the Monophysites. So it was that in the latter's reign al-Mundhir visited Constantinople, in 580, where he was triumphantly received and honored by the Emperor. Returning to the wars, al-Mundhir crowned Ghassanid success with the capture and devastation of Hira, the Lakhmid capital. Nevertheless, there was renewed friction between the Imperial government and its Arab allies. As suspicion against him mounted, al-Mundhir was seized and carried off to exile by the Emperor's orders. When his son also turned against his Imperial master, he was soon captured and treated in like manner. Though the Ghassanid principality continued even after this time, such repression severely reduced its power and value. It was a short-sighted policy on the part of Maurice's government, and one which was to have unexpected repercussions in the next generation.

With the Persian wars at last happily ended and the Eastern front pacified, Maurice was free to transfer his attentions and his troops to the Balkans. They were desperately needed there. The fall of the crucial fortress of Sirmium at the end of Tiberius' reign had brought with it the collapse of Imperial defenses in Illyricum. The Danubian lines were now definitely breached and the Avars could make inflated new demands with impunity. On his accession Maurice granted them increased tribute, but this did not long satisfy the Chagan Baian. In 583 the Avars secured further Danube strong points, including Singidunum (modern Belgrade), and ravaged the area. As long as he had his forces committed against the Persians there was little Maurice could do. In 584 he had to grant a new treaty, promising the Avars even greater amounts of tribute.

The fall of Sirmium had opened a path not only to the Avars. It was the Slavs who were even greater beneficiaries. Now that the Imperial defensive system was ruined, the Slavs poured southward and westward into Illyricum, Macedonia, Thrace, and even Greece. Unlike their Avar masters, they came not merely to raid but increasingly to settle. As the settlements spread, even into the far reaches of Greece itself, their grip on these areas became all but unbreakable. The Slavonization of the Balkan peninsula had begun. From their settlements the Slavs could also mount further raids beyond the lands they were absorbing. They devastated Thrace and reached the Long Walls of Anastasius. After the 584 treaty Maurice had taken the precaution of bringing some forces to serve in Europe. Under Comentiolus these troops had some success in driving the Slavs back at least as far as Adrianople.

While the Slavonic deluge continued, the Avars themselves did not long abide by their agreements. Treaties meant little to them. Within a year of the last one they were plundering and raiding Imperial lands again. Even though Comentiolus was able by 587 to launch a counteroffensive against them and defeat the Chagan, the situation was still critical as Slavonic raids continued in the face of inadequate Imperial defense. That was the situation when the peace of 591 with Persia enabled Maurice to concentrate fully on the Balkan sphere at last.

For a very brief period Maurice undertook personal command of the army, a bold and unpopular break with the tradition established since Theodosius the Great that the Emperor should leave the actual conduct of operations in the field to his generals. As it happened, Maurice soon abandoned this innovation. The campaigns of the ensuing years are not fully clear to us in all details, but they seem to have gone badly at first. Though the able general Priscus achieved some success, he was not maintained in command at all times. So precarious was the situation that in 597 the Slavs and the Avars mounted a massive assault on Thessalonica and were only barely driven off. Priscus was returned to command for a while, but Maurice unwisely insisted on associating him at various times with either Comentiolus, who was out of sympathy with the Emperor's plans, or with the Emperor's brother Peter, who was quite incompetent and who only helped increase the growing unpopularity of Maurice with the troops. There were reverses and a brief peace was arranged, but Maurice himself breached it. At last relieved of the millstone of his co-commanders, Priscus began to make renewed progress, so that by 602 the outlook was beginning to brighten. The goal of pushing at least the Avars back beyond the Danube once again appeared to be finally within reach. In this year, also, the Emperor won the Slavonic Antae as allies, obliging the Avars' to distract themselves in crushing this action by peoples whom they regarded as their own subjects. Such developments gave the Empire a further opportunity, and Maurice was determined to take it. Unfortunately for him, his decision would have results beyond his calculation.

Before we pursue this narrative, we should note something of the accomplishments of Maurice in other areas. For all his preoccupation with the Empire's Eastern situation, perforce the main concern of the Emperors after Justinian, Maurice by no means ignored the West. Indeed, during an illness in 597 he even went so far as to draw up a will in which he proposed a division of the Imperial office once again, giving the Western provinces as a sphere in its own right to one of his sons. The Emperor recovered, but he continued to be very much aware of needs in the West. North Africa remained subject to unrest and to attack by the Moors. Even more problematical, of course, was Italy. The Lombard advance there had largely come to a halt by Maurice's time, but even amid stalemate there was continued pressure on the remaining Imperial territory in the peninsula. To some degree the Bishop of Rome was able to exert a pacifying influence over the Christian Lombards, though they were Arians; nevertheless, even Rome was not free from danger.

Maurice's dealings with Italy were somewhat complicated by his relationship with Rome. The See of St. Peter was occupied at this time by Pope Gregory I, "the Great" (590–604), the most important Pontiff since Leo I and in some ways the real founder of the Papal position of spiritual power throughout Western Christendom. Maurice's ecclesiastical policy was for the most part a moderate one. In his concentration on military and administrative problems he followed a course of nonpersecution and mild conciliation towards the Monophysites during the early years of his reign. Nevertheless, he was cordially in agreement with his Patriarch that the See of Constantinople should recover its authority over the other Eastern Sees of Alexandria, Antioch, and Jerusalem. Correspondingly, the two were determined to resist any pretensions on the part of Rome to meddle in the Church affairs of the East. When Pope Gregory protested against the use of the title "Ecumenical" by the Patriarch of Constantinople, Maurice rebuffed the Pontiff. Emperor and Pope also quarreled over one of Gregory's particularly cherished institutions, monasticism. The Emperor wished to curb the drain on the Empire's military manpower by the monasteries. As a result, and in view of the Emperor's inability to spare any substantial forces to protect the Pontiff from the Lombards, Maurice could not expect much cooperation from Rome in the West. Conversely, the Pope was thrown increasingly on his own resources, a situation which was to continue with important consequences for the future history of the Papacy.

Nevertheless, it was in the period of Maurice that significant measures were taken to shore up Imperial control in the West. The result of these measures was the creation, or at least the completion of the creation, of the Exarchates of Ravenna and Carthage. A pattern of authority there had been established by Justinian, and by the time of Maurice the union of civil and military authority could be firmly embodied in administrative organization. The successors of Narses in Italy, charged with maintaining the Imperial position in that battered land, came to bear the title Exarch. Their rank made them in effect quasi-emperors in their assigned area, supreme in all spheres of authority, with Ravenna designated as their capital. Transferring the pattern to North Africa, Maurice early in his reign established a parallel arrangement for this territory, with Carthage as the seat of residence. In both cases these Exarchates were established to present a more effectively concentrated response to a specific military challenge (Lombard in one case, Moorish in the other) in distant provinces with which ready lines of communication or support were overstrained. These Exarchates were also to set the pattern for even more drastic overhauling of the entire Imperial system in the centuries to come.

In addition to his important administrative changes and his endeavors to put the finances of the Empire on a sounder basis, Maurice also instituted extensive reform of the military system. He attempted to improve discipline in the army and, above all, to establish more substantially native forces, free from the evils of mercenary recruitment which had plagued Justinian's era. His reforms provided the basic organizational form which was to last for centuries thereafter as a cornerstone of the Empire's military system. Further, he seems to have been the first Emperor to appreciate the value of the Armenian lands of Asia Minor as a source for recruiting reliable forces for the Empire within its own borders. Nevertheless, for all the constructive efforts of Maurice, he exhibited two essential faults as a reformer and as an Emperor, both of which we have already seen in operation. He often made poor choices in his commanders, persistently supporting them when their own inadequacy was proven, as in the cases of Comentiolus and his own brother, Peter. Secondly, for all the virtue of his reform measures, he had a poor sense of timing in imposing them — as we have seen in the previous occasions when such miscalculations won him the mounting hatred of the troops. It was this latter flaw that precipitated his disastrous fall.

The crisis came in 602. In view of the progress of Imperial forces at last in re-establishing the Danubian frontiers, Maurice decided to exploit his advantage. He ordered the army to spend the winter of 602–603 beyond the river in Avar territory. This would serve a double purpose: it would demonstrate the Imperial army's capacity to hold its own in Avar lands; and it would reduce expenses for supplies, since the soldiers would be living off the enemy's territory. To the troops, however, the plan was the final outrage. They were tired of fighting and wanted to enjoy a winter's repose in the security of home territory. Maurice's economies and arbitrariness had gone too far for their taste. A new mutiny broke out, and, as it turned into a rebellion, an obscure junior officer named Phocas emerged to lead it.

Maurice at first treated the outbreak lightly; he had mastered other mutinies. Only when Phocas and the army refused all negotiation did the Emperor look to his defenses. At this point the circus factions of the capital again emerged to prominence. Their resurgence had begun in the latter days of Justinian's reign, and their unruliness became a problem under Tiberius and Maurice. The latter tended to favor the Blues. In his need, the city militia which the demes of the capital formed were the only forces he could now muster. When a count was made of the demesmen of the city it was found that the Greens could reckon 1,500 men, the Blues only 900. The situation did not seem promising, but Maurice armed the demesmen of both factions and set them to guarding the Land Walls. The dissident army approached. Its immediate intention was to dethrone Maurice in favor of his eldest son, though an alternate candidate was the latter's father-in-law, the general Germanus. With the enemy finally at the gates, Maurice's position collapsed. Riots broke out and the demesmen abandoned the defense to join in. The Emperor and his family fled. Germanus now made a bid for the throne, but the Greens decided the issue by supporting Phocas, and Germanus acquiesced. The leader of the mutinous army was admitted to the capital and crowned Emperor. One final step remained to be taken in order to seal the change. Maurice had been halted on the Asiatic shore by illness during his flight. He and his sons were captured and brutally executed. Thus died the distinguished Emperor who, for all his faults, has been justly described by one historian as "a high-minded, conscientious, independent, hard-working ruler."[2]

The tragic fall and murder of Maurice had done more than cut short what might have been an important new dynasty in Constantinople. It also put a veritable monster in power. Crude, uneducated, coarse, half-barbarian, Phocas had as his sole concern the holding of his ill-gotten throne, to enjoy it as long as he could. He was utterly unequal to the tasks of his age, if even aware of them. A blood bath of executions cleared away all possible relatives and supporters of Maurice. When Phocas then attempted to assert his authority in the provinces he found that local officials and commanders would not accept him. Riots and repression became the rule on all sides. He could not be sure of the capital. Plots flourished everywhere, and Germanus made a new attempt

2. N. H. Baynes in *The Cambridge Medieval History*, IV, 284.

to seize power. Phocas retaliated brutally by instituting a reign of terror. The nobles particularly felt his severity. The social fabric of the East Roman aristocracy, as it had developed since Constantine and had endured through Justinian, was torn and trampled upon. Even Phocas' original supporters, the Greens, turned against him, and their strife compounded the blood bath. In the ecclesiastical sphere Phocas turned his tender mercies on the Jews as well as on the Monophysites in a new round of persecutions. The only one who had a kind word for Phocas was, of all people, the great Pope Gregory, who courted the new Emperor and won many favors from him. So it was that, while the tyrant presided over anarchy and barbarity at home, his name found honor in one place, in far-off Rome, where his actual power was nonexistent; and in his honor was erected the last public monument to be built in the old Forum, a column — torn from the ruins of an earlier building — which may still be seen there.

Amid such chaos, all that Maurice had been trying to do, and much more, was undone in a moment. His reign had brought the Empire close to controlling the forces unleashed since Justinian's death, forces which threatened its continued survival in the East. Phocas' accession ended the effort abruptly at a crucial juncture. With the Danubian campaigns cut off and with the Balkan provinces again left exposed by revolution, the barbarian attacks were redoubled. The Avars were able to extort heavy new tribute grants, while the Slavonic settlements multiplied. Against the flood of Slavonic migration and entrenchment the Imperial government could only hold isolated coastal areas and ports along the Adriatic coast and the shores and islands of Greece. As the seventh century advanced, Greece itself, the former seat of the Hellenic peoples, became part of an amorphous area known generally to contemporary writers as *Sklavínia*.

The crisis was to become even more acute in the East. In his flight the doomed Maurice had appealed for aid to the Persian King. The ambitious Khusru II found the new turn of events precisely to his taste. Upon the accession of Phocas, the Great King emerged in 603 as the avenger of his late Imperial benefactor. Once again the Empire was at war with Persia. To sustain the new struggle the Emperor had only one possible hope, an outstanding general with the not uncommon but most auspicious Armenian name of Narses. The outrages of Phocas had, however, driven Narses into rebellion in 603. Narses became for a while the supporter of a pretender who claimed to be the oldest son of Maurice, and he joined forces with Khusru when the Persian King led his army against the Empire's eastern territories in 604. Although Phocas denuded Thrace dangerously of soldiers in order to bolster his Asiatic defences, his measures were insufficient to stop the Persians. When Khusru returned home from his first campaign after capturing Daras, Phocas entered into negotiations with Narses. The general was lured into surrender by fair promises. Once he was in Phocas' hands the vengeful Emperor heaped treachery on short-sightedness by having Narses burned alive in the Hippodrome.

Delivered from the one opponent they might have feared, the Persians embarked on conquest in earnest. Armenia and Mesopotamia were overrun by 606, Syria-Palestine in 607, and in the following year the Persians moved through Cappadocia and westward across Asia Minor as far as Chalcedon, though they did not always occupy these more distant lands permanently. Repelled and afflicted by the Emperor's boundless cruelty, cities and provinces gladly surrendered to the Persians, or looked forward to doing so, while Phocas was occupied with conspiracies and suspicions at home. Khusru II found himself on the brink of achieving at last the Sassanid dream of restoring the old Achaemenian Persian Empire, while at the same time extinguishing what remained of its ancient foe, the Roman Empire. The surviving Imperial state, which three-quarters of a century earlier had been busily restoring itself in the West, appeared to be facing complete destruction in the East. So soon was Justinian's state and civilization falling to pieces.

It was amid this seeming catastrophe that salvation appeared, significantly from one of the recovered lands in the West. Eventually one of the numerous plots against Phocas was bound to succeed, and it was from North Africa that deliverance came. The Exarch there was Maurice's old general Heraclius. Under him the province had prospered in peace, and to him dissidents in Constantinople directed their appeals. Too advanced in years to seek the throne himself, he organized an expedition on behalf of his son, also named Heraclius, who was to proceed by sea against Phocas. A land force was organized under the Exarch's nephew, Nicetas, with the immediate task of securing Egypt and with the provision that the first one to reach Constantinople should take the throne from Phocas. It was, however, plain from the outset that Nicetas would serve essentially as the supporter of Heraclius. These forces set out in 608. During the following year, while Nicetas easily took control of Egypt, Heraclius occupied Thessalonica. Only in 610 was Heraclius finally ready to advance on Constantinople itself. In the first days of October his ships, bearing the image of the Virgin on their masts, appeared before the Sea Walls. Phocas' cruelty and suspicions had alienated everyone, including his son-in-law, Maurice's general Priscus, who now chose to cooperate with Heraclius. The scorned Greens also gave their support to the savior from Africa. On October 5, 610, the deposed Phocas was dragged before his conquerors and butchered. Heraclius professed to support Priscus for the throne, but the popular will would not be gainsaid. The conqueror mounted the throne himself as the new Emperor.

Heraclius: Survival, Transformation, and New Danger

It was a sorry prospect that the Emperor Heraclius (610–641) faced upon his accession. He might well have wondered if there was much that could be done to save the disintegrating Empire. Certainly no peace was forthcoming from the Persians. The fall of Phocas had theoretically ended the need for Khusru to carry on his professed war of vengeance, but the Great King quickly revealed his true motives. When Heraclius appealed to him to desist now that Maurice was avenged, Khusru ignored him, determined to press the advantages he had won. It was plain that the perilous Balkan situation would have to be left unattended for the time being as energies were concentrated on the new struggle with aggressive Persia. What forces the Empire had were put under Priscus and sent to oppose the Persian devastation of

Asia Minor. Priscus managed to recover Cappadocian Caesarea, but Persian gains continued elsewhere. A new danger arose: when in the light of continued danger Heraclius went to consult with Priscus at the front, he found the general haughty and overbearing. Priscus resented the Emperor's leaving his capital, where he belonged, and made it clear that his loyalty was uncertain. Heraclius was still only barely the master of his throne and had to proceed warily. In 612, when Heraclius seemed to be in better control of the situation, he was able to summon Priscus to Constantinople. There at the Emperor's mercy, the general was stripped of his command and confined to the peace and security of a monastery, a common form of sugar-coated imprisonment among the Byzantines.

In order to understand the continuing disasters which marked the early years of the reign of the Empire's new savior, one must appreciate the fact that he took over a state which was utterly bankrupt. Factional conflict was still rife; society was demoralized; the provincial administration was in complete disorder; the treasury was virtually empty; and there were few troops at hand, trustworthy or otherwise. It required years for Heraclius to establish his position firmly amid loose and shifting loyalties, let alone restore the state. Meanwhile, the Persian military effort pushed onward with increasing success, while the limited Imperial forces were powerless to halt it effectively. Khusru II had decided to concentrate on the eastern Mediterranean territories and to outdo the exploits of his predecessor Khusru I in the days of Justinian. Syria was formally invaded; Damascus fell in 613, while the Persians pressed to the northwest and occupied Tarsus in Cilicia. In the following year Palestine was attacked, and the Persian army swarmed down upon Jerusalem. After twenty days of siege the city was betrayed by the Jews, who were eager for revenge upon their Christian oppressors. The Holy City of Christendom was delivered over to three days of frightful massacre and pillage.[3] It was an ideological victory as well, for the Zoroastrian Persians

3. A vivid eye-witness account of this disaster by the contemporary writer known as Antiochus Strategus has been translated into English from the surviving Georgian text (the original Greek is lost) by F. C. Conybeare in *The English Historical Review*, 25 (1910), 502–517.

zealously desecrated the Christian shrines. Among their spoils they carried off the relic accepted by Christians as the Holy Cross on which the Saviour had been crucified and which, according to tradition, had been rediscovered three centuries earlier by St. Helena, the mother of Constantine the Great. In the wake of this success the Persians occupied all of Syria-Palestine, apparently receiving cordial encouragement and collaboration from the Monophysite Christians there. The union of theological dissent with local disaffection was now bearing its dreadful fruit.

The loss of Jerusalem was a frightful shock for the Christian Empire. Stunned, Heraclius sued anew for peace. Khusru undercut all negotiation, and his armies continued their progress into Asia Minor. To complicate matters further, the Avars took advantage of the Empire's tottering situation. With their help the Slavonic inundation of the Balkans progressed rapidly. About 614 Salona fell, and the Dalmatian coast in general was lost. The Slavs also raided northward around the headlands of the Adriatic. Meanwhile, deeper inland, they completed the process of driving the local and Hellenic populations to the coast in Greece; even the islands were not safe from their raids by sea. The Avars themselves became impossible in their demands for tribute from the exhausted Empire. At a peace parley with them the Emperor barely escaped from a treacherous attempt to capture him. In 617 the Avar Chagan led his hordes down upon Constantinople itself. The wall-girt city was proof against them, but its suburbs were mercilessly ravaged. While the capital was not placed under formal siege, the hardships of its population were increased.

Worse was to come. Within another two years the Persians launched the next phase of their offensive by invading Egypt. Here, again, the bitterly disaffected Monophysites seem to have aided the invaders willingly, welcoming their escape from the oppressive and Chalcedonian central government. After Alexandria was besieged and taken, the entire province fell. Its loss was a particularly severe one because it cut directly into the vital grain supplies for which Constantinople depended on Egypt. At the same time, Persian progress in Armenia deprived the Empire of the area which since Maurice had been its important recruiting ground. It appeared that nothing would prevent the Sassanid King from taking Asia Minor; after that he might even emulate Xerxes of a millennium earlier and cross to Europe.

In this desperate situation Heraclius contemplated an appropriately desperate measure. The one area of the shattered Empire which was still intact and prosperous was North Africa. From it Heraclius himself had come to purge the throne of the tyrant Phocas. To it he could now return to build up a new counteroffensive. And so, by 619, Heraclius was ready to abandon what was left of the East until he could recover it from a temporary base of operations in the West, at Carthage; such was the importance of the province Justinian had recovered. The plan, however, aroused a storm of protest in Constantinople. United at last in despair, the population of the city rallied behind the Patriarch Sergius, who exacted an oath from Heraclius that he would not desert the City of Constantine. Constantinople had long been the "spoilt child" of the Empire. Now the danger of ultimate abandonment brought it to its senses. The Eastern capital in effect rededicated itself to its mission. As a result, the Emperor changed his plan. He would make his stand in the East. He could now count on the hearty support of his aroused subjects. Since the Church had intervened, he could now draw upon it for what he desperately needed: money, from the Church's own vast wealth. The new effort would be a holy war against the unbelievers to avenge their desecration of Christianity's shrine. At its head would be God's deputy, the Emperor himself. To protests against the Emperor's abandoning his traditionally distant role in the capital, Heraclius could argue the brief precedent of Maurice, and the urgency of the situation. Once more the Roman sovereign would also be his own commander-in-chief in the field, a role which the Emperors would frequently assume thereafter.

The next five years were devoted to reforms and preparations, after an expensive peace had been arranged. Only in 622 was Heraclius fully ready. The capital was committed to the hands of the Patriarch Sergius, and after a public ceremony of religious dedication the Emperor crossed to Asia. The Persians had already made one brief raid on Constantinople, in about 619. They were not yet prepared to attack the capital in earnest, but they still threatened what was left of Imperial Asia Minor. It was here that they must be met first. In 622 Heraclius marched against and defeated them. For the moment Asia Minor was cleared of Persian invaders. During the winter the King and the Emperor exchanged messages, each indicating their respective determination to drive on to final victory.

In 623 the Emperor launched his new offensive. Directing his march towards Armenia, Heraclius boldly proceeded deep into Persian territory, to the city of Ganzaka (the modern ruins now called Takhti-Suleiman), as sacred a city to the fire-worshiping Zoroastrians as Jerusalem was to the Christians. Heraclius stormed Ganzaka and treated it as Jerusalem had been treated, in deliberate retaliation. The winter of 623–624 was spent in the Caucasus, where Heraclius built up his forces and made alliances with the Lazi, the Abasgians, and the Iberians there: the importance of this area, long a scene of struggle between Justinian and the Persians previously, was now more clear. In addition, two years later he made an even more crucial pact with the Turkish newcomers into the area, the Khazars. The year 624 was devoted to campaigns and maneuvering in Armenia, with some success. In 625 Heraclius worked his way westward to attempt the recovery of the Cilician and Cappadocian pathway into northwestern Asia Minor.

The year 626 brought a new peril. Since the interests of the Avars and the Persians so readily coincided, a coalition between them was natural. Disregarding their latest treaty with the Empire, the Avars threw themselves into a joint attack on Constantinople. The Persians made a new advance into western Asia Minor, which Heraclius was unable to block, and occupied Chalcedon, while across the Bosporus the Avars and Slavs invested the capital by land and sea. Presumably, the Persians hoped that the Emperor would thus be forced to abandon his Asiatic campaigns and return home. Heraclius, however, gambled on avoiding the distraction, though he did send a portion of his forces to aid in the defense of Constantinople. As events proved, he decided wisely, for the capital was in the capable hands of good commanders and, above all, the Patriarch Sergius. Under the Patriarch the population resisted bravely. The Empire still had the advantage on the sea, and the Imperial fleet succeeded in driving off the Slavonic ships. The Persians were obliged to watch helplessly while the Avars' land attack was repulsed — with the aid of the Virgin herself, the pious Constantinopolitans firmly believed. This victory was a crucial event in a context even beyond that of the Persian war, for the power and the prestige of the Avars were now broken. Their empire quickly began to crumble. Many of their subject peoples began to revolt, particularly the Slavs. The Empire was not in a position to take full advantage of this opportunity for the moment. Nevertheless, its prestige had been considerably enhanced, and it could certainly be cordial in its encouragement of Slavonic independence movements. Nothing could drive the Slavs out of most of their new positions in the Balkans, but at least Avar power south of the Danube was ended. The Avars' realm contracted to the area of modern Hungary, from which they continued to be the scourge of at least central Europe until they were finally destroyed by Charlemagne at the end of the eighth century.

For the Persian war itself, of course, the Avar-Persian repulse before Constantinople was the turning point. Heraclius could prepare his forces for the final effort once his capital was safe. In 627 he struck at Persian territory again. Driving deep into Mesopotamia, he met Khusru's army before the ruins of Nineveh, the ancient Assyrian capital. On December 12, 627, the battle fought there was a great victory for the Emperor. Heraclius pursued the fleeing Khusru, taking important points along the way and barely missing an opportunity to capture Ctesiphon itself. At this point fate intervened. Now tasting unwonted defeat, the Persian army mutinied. Khusru was overthrown and assassinated. Before the Emperor launched his new campaign in the spring of 628, he had the news of this change.

These developments marked the end of Sassanid ambitions. Khusru II was succeeded by his son Kavadh II Sheroë ("Siroës"). The new King lacked both the vigor and the good fortune of his father. He chose to sue for peace with the Empire. Heraclius had the pleasure of accepting terms by which all the conquests of Khusru were restored to him, the precious Holy Cross as well. A few months later the new Persian King was dying and appealed to Heraclius to be the protector of his own young son and successor. Persia was on the brink of collapse into anarchy. It was no longer a menace to the Empire.

The triumphant Heraclius spent the winter of 628–629 in Asia, clearing out the remnants of Persian invasion, and particularly courting the important Armenians. In 629 Heraclius finally returned to his capital for the first time since his six years of hard campaigning had begun. He was received with wild acclamation, as victor over the arrogant foe and as avenging champion of the Faith. Either before or after his entry into Constantinople he also entered the recovered Jerusalem: there, amid great religious exultation, he restored the True Cross to its shrine. This triumph was one which was long remembered in Christendom, Western as well as Eastern — for all believers, Heraclius was the first Crusader. In more practical terms, his spectacular victory over Persia had decisively ended the four centuries of struggle with the Sassanid power, a political, dynastic, and ideological conflict in which Justinian's unwilling entanglement had been but one of its several phases. The Empire had no intention of effecting an Alexander-like conquest of the Persian realm; but the latter was humbled and shattered, its capacity for aggressiveness ruined.

The triumph of Heraclius over Persia by 629, and the successful resistance of Constantinople in 626, had restored most of the Empire Justinian had known. True, by this time the last foothold in Spain had been lost; and the stalemate in Italy left the Lombards with a dangerously large portion of that province. In addition, though the collapse of the 626 siege had broken the power of the Avars and had removed them as a direct threat to the Empire, the problem of the Slavs in the Balkan peninsula continued to be an acute one. Nevertheless, it was still too soon for the Emperor to attend to European matters. The Eastern provinces were badly devastated and disorganized in the wake of the terrible Persian conquest, however ephemeral it had been. It was to the reorganization of these areas that the Emperor felt he must address himself before he could be free to turn elsewhere.

Heraclius' re-establishment of Imperial authority in the Eastern provinces assumes two aspects, one of which, the religious, will be considered later. The principal one, for the moment, was administrative. With the virtual collapse of the old governmental system by the beginning of the century it was clear that a drastic overhauling of the Empire's government was in order. This was to be more than a matter of redistributing the responsibilities of civil officials in the capital, and of giving them the new titles, such as Logothete, which begin to appear now. What was necessary was a complete reform of the system by which the Empire had been run since Diocletian and Constantine. It was required in part as a culmination of the developments which had made the old Diocletianic system obsolete. All parts of the Empire were now vulnerable to attack. Defense was no longer a matter of safeguarding the far-flung frontiers; no province was immune to enemy devastation. This was particularly evident in the case of Asia Minor. Recent events had indicated the importance of this area, not only as a pathway to the capital, but as a source of important revenues and above all of troops. It was indeed now the real heart of the Eastern Empire as it stood. It must at all costs be securely protected if the Empire were to continue to survive.

The immediate goal of strengthening the defenses in Asia Minor was achieved by what was, in some respects, a more drastic extension of processes already in motion since Justinian and his successors had experimented with the reunion of civil and military authority. The old provincial organization was to be superseded by a revised division of the Empire's territories. Each new province would be a military as well as an administrative unit, named a Theme after the Greek word for the "detachment" (the *théma*) of soldiers stationed there to defend it. These soldiers would be called by the Greek name of *stratiótai;* instead of being unreliable or expensive mercenaries they would be drawn from their respective provinces, or Themes, from people settled on, or supported by, land grants there linked to military service. The armies of the Empire thus became a chain of settled rural militias, identified with free small-holders, and with interests firmly rooted in the areas they were liable to defend. The supreme official, military and civil, over each Theme was given as his title the Greek word *strategós*, which of old meant merely "general," but which might in this usage be translated as "Governor-General." Obviously, this was an extension and elaboration of the rank of the

Exarchs, which had already taken shape in the Western provinces. In addition to these provincial arrangements, further troops (still likely to be mercenaries) would, of course, be stationed at the capital under a supreme commander, forming the nucleus of a mobile force which might draw upon troops from the Themes to serve where needed. Within this new military framework the army reforms of Maurice found an appropriate place. The new provincial and military system provided a flexible defensive arrangement which quickly proved its merits. It also gave the Empire a strong, dependable, and firmly rooted military (and, in the coastal Themes, naval) establishment, which was augmented by an extremely sophisticated service organization unparalleled elsewhere in medieval Christendom.

Two further observations should be made here. For one thing, it must be stressed that the reorganization of this era was, after all, really the culmination of processes which had been taking shape for several generations, as we have already seen. The Heraclian reforms represent in a sense merely the intensification and extension of these basic processes, under urgent pressures — not that this fact need detract at all from the significance of the achievement. Secondly, however drastic the innovations, it should be obvious that they had considerably conservative backgrounds in the past. Certainly the Romans in general and Heraclius in particular had the Persian system of satrapies at hand as a model, but there were indigenous precedents and foundations in abundance. The union of civil and military authority was, of course, a standard Roman practice of the period before Diocletian. The *stratiótai* were, in effect, merely a revival of the old Roman *limitanei*, or settled frontier forces, save that they were now deployed in the provinces deep within the Empire as well as on the borders. When we reflect on it, it is clear that the development of this Theme system is really a new example of the ancient Roman tradition of dealing with new situations in flexible and imaginative ways, combining conservatism, innovation, and boldness to a degree that is indeed worthy of the great days of the Roman Republic.

It should not be assumed that Heraclius simply imposed this system *in toto* on his Empire. Its full application would be completed under his successors in centuries to come. Indeed, there is even considerable debate as to whether or not Heraclius individually deserves any credit at all for the creation of the Theme system, or for the institution of the initial Thematic organization. Even those who salvage some of the credit for him do not agree on the extent or the precise beginnings of his measures. There has been some suggestion that he could not have begun such Thematic reforms until after his triumph over Persia, especially in consideration of some presumed imitations of the Persian institutions which he observed during his campaigning. It is arguable, however, that at least a good portion of such reforms could have been an essential part of his preparations for these campaigns. Hence it was natural that Asia Minor should have claimed primary attention; and it is precisely here that the reorganization supposedly achieved during his reign was carried out. To whatever extent Heraclius may have "begun" the Theme system there, however, he certainly would have intended to extend such reorganization to the Eastern provinces recovered from the Persians, but his subsequent distractions would have prevented him from carrying out the plan. We do know that Thematic organization elsewhere in the Empire was to come later.

Of course, the abandonment of the Diocletianic-Constantinian separation of civil and military authority raised anew the danger of overconcentration of power, and hence of usurpations. Heraclius himself was a living testament to this very danger. Certainly this problem could arise. At least one method of forestalling it was to divide large Themes into several smaller ones, as was subsequently done with the original four large Themes of Asia Minor. With the extension of the system throughout the Empire, and also with such subdivisions, the total number of Themes would ultimately reach forty and more. For all the perfection of the system still to come, however, it is to Heraclius that the credit has traditionally been accorded for its full-scale inception. If this tradition has any degree of merit, it is in this work, as well as in his repulse of the nearly fatal Persian onslaught, that he is the real author of the salvation of the Empire in the East. In such terms he might perhaps be reckoned an Emperor of even greater significance than Justinian.

Salvation through such drastic reorganization of the Empire thus meant a considerable transformation of the old Empire of Justinian into something quite different from what he had known. This transformation had implications more subtle and far-reaching than the physical organization itself. The reader may already have noticed in the foregoing discussion that the very titles used in the new system were not Latin in origin, as in the past, but Greek. Here, too, we have a completion of a process already seen emerging in the time of Justinian, as when that Emperor was obliged to issue *Novéllai*, his own New Laws, in the language which all his people and officials could understand, instead of in the traditional Latin. By the time of Heraclius, Latin seems to have died out all but completely in the East, even in administrative usage, its last stronghold. The Empire in the East could no longer avoid acknowledging its complete Hellenization even on the official level. The Emperor now adopted once and for all the title of *Basileús*. Originally the old Greek word for "King," this title might be translated as "Emperor." The actual Greek equivalent for the old Latin word for "Emperor" (*Imperator*), however, was *Autokrátor*. These two titles, *Basileús* and *Autokrátor*, now became the Emperor's formal style, translated more literally as "King and Emperor," as well as "Emperor and Autocrat." Indeed, the new assumption of the title *Basileús* has even been taken to celebrate Heraclian triumph at last over the *Basileús Basileúōn*, the "King of Kings" of Persia. Yet, it would be a mistake to overemphasize the influx of Asiatic ideas and autocracy from this period. The trappings and spirit of oriental monarchy had really been introduced by Diocletian and Constantine; Heraclius added little in this respect. It was the language of the title which triumphed at this juncture, not any oriental connotations. Moreover, the final Hellenization of the Empire in this period should not suggest the emergence of any more narrowly nationalistic or racial qualities. This was still a multi-national Empire. More specifically, it was still *the* Empire. Most specifically, it was still the *Roman* Empire. To be sure, it was a survival rooted essentially in the Hellenized East; but its essence was a fusion of the Roman Imperial idea with the idea of Christian polity. The citizens of the Empire were "Romans," and so they called themselves — not

"Greeks," for the word *Héllēn* meant "pagan." They were a part of the Christian Roman state, and they were the custodians of civilization, which had been reduced to its Greek essentials. We are already across the threshold of the civilization we call Byzantine.

For all the glory and achievement of Heraclius' reign, he was destined to end his years in disastrous failure. It had appeared that he had ended the age-old "Eastern question" once and for all. Unfortunately, he had not. True, the age-old enemy, Persia, was completely humbled, but Persia was in fact soon to be replaced by a new and mightier power. This is not the place to trace the emergence of the teachings of the Prophet Muhammad, or Mohammed, or "Mahomet" (570–632). What is important for us to bear in mind, above and beyond the intangible circumstances of the birth of one of the great world religions, is that its origins did coincide significantly with a ferment among the Arab peoples. These peoples had a long history before the rise of Islam, and a restless one. In some areas of more formal settlement important cities had developed and had become major centers of mercantile activity and of worship. The bulk of the peninsula, however, was occupied by nomadic tribes of Bedouin, whose way of life was the *razzia*, the raiding of settlements and the pillaging of caravans. We have already noted the old danger of these raids on Imperial frontiers in the past, and it was to control or channel such raiding, as well as to provide for opposing buffers, that the Empire and Persia had each developed its respective Arab client state, the Ghassanids and the Lakhmids. Unfortunately, both the Empire and Persia had committed the miscalculation of repressing these clients or allowing them to decline. This blunder removed what might have been important barriers for both realms against at least some of the initial impact of the Arab conquests. In addition, circumstances had not favored the spread of Christianity (though it would have been the suspect Monophysite brand) through the rest of the Arabian peninsula by the zealous Ghassanids. Instead, the sixth century had also seen the failure of Christianity to take firm root in Yemen in the south. As a result of the decline of San'a', the Yemenite capital, the great pagan center of Makkah, or Mecca, was freed of its rivalry, and emerged as the uncontested chief city of the Arabs, just at the time of the youth of its greatest citizen, the Prophet himself. The emergence of his teachings and leadership is in part the history of a religious reform movement which that city — then at the height of new prosperity — and its neighboring territories underwent, and which began to win the adherence of all the Arabs. For the Bedouin it became a unifying, rather than a motivating, force in extending the scope of their raids northward.

Exactly how much of a plan of conquest the Prophet himself envisaged is uncertain. In his final years, major raids were launched against Imperial territories, but they were probably intended at first as no more than that. It was not long, however, before they assumed a new character. So it was that the Arab conquests burst upon the startled Mediterranean world. This movement was a vast outpouring of the long pent-up energies of the Arab peoples.[4] An ideological element was definitely there, but conversion was not the goal of conquest. The tolerant Arabs allowed free exercise of worship in their new possessions on payment of special taxes, thus making religious tolerance pay. That the conquests should overrun Persia and destroy the Sassanid kingdom is perhaps not so surprising. It was a state that had been shattered and demoralized since 628. An initial raid against it in 630 was followed by a setback in the next year; but a major expedition was launched in 636, and in the following year Ctesiphon was captured. The ensuing years were devoted to mopping up the remnants of Persian resistance, though the last King, Yazdigerd III, lingered on as a fugitive until he was killed in 651 or 652. More striking than success against Persia, however, were the devastating blows which the Arabs managed to inflict so quickly on the Empire.

In spite of its glorious triumph under Heraclius by 629, the Empire was itself exhausted. It had put forth an extreme effort which had left it as weakened in its way as was Persia. As a result, it lacked the full resources necessary to stave off the unexpected

4. For a penetrating analysis of the basic nature of these conquests, see P. K. Hitti's *History of the Arabs* (2nd ed. rev., London, 1940), pp. 143–146. This book provides perhaps the best general history of these peoples for the English reader.

Arab onslaughts. These were, in addition, badly misunderstood at first. After all, Arab raids were an old story. The first one was actually joined by Christian Arabs, angry over the withdrawal of Imperial subsidies by the economizing government. Pressure mounted, however, and in February of 634 the great Arab general, Khalid, defeated an Imperial army. Alarmed, the Emperor sent against Khalid his own brother, Theodore, but the able Arab defeated Theodore in the battle of Ajnadayn on July 30, 634. As a result, Palestine was left open and defenseless to Arab devastation, though some fortified towns held out behind their walls. The Arabs were by this time becoming aware of their prospects for full-scale conquest and permanent settlement, beyond mere raiding. Another victory in February of 635 prepared the way for the siege of Damascus, which fell that autumn, followed soon after by Emesa. The desperate Emperor gathered forces for a last major effort against the invaders. Thanks, however, to disorganized command, disloyalty, and desertions, the Imperial army was decisively defeated in the great battle on the River Yarmuk on August 20, 636. The Imperial position collapsed, and Heraclius had to view in despair the second and now irretrievable loss of part of the provinces he had heroically saved. Thus isolated, the remaining major cities eventually capitulated to the Arabs: Jerusalem in 638, and Caesarea two years later.

The spectacular progress of the Arab invasion of Syria-Palestine was partly the result of the failure of Byzantine military defenses. Again, however, large elements of the local population welcomed the invaders as liberators; and in view of the great moderation of the new Arab regime, they were not disappointed. The role of the Jewish elements is understandable. Nevertheless, the general Christian population also had no love for the Imperial government, in view of its oppressive taxation and administrative system, and above all because of the extensive Monophysite sentiment in this area.

Amid all that Heraclius had tried to do to cope with the Arab conquest, he particularly had exerted himself in this last regard. Actually, the exertions had begun earlier, in the Persian war, when he had seen all too clearly the terrible consequences of Monophysite and local dissent in undermining Imperial resistance during Khusru II's conquest of Syria-Palestine and Egypt. He therefore had earnestly sought a means of soothing Monophysite feelings in order to win back their loyalty to the Empire. Once again, an Emperor was trying to bridge the gap between Chalcedonians and their foes. In this labor he was aided by his Patriarch, the great Sergius, a Syrian himself. Sergius worked out a compromise scheme in which the Two Natures of Christ, the Human and the Divine, would both be acknowledged, but as involved together in only a single Operation or Active Force (*enérgeia*). This was the essence of the so-called *Eirēnikón*, or "Peace Formula." In his Persian campaigns Heraclius used every contact he had with Asiatic churchmen to advance the formula. Its promotion became one of the key elements of his re-establishment of Imperial authority in the Eastern provinces after the defeat of Persia. The new Patriarch of Alexandria, Cyrus, became the particular adherent of the policy upon his appointment in 630 or 631, and he had some momentary success in working out a compromise on its basis with moderate Monophysites in Egypt. Even the Pope in Rome seemed well-disposed. Nevertheless, orthodox opposition rallied under the leadership of the monk Sophronius, who became Patriarch of Jerusalem in 634. Then the Pope began to waver. Sergius responded to criticism by modifying his doctrine to encompass the Two Natures no longer within a single theandric Energy, but within One Will (*thélēma*). In this form the doctrine of Monotheletism finally emerged.

Resistance and wrangling continued, however. The new doctrine had seemed to offer for the first time a workable incorporation of the impossible equation "one equals two" within an Imperial formula of compromise. Even so, it was doomed to failure, along with all previous attempts. Unlike Justinian's efforts, Monotheletism represented not so much a disruption of Chalcedonian dogma as an unwarranted imposition upon it. As such, however, it was no more acceptable to the orthodox than any previous compromise. Neither could the bulk of the Monophysites accept it — though an element of them would, forming the Melkite, or Royalist, Church in Syria-Palestine when they came under Arab rule.

Nor was it to be of much help in Egypt, where the dissidents were antagonized the more by the high-handedness of Cyrus. As time ran out, Sergius, just before his death, helped the Emperor draft the formal manifesto of Monotheletism, the Imperial *Ekthesis*, in 638. It was a lost cause: the Pope rejected it, and the Egyptian Monophysites were unreconciled to it. Meanwhile, the Arabs had recognized the strategic and economic desirability of Egypt, and in 639 they invaded it. The provincial defenses were disunited and disorganized, while the disaffection of the population was beyond amending. The Arabs swept over Egypt with a few quick victories in 640. Imperial relief was difficult, especially when the Emperor died in the following year, leaving the government in a state of considerable flux. In September of 642 Alexandria capitulated. Thus was Egypt added to the new Arab domains, and the conquerors next began their pressure further westward across North Africa. Though an Imperial fleet took advantage of a brief revolt in Alexandria in 645, the city was retaken by the Arabs in the following year. The great metropolis was thus definitely lost to the Empire and began its decline from its former glories.

In tearing away and devouring huge chunks of the Empire of Justinian, the Arab conquests in effect finally resolved the terrible Monophysite problem which had vexed him and other Emperors. Certainly the loss of Syria-Palestine and Egypt, and presently of North Africa, were terrible blows to the Empire. These had been its particularly important commercial areas. Palestine, of course, contained the chief shrines of the Faith. In addition vital adjustments would have to be made in regard to the provisioning of Constantinople since its Egyptian grain sources were gone. Finally, the unity of the Mediterranean world was ended, now that its shores were being divided between Christendom and Islam. In retrospect, however, the loss of these provinces was in some ways a blessing in disguise for the Empire. Given the religious and political circumstances of the time, the Monophysite problem was probably an insoluble one. By relieving the Empire of the very provinces most involved with the controversy, the Arabs reduced it to a more compact and viable entity, whose energies were more urgently aroused, whose processes of self-regeneration were quickened, and whose prospects of united survival were far better than they might have been otherwise.

Ironically, the last of the Imperial compromise formulas, Mon-otheletism, would, as we shall see, linger on in that surviving entity to cause further controversy, even after the disappearance of the problem it was meant to solve.

The Pangs of Regeneration

Broken and dispirited by the disasters of his closing years, Heraclius died in 641.[5] The months immediately following his passing were occupied by the confused struggle for succession, out of which emerged his grandson, Constans II (641–668), who was then followed by his own son, Constantine IV (668–685), and the latter's son and successor Justinian II (685–695). These successive representatives of the Heraclian house faced manfully the terrible challenges which confronted the Emperors through the rest of the seventh century.

The most urgent challenge remained the Asiatic situation. The initial interest of the Arabs was land conquest, and so the major thrust of their expansion was eastward across Mesopotamia and the Iranian plateau, northward into Syria-Palestine and beyond, and westward into Egypt and across North Africa. Once in possession of Syria and Egypt, however, with great ports, shipyards, and maritime resources there, the Arabs began to turn their eyes seaward. They came to understand that development on their part of sea power was both essential for holding the Mediterranean coastal areas they had won, as well as the key to greater conquests beyond. Credit for this broadening of perspective is due primarily to the new Arab governor of Syria, Mu'awiya, a man of great ability and vision, and to a somewhat lesser extent to his counterpart in Egypt, Abdullah. To be sure, Mu'awiya maintained Arab attacks: his armies assailed Asia Minor, ravaging Armenia in 642–643 and invading Cappadocia in 644–646, capturing Caesarea in the latter region. Arab forces also penetrated deeper and more perilously into the heart of western Asia Minor. At the same time,

5. For a good characterization of this Emperor's complicated personality, see Baynes in *The Cambridge Medieval History*, II, 300–301.

however, Mu'awiya began to develop a fleet, taking advantage of the shipyards and maritime skills of his new subjects. In 646 he was able to mount a raid on the island of Cyprus, the first water-girt target of Arab expansion. Then, in 652, in conjunction with Abdullah, the first Arab raid was launched upon the island of Sicily from Mu'awiya's bases. For the first time since the days of Vandal power, the Empire was challenged seriously on the seas. In the ensuing years the ships of Mu'awiya and Abdullah began to devastate the Aegean islands and the Asia Minor coast: in 654, in an attack on Rhodes, its long-fallen Colossus, once one of the Seven Wonders of the Ancient World, was dismantled and carried off. As the Arabs approached by land, and as their power surged formidably on the sea, they began to dream of capturing the Imperial capital itself. Realizing the danger, Constans II boldly endeavored to oppose them. In 655, off the coast of Asia Minor, the Imperial fleet under the Emperor's personal command met the Arab squadrons in the so-called "Battle of the Masts." The Imperial fleet was disastrously defeated, and Constans himself barely escaped with his life. The Empire's naval supremacy was broken.

Fortunately for the Empire, the Arabs were not able to make full use of their triumph immediately. For one thing, their own losses in the battle were heavy. More important Mu'awiya became embroiled in the wars attending the collapse of the initial line of Caliphs, who had succeeded the Prophet as temporal rulers. Bidding for power himself, Mu'awiya finally became Caliph in 661, and established the Umayyad (or Omayyad) dynasty in hereditary control of the Muslim Caliphate. Its capital was moved to Damascus, and one of its main goals became the destruction of the Empire of the Christians. Coastal harassments were increased, while a major effort against the Empire was prepared. The Arab armies pressed closer by land to Constantinople, wintering on Imperial territory, reaching Chalcedon by 699, and mounting the first Arab siege of the city. This siege proved brief and ineffectual. Again Mu'awiya understood the need for full-scale naval strength. As the 670's began the Arab fleets commenced carving a path of bases for themselves along the Aegean coasts and islands. In 674 Crete was briefly occupied, and in that year the new effort began in earnest. Constantinople was blockaded and attacked, most fiercely by sea. The Arab forces withdrew each autumn to winter in nearby Cyzicus and then returned each spring to continue the beleaguerment. Under the vigorous new Emperor Constantine IV, however, the city resisted successfully. By 677–678 the Arab siege was broken. One of the principal aids in this achievement was the newly-perfected combustible weapon, maritime fire, or "Greek fire" as it is most commonly called; it was employed by the Imperial ships against the Arabs with devastating effectiveness. The Byzantine rebuff of this Arab attack was an event of great significance in stemming the Arab advance, which found itself severely checked for the first time. Mu'awiya was forced to accept the failure of his grand design, and he granted a treaty in 680 by the terms of which the Arabs withdrew from their advanced position. In the following year the Emperor could begin to chip away at the Arab holdings by land on his own initiative.

In the intervals of repose which the Heraclian Emperors were granted during the Arab assaults, attention could be turned at last to the frightful situation in the Balkans. It was Constans II who made the first effort to reassert Imperial authority over some portion of these areas, at least in Greece, in the course of a campaign in *Sklavínia* about 658. We know painfully little about this campaign, though it is reported that Constans deported large numbers of Slavonic captives to Asia Minor as settlers for the reorganized and depopulated Themes there. Another Balkan effort was made by his successor, Constantine IV, in view of a still further threat. In the early years of his reign one of the many remnants of the Hun peoples, the Onogurs, who were also known as Bulgars, crossed the Danube and settled on Imperial territory. About 680, Constantine IV sallied forth to reduce them in a major land and sea campaign. It failed, and the Emperor was obliged to agree to a treaty with the Bulgars, promising tribute and acknowledging their independence. This was the first time the Empire formally recognized a new state south of the Danube, on what was supposed to be its own Balkan territory. However, the establishment of the Bulgar state was to have far-reaching consequences. In the next two centuries the Asiatic "Old Bulgars" would be assimilated and quite Slavonicized ethnically and linguistically, emerging as the ancestors of the modern Bulgarian nation. In addition, the Bulgar kings would increasingly threaten the Empire, at times with nearly fatal intensity. For the next three and one-half centuries Bulgaria and the Empire would enter into a deadly rivalry that would be resolved at last only through the laborious conquest of Bulgaria by the Empire, during the period of a great Byzantine military zenith.

Meanwhile, the re-establishment of Imperial authority elsewhere in the inland Balkan territories among the Slavs was to be a slow process. Only in the ninth century could the bulk of Greece be restored finally to the Empire, and then be re-Hellenized linguistically, culturally, and ecclesiastically, if not ethnically. The recovery of Greece, however, should not be looked upon as any reflection of Hellenic sentiment for nationalistic "liberation." Greece had been a province of the Empire, and was recovered as such. The Empire never forgot its own. Though many of the losses it sustained in its long history were permanent, it was often able to recover lost territories with surprising frequency and resiliency. Justinian's Reconquest program was far from unique in its conception: it was, in fact, only the first such expression of this "irredentist" attitude. However much the Empire changed after him, and whatever harm was done by his implementation of such irredentism, the attitude was never abandoned by the Emperors as the centuries passed. To do so would have been to compromise the entire Imperial idea. The difference is that recovery in the centuries after Justinian was more practicable when applied within reason in the Eastern spheres; whereas the Justinianic all-Mediterranean outlook had been too ambitious even for its own time.

Therefore the Balkan recovery would proceed. Its key would be the terrible struggle with the Bulgarian state. When the stalemate was broken in the early eleventh century, however, Imperial influence would at least overshadow the various local Slavonic principalities beyond, bringing them into some degree of subjection to the Emperor in Constantinople. As late as the twelfth century the Emperor Manuel I Comnenus (1142–1180) could claim with reasonable justice that his Balkan frontier was the Danube River as far as its reaches in distant Croatia, as it had been, at least in theory, in the days of Justinian. Meanwhile, the first attempts of the Heraclian Emperors to recover Balkan territory from the Slavonic invaders, or at least to assert hegemony over them in the Imperial regions they had settled, had a deeper significance. In reclaiming these territories, the Emperors also, consciously or otherwise, committed themselves to some extent to responsibility for the fate of the Slavonic peoples who were becoming firmly planted in them. The Empire never attempted to drive out the Slavs, but rather to overcome them and to recover some degree of control over the land they now occupied. In the ninth century, as an extension of military and diplomatic effort, the Empire would thus launch its full-scale program of Christianizing and civilizing the Slavs. Its remarkable measure of success in this sphere was of vast significance for the history of Europe and of Western civilization, and was to become one of the Byzantine Empire's greatest achievements.

For our purposes the Heraclian era has still another point of great interest. Despite all the innovation and transformation which the Empire underwent in this period, it is noteworthy how much remained of the world outlook of Justinian. It is true that the Emperors had recognized the critically Eastern nature of Imperial survival, and that their efforts were of necessity concentrated mainly on assuring it. Nevertheless, the Empire had no intention of abandoning either the pretensions of Justinian, or the Western territories which he had recovered for it at so great a cost. This enduring interest in the West, in spite of perils in the East, is reflected among the Heraclians by Constans II above all.

Hated in his time for his arrogance and tyranny, often misunderstood by modern historians, this man was nonetheless a remarkable Emperor indeed. He seems to have developed a particular interest in preserving the Empire's position in the Western Mediterranean, to the extent of neglecting the East. For various reasons he ceased to reside in Constantinople, thus carrying out to a degree his grandfather's erstwhile scheme. In spite of renewed Arab dangers in the East, he set out with an army for Italy, deciding to try to end the stalemate against the Lombards. Unfortunately, his action against them in 662–663 produced no genuine results. The outstanding episode of his Italian sojourn was rather his visit to Rome in 663 — the first such since Theodosius I almost two centuries before. He celebrated the occasion by stripping bronze roofing off public buildings as though he were some barbarian plunderer. He then removed himself to Sicily, which he seems to have decided to use as a base for stopping the Arab advance in the central Mediterranean area. He is even supposed to have contemplated moving his capital formally to Syracuse. Whatever his actual plans and achievements, however, his harsh and arbitrary personality won him assassination in 668. He died discredited, but still distinguished by impressive qualities: he was the first Emperor to fight back against the Arabs at the peak of their tide of conquest; the first to check and subjugate the Slavs in the Balkans to some extent, at least in Greece; and the first, as well as the last, Eastern Emperor to concern himself personally with saving the remnants of Imperial holdings in the West.

The familiar Justinianic pattern can be observed even more strikingly in another aspect of Constans II's reign, his religious policy. On his accession the problem of Monotheletism, though rendered largely futile by the Arab conquest of the Monophysite provinces, was still unsettled. The Papacy had rejected Monotheletism, and the new Emperor was faced with strong pressures to abrogate the *Ékthesis* of Heraclius. The Papal efforts in that direction even seem to have been involved in a brief and untimely revolt by the African Exarch Gregory. Meanwhile, the Chalcedonian orthodox hatred for the Monothelete compromise found its most eloquent spokesman in the great theologian, Maximus, called "the Confessor." Unlike Justinian, Constans II himself seems to have had little interest in or sympathy for theological controversy. For him the Monophysite problem was dead, and he had many other problems to cope with as it was. Therefore, in 648 he issued his pronouncement, the *Týpos*, in which he formally withdrew the *Ékthesis*, but refused to make a complete condemnation of Monotheletism, and forbade any further discussion of the matter of the Energy or Will of Christ. In effect, he declared a moratorium on theological debate, which was designated as "off limits" until circumstances allowed a better opportunity to renew it. The orthodox were furious. The new Pope, Martin I (649– [654], d. 655), himself illegally consecrated, defied the new Imperial policy. Constans may not have shared Justinian's interest in theology, but he did share Justinian's concern for guarding Imperial prerogatives. In 653 he was able to have Pope Martin arrested and conveyed to Constantinople. Humiliated and mistreated, the Pope refused to comply even under pressure. In 654 he was deposed and exiled to Cherson in the Crimea, where he died. Next it was the turn of Maximus the Confessor, who was also subjected to terrible pressures, which he resisted courageously. Condemned to mutilation, he was then sent to exile in Lazica. There he died in 662, a martyr to Imperial caesaropapism, and in some ways the first of a line of Eastern Orthodox Church leaders who opposed Imperial intervention in affairs of the Church. So it was that, after a century, it was still possible for the Eastern Emperor to emulate Justinian's domineering Church policy, especially in overawing the still-subject Papacy.

Such a situation was not long to continue, however. The new Emperor, Constantine IV, chose to follow a different course. Friction and pressure over Monotheletism had not been stopped, even though the issue had become by this time, after all, a dead letter. Constantine therefore decided to yield to the Papal and orthodox position and reunify the Church, hoping also that this step would strengthen the weakened Imperial position in Italy. A reversal of policy followed, culminating in the Sixth Ecumenical Council of 680–681, which met in the palace under the Emperor's presidency. Representatives of the Arab-controlled Patriarchates were present to defend Monotheletism, but it was finally condemned. The strict Chalcedonian doctrine of Christ's Two Natures, and by extension His Two Energies and Two Wills, was reaffirmed. Monotheletism was anathematized and forthwith disappeared. The Partriarchate of Constantinople, however, lost its last possible link with the captured Monophysite Churches, which thereafter went their own way beyond recall. Nevertheless, the vexing question of doctrine was at last ended with the definitive triumph of Chalcedonian orthodoxy in the Christian world. The time of arbitrary Imperial compromise doctrines imposed on the Church was past. Nor could the Emperor again act in so highhanded a fashion with regard to the Papacy as circumstances changed. The last of the Heraclians, Justinian II, chose to break

the new peace with the Papacy and to foster new dissent, foment-
ing ominous new differences between the Eastern and Western
Churches in the process. When this Emperor attempted to answer
renewed Papal defiance with the methods of his grandfather
Constans II, and of the first Justinian, he found that he was no
longer able to do so. The Emperor's power in Italy was more precarious than ever, and he could do nothing against the Pope. His
Exarchs were either powerless to carry out his wishes or else
defied him to make common cause with the Pontiff. Ultimately,
Justinian II was forced to swallow his pride, reverse himself, and
curry favor with the Papacy.

Of all the Heraclians, however, Justinian II is perhaps the most
interesting for us. His name was to be more than a coincidence;
or so, at least, he was determined. Justinian II seems to have
been consciously eager to emulate his great namesake and predecessor in the latter's own terms. Thus we find Justinian II becoming a particularly active builder. When he later took a barbarian
bride, he renamed her Theodora, with an all-too-obvious back-
ward glance to the past. His would-be caesaropapistic Church
policy may also have involved some imitation of the great
Justinian.

In his way Justinian II was indeed an important Emperor. He inherited the vigor and perception of his family in great abundance,
and he understood many of the requirements of his time. He undertook some aggressive steps against the Arabs in Syria which,
though at the time ill-advised and unfortunate, at least showed
that the Empire could take the offensive under the right conditions. He also led a new Imperial campaign in *Sklavinia*, about
688–689. Whatever its limitations, it succeeded in clearing a path
through Slavonic-held land, in relieving threatened Thessalonica
again, and in imposing new subjection on the Slavs in Greece.
Another large number of Slavs was transported to Asia Minor
to serve the Empire there. Justinian II was in fact a particular
exponent of this Byzantine practice of resettlement of peoples,
and in many cases he moved populations from one area to another
to fit current needs. It was a harsh policy which bore severely on
the people involved, but it was often an effective measure for
meeting new dangers to which menaced and ravaged parts of

the Empire were exposed. It is perhaps to Justinian II's time, also, that many important administrative, social, and economic reforms can be dated, reforms which vitally supplemented the previous Heraclian overhauling of the Imperial governing system, and which laid the basis for a new and coherent Byzantine society. Further, though the application of the Thematic organization to Europe had already begun — Thrace was thus organized under Constantine IV in the face of the Bulgar threat — Justinian II began a new extension of it westward into Greece.

It was, as a matter of fact, just such a step in this last regard that precipitated Justinian's fall. In 695 he established the new Theme of Hellas; a territory which, however, included only a portion of what we think of as Greece. As its first *Strategós* he appointed the general Leontius, who had spent the previous few years in prison by reason of Imperial disfavor. Instead of proceeding to his new post, Leontius took advantage of his change in fortune to lead a revolution. The situation was ripe: if he had inherited the good qualities of his house, Justinian II had also inherited and even magnified the evil ones. He was autocratic, arrogant, and despotic; his punishments were arbitrary, and his conduct extravagant. His favor to unscrupulous and oppressive ministers had — in the best Justinianic tradition — won his government much hatred, while many of his radical reform measures had earned him bitter enemies, especially among the powerful aristocrats. By 695 virtually all elements of society were antagonized, justly or not. Nor was the revolt that broke out against him that year a mere Nika Riot. Justinian II was seized and deposed. His life was spared, but in order to render him unfit to occupy the throne thereafter he was mutilated. This was not done by blinding, the method soon to become common among the Byzantines, but by having his nose slit and his tongue cut out, though the latter operation was not performed very thoroughly. Thus degraded, Justinian was then sent into exile in the Crimea.

His successor, Leontius (695–698), did not long enjoy his precarious throne. Internal dissension raged everywhere. When Carthage fell to the Arabs and Moors he sent an expedition to retake it, which was only briefly successful. Amid the ensuing dissatisfaction a revolt broke out in the expeditionary fleet, and its commander, Apsimar, was proclaimed Emperor. Sailing to Constantinople, he deposed Leontius, who suffered the slitting of his nose in his own turn and who was then encloistered. Apsimar was one of two men in Byzantine history who rose from the ranks of naval service, instead of the army, to become Emperor — indicating something of the unique importance of the fleet in the Empire in contrast to the situation in other medieval Christian states. Taking the official name of Tiberius III (698–705), he seems to have possessed genuine ability, and he exerted himself earnestly. Nevertheless his possibilities as a worthwhile Emperor were cut short all too soon. For Justinian II would not resign himself to his deposition. His mutilation had incapacitated him far less than expected, only feeding his fury. After a romantic history of escapes and escapades in the far reaches of the Black Sea and Steppe areas, exploits which reveal his iron will and determined ability, Justinian secured Bulgar support and finally managed to march on Constantinople to regain his throne. Though lacking popular sympathy, he succeeded in entering the capital. Tiberius III was deposed and was executed, together with the fallen Leontius. Justinian II proceeded to devote the years of his restoration (705–711) to avenging himself on the fortune which had given him his popular surname of *Rhinotmétos* ("Slit-Nosed"). He launched a fantastic orgy of retaliation in all directions, regardless of the practical consequences for the Empire. One can only conclude that the man had lost his sanity in his passion for vengeance. His new regime made a shambles out of the Empire. The aristocracy particularly suffered, and the work of Phocas in destroying what was left of Late Roman society was completed. The outcome was only a matter of time: Justinian II was finally deposed by a rebellious general. The last Heraclian Emperor and his family were butchered.

It is tragic that the great Heraclian dynasty should have ended in such bloody disgrace and chaos. In spite of the final stain of Justinian II's excessive tyranny and insane vengefulness, it had been a brilliant house, one whose record could be matched by few others in Byzantine or other history. Of its four actual rulers, all were men of irreproachable morality, vigor, and genius, for all their progressive tendency to brooding and fanatic despotism. They led the Empire through two nearly fatal crises, against the Persians and the Arabs, and they gave it a new institutional and internal life. Even if their age was the bleakest and most debased in cultural life, it had given the Empire a new basis for flourishing in revised frames of reference. Whatever else they did, the Heraclians had saved and transformed the collapsing Empire of Justinian, and their era marks the real beginnings of a mature Byzantine state.

The immediate successors of Justinian II were a mean and unfortunate lot. The rebellious general Philippicus Vardanes (711–713) proved to be a worthless ruler whose debauchery soon provoked a revolt and his overthrow. His successor was an obscure official named Artemius, who chose to rule as Anastasius II (713–715), in memory perhaps of the previous civilian-Emperor of that name. As in the case of Apsimar/Tiberius III, he seems to have been a person of ability and initiative, but he was the captive of circumstances which undermined his opportunities and betrayed his potential. Another revolt placed on the throne a frightened tax-gatherer who reigned as Theodosius III (715–717), but who was in no position actually to rule. As a figurehead ruler, and devoid of any genuine personal capability, he was helpless on his throne as disaster approached.

Disaster came in the shape of a formidable new effort by the Arabs. The chaos in the Empire since 695 did not pass unnoticed by the Umayyad Caliphs, and in due time they moved to take advantage of it. As a new drive was launched in Asia Minor by 715, it began to appear as if the Arabs might at last realize their great dream of capturing the Christian capital. Fortunately, as it was so often able to do, the Empire produced another savior in an hour of peril. Leo, the *Strategós* of one of the important Asiatic Themes, led a successful coup and took the throne. It was a triumph for the Asiatic aristocracy of the Empire and for the interests of strong centralized government. It was also a victory for the elements in the Empire most capable of organizing effective resistance to the enemy. When in the summer of 717 the Arabs gathered around Constantinople for their greatest siege of it, the Empire at last had a leader who could save it. The resistance was brilliantly organized, utilizing all the benefits of the city's defensive advantages. As their failure turned to misery and hardship, the Arabs became demoralized; finally abandoning their siege after a year, they withdrew in disorder. It was a triumph in the tradition of 626. The Arabs' tide of conquest was ended, and the Empire could now begin its painful progress towards forcing them out of its lands. There would be a long period of precarious stasis on the Asiatic frontiers. The replacement of the Umayyad dynasty in 750 by the new Abbasid house would bring some new and capable Arab rulers to the throne. Nevertheless, the Abbasid Caliphs would begin to decline and lose their grip after the middle of the ninth century, by which time the Byzantines could begin to take the initiative. To be sure, the loss of the islands of Crete and Sicily in the third decade of the ninth century would spawn a new phase of Arab maritime depredation, this time from semi-independent and highly organized corsair powers whose pirate bands devastated the Empire's coasts. Within another century, however, the Arabs would be thrown back decisively on sea and land as Byzantium reached its zenith of military might and initiative at the end of the tenth and early eleventh centuries. Thereafter the Arabs would decline irrevocably and new Islamic peoples would rise to prominence in their place.

The significance of the 717–718 siege for Europe as a whole should not be underestimated. This had been the greatest single effort which the Arabs ever launched against Christian power. Had this bastion of Christendom, Constantinople, fallen to them, the course of medieval history would have been much different. It stood fast, holding the Eastern flank of Europe. The siege also coincided with the general ending of the first great tide of Arab conquest. By the end of the seventh century the Arabs had finally broken down the Imperial defense of North Africa, and had won the Moors to their cause — a process of amalgamation in which the Roman and Vandals and Byzantines before them had failed. With the Moors as the new Islamic spearhead, the Arabs subjugated Spain in the second decade of the eighth century, destroying the decayed Visigothic kingdom, against which Justinian's own effort had failed. The raids of the Arabs northward carried them across the Pyrenees into Frankish territory. The old Merovingian dynasty of the Franks had by this time sunk into impotence. The real holder of the power vacated by the figurehead kings, the Mayor of the Palace, Charles Martel, was able to organize resistance to the Muslims' raids and defeat them at Tours in 732. This victory has long been much exaggerated at the expense of the more significant breaking of the siege of Constantinople in the 670's and in 717–718. Martel defeated massed raiders, not a concentrated expedition of conquest; moreover, more than a quarter of a century ensued after the Battle of Tours before Arab raids between the Loire River and the Pyrenees really ceased. This battle did at least mark the end of actual Arab expansion to the northwest. Within the next century the untenably vast Arab Caliphate would begin to break up into its component areas. What further Arab conquests were made were generally the efforts of the individual North African states and were concentrated in southern Italy, where the Byzantines themselves led, successfully, the bulk of the resistance to them. Nevertheless, whatever barriers were erected and maintained against the Arabs, by the ninth century they had completed their work of splitting the Mediterranean — once the symbol of unity of the ancient world — between the hostile worlds of Islam and Christendom.

The reign of Leo III (717–741) marked the beginning of a new era for the Empire. The previous processes of reorganization and regeneration continued, but it was by this ruler that the Iconoclastic controversy was first initiated. A new cultural and esthetic life was taking shape on the old foundations. Iconoclasm was a great new spiritual ordeal for the Empire, concerning the use of images in the Christian Church, but involving social, economic, and even anti-monastic issues as well as theological ones. It was also the crucial struggle, foreshadowed by Maximus the Confessor, against the Emperor's power in the Church by those who believed that the sovereign should not interfere in ecclesiastical and doctrinal matters. The Iconoclastic policies of the Emperors would be defeated at the Council of Nicaea in 787, the Seventh — and for the Eastern Orthodox Church the last — of the ecumenical councils; and this verdict would be reaffirmed in 843. In both cases, however, the repudiation would originate from the throne itself. Significantly enough, it would be women, regents for their sons, who would take the step: respectively, the remarkable Irene in 787, and then in 843 the later Empress with the by-now-common name of Theodora. Nevertheless, the Emperor's power in the Church would not be broken, even if such caesaropapism as that of Justinian I would be more controlled. Indeed, the spirit of Justinian would never be very far below the surface in the Empire's Church-State relations thereafter.

The Iconoclastic controversy would, however, leave its imprint even on the West, though those regions were theologically unaffected by it. For the Imperial Church policy in this direction served as the final irritation which completed the alienation of the Papacy from the Eastern court that had previously dominated it. Imperial power in Italy was drastically limited. Occupied with their own problems at home, the Emperors could give little effective aid to the isolated Papacy against the revived aggressiveness of the Lombards. In the year 751 the Lombards succeeded in capturing Ravenna. With the loss of this last great stronghold in northern Italy, the Exarchate ceased to exist, and the Empire's power in the peninsula was reduced to some precarious holdings in the south. It was amid these conditions that the Popes finally turned in their need to the one surviving barbarian state in the West, the only orthodox catholic German power in the West which had any promise: the Frankish kingdom. The alliance of the Pope with the Carolingian royal house, newly established after its removal of the last Merovingian puppet king, led to the campaigns of Pepin I in 754 and 756, and then to those of 774–775 by Charles the Great, or "Charlemagne." Out of them came the absorption of the Lombard kingdom by the Franks; the establishment of the Papacy as a territorial power in central Italy; the perfection of the Carolingian Empire, that first attempt as a medieval all-European state; and the laying of the basis for the cardinal institution of the Middle Ages, the German or "Holy Roman" Empire. From here medieval European history may be said to have begun. For the Latin West was by then no longer a backwater of the East, but a sphere all its own, with a long and glorious life ahead of it.

As the West began to go its own way, in the surviving Eastern Empire the heirs of Augustus, Constantine, and Justinian continued their tradition as they recognized it. Byzantium had its foundations firmly laid. It had settled into its magnificent triple role of preserving what remained of Classical Greek civilization in a world that had otherwise lost that heritage, of holding the eastern flank of Europe against Islam, and of civilizing the Slavonic peoples.

The emergence of a new order out of the remnants of the Late Roman world, as Justinian had known it, was in full progress.

Justinian after Justinian

The foregoing sketch of the centuries of Imperial history immediately after Justinian's time may already have suggested a few of the ways in which the Emperor's example endured even after his society and state had undergone extensive transformation. Some further comments in this regard, however, may serve to conclude our consideration appropriately.

The history of the Roman, Late Roman, and Byzantine Empires — the distinctions among which, obviously, cannot be clearly drawn — is all a single process. The subjects of the Empire were themselves generally unconscious of the underlying currents of change and evolution to the extent that we can appreciate them now in restrospect. Once the generation which had suffered under the oppressions of Justinian was dead, it was easy to forget how hard his times had been. Nor could the problems and mistakes of his reign seem so glaring then as they now do to the historian. There was splendor and glory in the age of Justinian as well as failure, and it was the former aspects which were remembered. The splendor was not merely a matter of records and memory. All around them the Byzantines had reminders of it, especially in Constantinople. Throughout the city there were his great buildings, especially churches, some of which still stand in their beauty to our own day. For centuries after him his successors were buried in the magnificent Church of the Holy Apostles, which he had built in its final form. In the *Augoustaîon* — the great public square near the Palace, the Hippodrome, and Haghía Sophía — there was the colossal equestrian statue of the Emperor perpetuating the image of his glory and pretensions long after their consequences were forgotten. And above all there was Haghía Sophía itself, at once a unique architectural achievement, and at the same time the very pivot of life in the capital. Within its walls were enacted centuries of drama, triumph, violence, piety, everyday routine, unheard-of spectacle, and heartbreaking disaster, all of which made up the long and fascinating history of the civilization which called this building its *Megalé ekklēsía*, the "Great Church." As we see it today we might well wonder with Justinian if Solomon's Temple in Jerusalem could have matched it for either beauty or historical meaning.

Symbolic of the Byzantine appreciation of what Justinian had given them is a mosaic still to be seen in the Haghía Sophía (see Plate IX). It is in the south vestibule, and it is significantly not of Justinian's own age, but of a later period, the end of the tenth century. In it is portrayed, as it were, the heritage of the Christian Imperial tradition, as the Byzantines understood it. The Virgin sits enthroned in glory, her Son on her lap, receiving from two Emperors their choicest offerings. On her left is Constantine the Great, the first Christian Emperor, the founder of Christian Imperial polity. Represented in his hands in quaintly stylized form is his offering: Constantinople, the Imperial City Guarded by God, the seat of the Christian Imperial mission, and the special beneficiary of the Virgin's protection, the City unmatched in the world of its time. But on her right — and is that placement itself of significance?— stands Justinian, "the celebrated *Basileús*," as the mosaic inscription labels him. In his hands, again in miniature stylized representation, is his contribution: Haghía Sophía, the supreme center of Christian worship in the *oikouménē*, or "Inhabited World." The City and the Great Church, these were the two Imperial accomplishments which the Byzantines remembered as their sovereigns' greatest achievements, at least as represented here. Being held the peer of Constantine the Great, the "Thirteenth Apostle" and "Equal of the Apostles," was the measure of Justinian's greatness in Byzantine eyes.

It is small wonder, then, that generation after generation of Byzantine writers and historians signalized their remembrances of this Emperor by calling him "The Great Justinian." The designation implied more than a distinction between him and the Lesser or Later Justinian II. One is almost tempted to suspect that the phrase might have been used to describe Justinian I even if Justinian II had never lived. Against this remembrance might be placed the fact that no Emperor after 711 bore his name. Perhaps some analogy might be made in this regard to the effects of the reputations of Kings Richard II and Richard III, which, although they have discouraged the further use of the name by later members of the English royal house, have not diminished the popular regard for Richard I. In addition, Justinian was a Latin name and as such passed out of usage in the East in later, more Hellenized generations. Actually, it continued to be popular in the Latin West, particularly among the later Italians (especially the Venetians), for whom it was common as both a given and a family name. And so we find, ironically enough, that the chief commander of the final defense of Constantinople against the Turks in 1453 was a Genoese adventurer named Giovanni *Giustiniani.*

We have seen in Justinian II at least one Emperor who consciously strove to imitate the Great Justinian. He was by no means the only one. As anachronistic as Justinian's Reconquest program may have been as applied in its time, it was characteristic of an outlook which could not but continue to be a part of the Imperial idea as long as the Empire endured, even without an Emperor of such a specifically Latin-minded orientation. We may thus see as perhaps its last great exponent so late an Emperor as Manuel I Comnenus (1143–1180). His perspective still embraced much of the Western Mediterranean, specifically Italy, in terms of obviously Justinianic background. The Byzantines had lost their last hold in Italy in 1071. Yet, nearly a century later, Manuel I made a serious effort to recover Italy, as Justinian had done. He likewise made the last attempt of any Byzantine Emperor to restore his state to the rank of a great Mediterranean power. By the end of his reign, however, his attempts and pretensions collapsed about him like a house of cards, to an even greater extent than Justinian's had. Thus, if the Empire had long lost its capacity to practice a Justinianic external policy, it had still not lost the desire to follow his example.

In the Empire's twilight, as the centuries passed, the memory of Justinian was still very much alive. One of the most bizarre reminders of him came in the tragic year of 1204, when the pious brigands of the Fourth Crusade, after their capture of Constantinople, rifled the Imperial tombs in the Great Church of the Holy Apostles, Justinian's among them. It was specifically recorded that, to everyone's amazement, this Emperor's corpse was still fully intact.[6] Less grisly is an episode which occurred in 1415. In that year the Emperor Manuel II Palaeologus was attempting to protect one of the few territories still left to the Empire by rebuilding the old wall, the Hexamilion, across the Isthmus of Corinth, to keep the Turks out of the Peloponnesus, just as Justinian had built it earlier for similar protective purposes. While this work was in progress an inscription was discovered which had been a part of Justinian's structure. Its invocation of divine aid, as appropriate then as it had been nine centuries earlier, and the prestige of Justinian's name, made the discovery of this inscription a kind of omen that was faithfully recorded in almost all the contemporary Byzantine accounts of the event, however brief they were.[7]

That the memory of a long-dead ruler should have such meaning for people nearly nine centuries after his time may strike us as strange until we realize how indicative this is of the very durability of the Imperial tradition and of the so-called "Byzantine" Empire. In an age when nations wax and wane in a brief span of years, the example of a society more than a millennium old seems unusual to us, especially in such stable form. Yet, the Empire of the fifteenth century was still, in reality as well as in contemporary consciousness, in the direct tradition of which Justinian was a part. This very durability of his memory in his civilization testifies to the vitality of the state and society which he had ruled and helped to maintain.

6. Marvelous as it was, it did not stop the greedy Latin plunderers from throwing the body out of its sarcophagus to get at the ornaments they sought, as we are told by the great Byzantine historian of that period, Niketas Choniates, *Historia* (ed. Bekker, *Bonn Corpus*, 1835), pp. 855–856.

7. The inscription is still preserved in the Corinth Museum. Its text, beginning with a liturgical invocation, may be translated as follows: "Light from light, true God from true God: guard the Autokrator Justinian and his faithful slave Victorinus, together with those dwelling in Hellas, those living according to God's will." Victorinus was presumably the Imperial official who carried out the construction of the fortification in the Emperor's name. The reference to this construction by Procopius is quite terse, if admirably to the point: see *Buildings*, Book IV, chap. ii, sec. 27. For the sources on the episode of this inscription's rediscovery, see my own article, "On the Chronology of the Activities of Manuel II Palaeologus in the Peloponnesus in 1415," in *Byzantinische Zeitschrift*, 55 (1962), 39–55.

In a way, the durability of his memory seemed to mock that state and society even after the Empire had perished. The huge equestrian statue of the Emperor remained in its place of glory at least partly intact as late as the sixteenth century, long after the Turkish conquest. (See Plate X.) It was seen then by a French traveler, Pierre Gilles, who witnessed its destruction, ingloriously melted down to make cannon. Yet, perhaps we may trace just a suggestion of the great Emperor's spirit still living on even among the Turks. For the dates of power of Justinian I the Great (518/527–565) are duplicated after almost exactly a millennium in the reign of the famous Turkish Sultan Suleiman I the Magnificent (1520–1566), among whose appellations was *el-Kanuni*, "The Lawgiver," a title that encourages further reflection on the parallelism.

That Justinian's memory should survive powerfully in the East is not strange, though the length of time involved does heighten our interest. Yet, even elsewhere his reputation was great. For the builder of Haghía Sophía was also the compiler of the *Corpus juris civilis*. The medieval descendants of the barbarian peoples in the West might have only limited or occasional understanding of Justinian and his reign, but they could appreciate Justinian the Lawgiver perhaps even more than later Byzantium could. The rediscovery of Justinian's great legal compilation in the Latin West in the twelfth century was a vital part of the intellectual flowering of that period, and was of profound significance for the development of European political institutions thereafter. The German Emperors, and then after them the national monarchs, who sought to buttress their power by all means found the Roman *Body of Civil Law* an ideal source of support for their centralizing ambitions. In essence, what Roman Law meant for them was summed up admirably by the statement of the third-century jurisconsult Ulpian, included by Justinian's commission in the *Institutes*. It is a statement which reveals pointedly both the basic implications of the old Imperial legal tradition and the reason for medieval interest in it: *Quod principi placuit legis habet vigorem* — "What pleases the prince has the force of law." [8] Here is the foundation of European absolutism distilled to its essence.

8. *Institutes*, Book I, chap. ii, sec. 6.

Remembering this background of Western appreciation of Justinian, we can understand the full significance of the appearance of this Emperor in that epitome of medieval concepts, the *Divina Commedia* of Dante. The great Florentine poet (1265–1321) was throughout his life a Ghibelline, a devoted partisan of the claims of the German, or "Holy Roman," Emperors to their old lands in northern Italy. For Dante as for the medieval mind in general, the unity of the Faith and of the Divinity required the unity of power on earth, and the Emperor must be that ultimate authority over all men. The prop and symbol of that authority was the Law, as gathered and synthesized for all ages by the Emperor whose name was affixed to the *Corpus juris civilis*. So it is that, as Dante begins his journey through Paradise, he finds on the second level (that of Mercury, the seat of those distinguished by lofty ambitions) a glowing spirit who identifies himself thus:

> Caesar I was, and Justinian I am,
>> Who, through the will of the Prime Love which I can now sense,
>> Out from the Laws did purge all superfluity and ineffectuality. . . .[9]

The Law for the medieval Westerner, Haghía Sophía and memories of glory for the medieval Easterner — these were the living monuments of Justinian for those who came after him. Their luster has still not entirely faded today. To us Justinian appears as a ruler with grave flaws, and his reign was not a happy one for either those who had to endure it or for those who had to bear its consequences thereafter. Yet, history is often charitable to those who have erred, as long as they have done so in lofty terms. Justinian was a ruler who thought and acted on a grand scale. Many of his achievements were indeed worthy of his aspirations. For what he meant to do as well as for what he succeeded in doing, Justinian well deserved the memorial appellation of "the Great."

---

9. *Paradiso*, Canto vi, ll. 10–12. Justinian first appears in the preceding canto. Canto vi is devoted to this former Emperor's narrative, and reveals something of the medieval Westerner's understanding, or supposed understanding, of Justinian's history.

REFERENCE
MATTER

CHRONOLOGY OF
THE REIGN
OF JUSTINIAN

c. 482   Justinian born, as Flavius Petrus Sabbatius, son of Sabbatius and Vigilantia, of Thracian-Illyrian peasant background.

c. 502–   Justinian is brought to Constantinople by his uncle, Justin;
518   there, with some cousins, he is given a thorough education. Justin adopts him and changes his name to "Justinianus." He receives a commission in the Imperial bodyguard.

518   Justin I becomes Emperor; Justinian is promoted. Schism with Rome is ended; persecution of Monophysites and other dissenters begins.

519   Eutharic, son-in-law and heir of Theodoric the Ostrogoth, is made Consul in Italy.

520   Amid riots by circus factions, the former rebel and rival Vitalian is assassinated by Justin and Justinian. The latter emerges as the power behind his uncle's throne.

521   Justinian holds the Consulship, currying popular favor.

522   Eutharic dies; Theodoric is allowed to make Boethius and Symmachus Consuls.

523   The Lakhmid Arabs of Hira, vassals of Persia, raid Imperial territory. The Jewish Himyarite King of Yemen massacres Christians, and the survivors appeal to the Empire. Accession of Hilderic to the Vandal throne; cultivated by Justinian, he begins a new pro-Imperial, anti-Ostrogothic policy. Suspicious of the Empire, Theodoric the Ostrogoth adopts an anti-Imperial policy in his last years. About this time

Slavonic attacks on Balkan provinces begin seriously; Germanus, Justinian's cousin, defeats the Slavonic Antae.

524   King Kavadh I of Persia opens war on the Empire, driving the Romans out of Caucasian Iberia. Theodoric executes Boethius and Symmachus.

525   Justinian is made Caesar by Justin, marking him as successor. The Empire supports the Abyssinian conquest of Yemen.

526   Pope John I visits Constantinople (spring), on behalf of Theodoric; failing in his mission, he dies on his return (May). Death of Theodoric (Aug. 30), leaving his grandson Athalaric under the regency of his mother Amalasuntha, who follows a pro-Imperial policy. Emergence of Belisarius in war with the Persians. A disastrous earthquake ravages Antioch.

527   Justinian is made co-Emperor (Apr. 4); by this time he has married his paramour, the former actress Theodora. Persecution of the Monophysites is renewed. Justin I dies (Aug. 1), leaving Justinian in full power. Belisarius is elevated to major command in Mesopotamia against the Persians; the historian Procopius is made Belisarius' private secretary.

528   Justinian begins the recodification of the legal system.

529   The first version of Justinian's *Code* is issued (Apr. 7). In a persecution of paganism, Justinian closes the schools in Athens; an emigration of pagan scholars to Persia begins. The Arab prince al-Harith is made the Ghassanid Phylarch and auxiliary of the Empire.

530   John of Cappadocia is made Praetorian Prefect. Victory of Belisarius at Daras (June) over the Persians. The Vandal King Hilderic is deposed by the usurper Gelimer, reviving Vandal anti-Imperial policy. The general Mundus defeats Slavonic raids in the Balkans. The Fifty Decisions are issued as part of the legal classification program; a commission under Tribonian is appointed (Dec.) to harmonize the writings of the ancient jurisconsults.

531   Defeat of Belisarius by the Persians at Callinicum (Apr.). Death of Kavadh I, who is succeeded by Khusru I (Sept.).

532   Outbreak of the Nika Riots (Jan.) by united circus factions and discontented elements; Justinian attempts appeasement by dismissing unpopular ministers; the rioters become bold and attempt a revolution; contemplating flight, Justinian is inspired to stay by Theodora's courage; Belisarius and Mun-

dus massacre rioters in the Hippodrome, crushing the rising; Justinian's autocracy increases. Plans are prepared for rebuilding the damaged capital, especially the Church of Haghía Sophía. The "Perpetual Peace" is signed with King Khusru of Persia (spring).

533   Justinian, seeking to conciliate rather than persecute the stubborn Monophysites, sponsors the Theopaschate doctrine as a compromise formula. A small expedition under Belisarius sails to Sicily (June), from which a surprise attack is launched on the Vandal King Gelimer; Belisarius lands in North Africa, defeats Gelimer in the Battle of the Tenth Milestone (Sept. 13), occupies Carthage, and shatters Gelimer's army at Tricamaron (Dec.), beginning the dissolution of the Vandal nation. Tribonian's commission completes and issues (Dec.) the Digest, or Pandects; he and colleagues prepare the Institutes.

534   Belisarius sends a force to Spain where it briefly occupies Septum on the Straits. The fugitive Gelimer surrenders (March); Belisarius leads him in his "triumph" in the Hippodrome on his return to the capital. Solomon takes command in Africa, beginning the struggle with the Moors. Amalasuntha negotiates to surrender Ostrogothic Italy to Justinian; but on the death of Athalaric (Oct. 2) she instead marries her kinsman Theodahad to retain power. The revised second version of Justinian's *Code* is completed under Tribonian and is issued (Nov. 16), completing the first three Latin sections of the *Corpus juris civilis* in its final form; Justinian's *Novéllai* (New Laws) thereafter are issued in Greek.

535   Theodahad imprisons Amalasuntha in a coup; amid his negotiations with Justinian, the Queen is murdered (Apr.); Justinian prepares for war. Mundus invades Ostrogothic Dalmatia; Belisarius is sent (summer) with a very small force to assay Ostrogothic Sicily; the island is surprised, Syracuse is taken (Dec.), and the occupation of the island begins. Justinian negotiates with the Franks for cooperation against the Ostrogoths.

536   Theodosius, a pro-Monophysite, imposed as Patriarch of Alexandria. Visiting Constantinople on Theodahad's behalf, Pope Agapetus deposes its pro-Monophysite Patriarch Anthimus, and dies soon after. Mutiny breaks out in North

Africa, and Solomon has Belisarius intervene. Theodahad attempts to avoid war and vacillates over surrendering Italy to Justinian, but his forces recover Dalmatia, killing Mundus. Belisarius invades Italy, progresses rapidly northward, and takes Naples (autumn); Theodahad is deposed, murdered, and replaced by Wittigis; Belisarius enters Rome.

537   The North African mutiny under the rebel Stotzas is finally put down by Germanus; Solomon renews the war there against the Moors. At the instigation of Theodora, Belisarius has the Gothic-appointed Pope Silverius deposed on charges of collaboration with the Goths, replacing him with the treacherous Vigilius (March); Wittigis begins his siege of Rome (late winter), which Belisarius defends brilliantly. Theodosius of Alexandria is deposed. Haghía Sophía is completed by Anthemius of Tralles and Isidore of Miletus, and is dedicated by Justinian (Dec. 26).

538   Unsuccessful before Rome, Wittigis abandons his siege of it (March), and instead besieges the Imperial general John in Ariminum; Narses arrives in Italy and sows dissension in the Imperial command; Ariminum is relieved; Liguria and Milan are occupied by Imperial forces.

539   With Frankish help the Ostrogoths retake Milan and massacre its populace (March); Narses is recalled. Wittigis appeals to Khusru of Persia to make war on the Empire. The Franks invade the Po Valley and fall on the Goths until famine and disease drive them back. Belisarius takes Auximum; Wittigis negotiates for liberal peace terms.

540   King Khusru of Persia breaks the peace and invades Syria, storming and devastating Antioch, and attacking other points. Belisarius negotiates a Gothic surrender and occupies Ravenna; he is recalled by Justinian; Ostrogothic unrest continues. As Slavonic attacks increase in Illyricum, a mixed barbarian force threatens Constantinople and then ravages Greece.

541   John of Cappadocia falls from power. Khusru of Persia invades Roman Lazica, and takes Petra; Belisarius is restored to command in Mesopotamia. Totila is made the new Ostrogothic King (autumn) and renews the war successfully against disorganized Imperial forces.

542   Khusru menaces Palestine and is halted by Belisarius, who is recalled thereafter. On the suggestion of the finance min-

ister Peter Barsymes, the silk industry is made a state monopoly. The Consulship is allowed to lapse. A terrible plague begins in Egypt (summer), spreads through the Empire, and continues into the following year, Justinian himself being briefly stricken.

543   Under Theodora's sponsorship, Theodosius, former Monophysite Patriarch of Alexandria, consecrates Jacob Baradaeus as Bishop of Edessa; the latter begins his rebuilding of the Syrian Monophysite (Jacobite) Church. Orthodox elements persuade Justinian to condemn neo-Origenist heresies. Making rapid progress through Italy, Totila takes Naples (spring).

544   Solomon is killed in wars against North African Moors. Belisarius returns to command in Italy (summer).

545   After long and uncertain hostilities, a truce is bought by Justinian from Persia. Totila begins a new siege of Rome (end of year).

546   Persuaded by Theodore Askidas, Justinian condemns the writings of three earlier theologians, Theodore of Mopsuestia, Theodoret of Cyrrhus, and Ibas of Edessa, in his "Edict of the Three Chapters," in hopes of placating the Monophysites. Areobindus, husband of Justinian's niece and commander in Africa, is assassinated in a new mutiny there, which is put down by the loyal Artabanes; John Troglita is appointed to command there against the Moors and begins their reduction. Belisarius is unable to relieve Rome, which falls to Totila (Dec. 17); Justinian rejects Gothic peace overtures.

547   Pope Vigilius is brought to Constantinople, but resists pressure to support Justinian's Three Chapters policy. Totila abandons Rome (late winter), but Belisarius enters and again fortifies it (spring), resisting Totila's return; Belisarius otherwise despairs of his position. The octagonal church of San Vitale in Ravenna is completed. Beginning of new circus faction riots in the capital.

548   Death of Theodora (June 28). Belisarius' wife, Antonina, has her husband recalled from his hopeless command; Belisarius leaves Italy (summer) to go into retirement. The conspiracy of the disaffected Artabanes is discovered and checked. John Troglita brings the Moorish wars in North Africa to a successful conclusion. Slavonic raids on the

Adriatic coast reach Dyrrachium. New riots by the circus factions break out.

549   Totila again besieges Rome. The Church of San Apollinare in Classe, near Ravenna, is completed.

550   Totila takes Rome (Jan.). Germanus prepares to take command in Italy; he drives invading Slavs away from Thessalonica; but he dies (autumn) before leaving for Italy. The Slavs continue to ravage Thrace. Totila is at his peak, and attacks Sicily; but he is forced to acknowledge Frankish annexations in northern Italy. Narses is appointed new commander in Italy and begins preparations. Justinian's forces occupy the southern coastal area of Visigothic Spain on both sides of the Straits. About this time, the embittered Procopius writes his *Anékdota* (*Secret History*), before writing the final book of his official *History of the Wars*.

551   Pope Vigilius, still kept in Constantinople, is harassed to win his support for Justinian's Three Chapter policy. Imperial forces under Bessas retake Petra in Lazica from the Persians (spring); a second truce is bought from Persia (autumn), causing much popular indignation. Totila besieges Ancona, but is driven off by an Imperial naval victory at nearby Sena Gallica (autumn); Totila renews peace offers, which are rejected by Justinian. About this time the Kotrigur Huns ravage Imperial territory; Justinian distracts them by inciting the Utigur Huns against them. More circus faction rioting occurs in Constantinople.

552   Narses marches to Italy and defeats Totila at Busta Gallorum, or Teginae (spring); Totila dies and is succeeded by Teïas; Narses recovers Rome, and then defeats and kills Teïas at Mons Lactarius, near Mt. Vesuvius (autumn), beginning the destruction of the Ostrogothic nation.

553   The Fifth Ecumenical Council meets (May) and condemns the three contested theologians, despite Pope Vigilius' continued opposition; later the Pope yields (end of the year). Franks and Alemanians invade Italy (spring) and begin ravaging it.

554   Narses confronts the Franko-Alemanian forces and annihilates them; he begins the slow pacification and reviving of Italy. Al-Harith, the Ghassanid Arab ally of the Empire, defeats and kills his Lakhmid rival, al-Mundhir. The Visigoths check expansion of the Imperial foothold in Spain, which

begins to contract rapidly. About this time silkworms are smuggled from the Far East, enabling Justinian to develop full-scale native silk production.

555   Pope Vigilius dies while returning to Rome (June). The King of the Lazi is assassinated by Roman authorities there, endangering Lazian loyalty until the culprits are brought to justice in the following year.

556   More rioting by circus factions (May).

557   A new truce with Persia.

558   The original dome of Haghía Sophía collapses and Isidore the Younger is charged with building a new one. A new plague strikes the Empire. Remnants of the Asiatic Avars under the Chagan Baian approach Imperial frontiers and enter into contact with the Emperor. The Kotrigur Khan mounts a three-pronged attack on Imperial Balkan territories.

559   Belisarius emerges from retirement and saves Constantinople from the Kotrigurs; the remaining Kotrigur forces are finally driven back, and the Utigurs are again incited against them. New rioting and destruction by the circus factions occur (May).

560   About this time Procopius composes his panegyric, *On the Buildings*, celebrating the Emperor's vast construction program.

562   A Fifty-Year Peace is arranged with Persia, the Empire paying tribute. A conspiracy to assassinate Justinian is discovered (Nov.), implicating Belisarius, who is disgraced. More rioting by factions. The second dome of Haghía Sophía is completed, and Justinian reinaugurates the church (Dec. 24).

563   Impressive visit of the Ghassanid Phylarch al-Harith to Constantinople. A brief rising of the Moors occurs in North Africa. Narses progresses in his final pacification of Italy. Belisarius is reinstated at court (July). Renewed circus faction rioting.

564   About this time the Avars negotiate with Justinian to win concessions.

565   Justinian attempts a new compromise with the Monophysites, sponsoring (Jan.) the doctrine of Aphthartodocetism; there is wide resistance to it, and he plans new persecutions. Belisarius dies (March). Justinian dies (Nov. 14), and is buried in the Church of the Holy Apostles; his nephew Justin II secures the throne amid great rejoicing.

HISTORICAL
LISTS

I. *Emperors*

(From the last of the Severan Dynasty, through the Byzantine succession, to the beginning of the so-called Isaurian, or Iconoclast, Dynasty. The parallel columns indicate the phase of simultaneous Western and Eastern succession, and the subdivisions throughout represent the various dynastic divisions.)

Caracalla	211–217
Macrinus	217–218
Elagabalus (Heliogabalus)	218–222
Alexander Severus	222–235
Maximin	235–238
Pupienus, Balbinus, Gordian I, and Gordian II	238
Gordian III	238–244
Philip "the Arab"	244–249
Decius	249–251
Gallus	251–253
Valerian	253–259
Gallienus (and various pretenders, the "Thirty Tyrants")	259–268
Claudius II "Gothicus"	268–270
Aurelian, *Restitutor orbis*	270–275
Tacitus	275–276
Probus	276–281
Carus	281–283
Numerianus and Carinus	283–285
Diocletian	284–305

TETRARCHY

Maximianus, 286–305, 307–308;
Constantius I Chlorus, 293–306;
Galerius, 293–311;
Severus, 305–307;
Maximin Daia, 305–313;
Constantine I, 306–324;
Maxentius, 306–312;
Licinius, 308–324

CONSTANTINIAN HOUSE

Constantine I "the Great" (alone)	324–337
Constantine II, 337–340;	
Constans I, 337–350;	
Constantius II, 337–353;	
Magnentius (usurper), 350–353	
Constantius II (alone)	353–361
Julian "the Apostate"	361–363
Jovian	363–364

VALENTINIAN HOUSE

West		*East*	
Valentinian I	364–375	Valens	364–378
Gratian	375–383	Theodosius I	379–395
Maximus (usurper)	383–388		
Valentinian II	378/383–392		
Eugenius (usurper)	392–394		

THEODOSIAN HOUSE

Theodosius I "the Great" (alone)	394–395

West		*East*	
Honorius	395–423	Arcadius	395–408
co-Emperor Constantius III, 421		Theodosius II	408–450
John (usurper)	423–425		
Valentinian III	425–455		
Petronius Maximus	455	Marcian	450–457

Avitus	455–456	Leo I	457–474
Majorian	457–461	Leo II	474
Severus	461–465	Zeno	474–475
Anthemius	467–472	Basiliscus (usurper)	475–476
Olybrius	472		
Glycerius	473–474		
Julius Nepos	474–475		
Romulus Augustulus	475–476		

Zeno (restored; alone)	476–491
Anastasius I	491–518
Justin I	518–527
Justinian I "the Great"	527–565
Justin II	565–578
Tiberius II Constantine	578–582
Maurice	582–602
Phocas	602–610

HERACLIAN HOUSE

Heraclius	610–641
Constantine III and Heraclonas	641
Constans II	641–668
Constantine IV ("Pogonatos"?)	668–685
Justinian II	685–695
Leontius (usurper)	695–698
Apsimar/Tiberius III (usurper)	698–705
Justinian II (restored, "Rhinotmetos")	705–711
Philippicus Vardanes	711–713
Artemius/Anastasius II	713–715
Theodosius III	715–717

ISAURIAN HOUSE

Leo III "the Isurian"	717–741
Constantine V "Kopronymos"	741–775
(etc.)	

II. *Patriarchs of Constantinople*

(From the establishment of the See of Constantinople, previously an arch-bishopric, as an avowed partriarchate, through the succession to the beginning of the eighth century, at the outset of the Iconoclastic controversy; numbers in parentheses indicate that there were predecessors of the same name before the See's elevation to a patriarchate.)

Nectarius	381–397
John I Chrysostom	398–404
Arsacius	404–405
Atticus	406–425
Sisinnius I	426–427
Nestorius	428–431
Maximian	431–434
Proclus	434–446
Flavian	446–449
Anatolius	449–458
Gennadius I	458–471
Acacius	472–489
Fravitas	489–490
Euphemius	490–496
Macedonius (II)	496–511
Timotheus I	511–518
John II Cappadoces	518–520
Epiphanius	520–535
Anthimus I	535–536
Menas	536–552
Eutychius	552–565
John III Scholasticus	565–577
Eutychius (restored)	577–582
John IV "the Faster"	582–595
Cyriacus	596–606
Thomas I	607–610
Sergius I	610–638
Pyrrhus	638–641
Paul (II)	641–653
Pyrrhus (restored)	654
Peter	654–666
Thomas II	667–669
John V	669–675
Constantine I	675–677
Theodore I	677–679
George I	679–686
Theodore I (restored)	686–687
Paul (III)	688–694
Callinicus I	694–706
Cyrus	706–712
John VI	712–715
Germanus I	715–730
(etc.)	

III. *Patriarchs of Alexandria*

(From the first clear emergence of a strong patriarchate, to the early era of Arab domination. The parallel columns illustrate the separate, schismatic lines of the loyalist, anti-Monophysite succession, and the anti-Imperial, nationalist, Monophysite succession.)

Athanasius I	328–373
(and various Arian rivals)	
Peter II	373–380
Timotheus I	380–384
Theophilus	384–412
Cyril	412–444
Dioscorus	444–451
Proterius	451–457
Timotheus II Elurus	457–460
Timotheus (II) Salofaciolus	460–475
Timotheus II Elurus (restored)	475–477
Peter III Mongus	477
Timotheus (II) Salofaciolus (restored)	477–482
John (I) Talaia	482
Peter III Mongus (restored)	482–489
Athanasius II Keletes	489–496
John I	496–505
John II	505–516
Dioscorus II	516–517
Timotheus III	517–535

MELKITE SUCCESSION		COPTIC SUCCESSION	
Paul of Tabenna	537–540	Theodosius	535–566
Zoilos	540–551	(and various rival claimants)	
Apollinarius	551–570	Peter IV	575–578
John (II)	570–580	Damian	578–607
Eulogus	581–608	Anastasius	607–619
Theodore Scribon	608–609	Andronicus	619–626
John (III)	610–619	Benjamin	626–665
"the Alms-Giver"		Agathon	665–681
George	c. 620–c. 630	John III	681–689
Cyrus	631–643	Isaac	690–692
Peter (III)	643–651	Simon I	692–700
(various Imperial agents and titular appointees thereafter)		(various rivals, vacancies, and continued succession)	

IV. *Popes of Rome*

(From the period of the Pontiffs' first emergence to political significance, under Constantine the Great, through the succession to the early eighth century.)

Sylvester I	314–335
Mark	336
Julius I	337–352
Liberius	352–366
Damasus I	366–384
Siricius	384–399
Anastasius I	399–401
Innocent I	401–417
Zosimus	417–418
Boniface I	418–422
Celestine I	422–432
Sixtus III	432–440
Leo I "the Great"	440–461
Hilarius	461–468
Simplicius	468–483
Felix III	483–492
Gelasius I	492–496
Anastasius II	496–498
Symmachus	498–514
Hormisdas	514–523
John I	523–526
Felix IV	526–530
Boniface II	530–532
John II	533–535
Agapetus I	535–536
Silverius	536–537
Vigilius	537–555
Pelagius I	556–561
John III	561–574
Benedict I	575–579
Pelagius II	579–590
Gregory I "the Great"	590–604
Sabinian	604–606
Boniface III	607
Boniface IV	608–615
Deusdedit I	615–618
Boniface V	619–625
Honorius I	625–638
Severinus	640
John IV	640–642

Theodore I	642–649
Martin I	649–654
Eugenius I	654–657
Vitalian	657–672
Deusdedit II	672–676
Donus	676–678
Agathon	678–681
Leo II	682–683
Benedict II	684–685
John V	685–686
Conon	686–687
Sergius I	687–701
John VI	701–705
John VII	705–707
Sisinnius	708
Constantine	708–715
Gregory II	715–731
(etc.)	

V. *Vandal Kings of Africa*

(Complete.)

Gaiseric	428–477
Huneric	477–484
Gunthamund	484–496
Thrasamund	496–523
Hilderic	523–530
Gelimer	530–533

VI. *Ostrogothic Kings of Italy*

(Complete, including the pre-Ostrogothic barbarian ruler.)

(Odovacar	476–493)
Theodoric	493–526
Athalaric (Amalasuntha, regent)	526–534
Theodahad	535–536
Wittigis	536–540
Ildibad	540–541
Eraric	541
Totila (Baduila)	541–552
Teïas	552–553

VII. *Imperial Exarchs in Italy (Ravenna)*

(Complete, so far as has been established.)

Narses	552–568
Baduarius	575–577
Smaragdus	585–589
Julianus	589
Romanus	589–596
Callinicus	596–603
Smaragdus (restored)	603–*c.* 610
John I	*c.* 610–616
Eleutherius	616–619
Gregory I	619–625
Isaac I	625–643
Theodore I Calliopas	643–*c.* 645
Platon	*c.* 645–?
Olympius	649–653
Theodore I Calliopas (restored)	653–?
Gregory II	?–666
?	?
Theodore II	678–687
John II	687–?
Theophylact	701–(705)
John III	(700)–710
Eutychius	710–713
Scholasticius	713–?
Paul	723–726
Eutychius (restored)	727–751

(Ravenna occupied by the Lombards, 752–756; annexed by Pepin the Short to the See of Rome, 756)

VIII. *Imperial Exarchs in Africa (Carthage)*

(Complete, so far as has been established.)

Gennadius	*c.* 585–*c.* 598
Heraclius the Elder	*c.* 602–*c.* 610
Caesarius	?
Nicetas	*c.* 620–633
Peter	633–?
Gregory (*Patricius*)	?–648
?	

(Conquest by the Arabs, culminating in their capture of Carthage, 697)

IX. *Sassanid Kings of Persia*

(Complete, from the re-establishment of the Persian empire, to its destruction by the Arab conquest.)

Ardashir I	226–241
Shapor I	241–272
Hormizd I	272–273
Vahram I	273–276
Vahram II	276–293
Vahram III	293
Narses	293–303
Hormizd II	303–310
Adharnarses	310
Shapor II	310–379
Ardashir II	379–383
Shapor III	383–388
Vahram IV	388–399
Yazdigerd I	399–420
Vahram V	420–438
Yazdigerd II	438–457
Hormizd III	457–459
Firoz	459–484
Valash	484–488
Kavadh I	488–498, 501–531
Khusru I "Anosharvan"	531–579
Hormizd IV	579–590
Vahram VI (usurper)	590–591
Khusru II "Parviz"	590–628
Kavadh II " Sheroë"	628
Ardashir III	628–630
(Regency	630–632)
Yazdigerd III	632–651/652

(Arab conquest, from the capture of Ctesiphon, 637, through the following years)

X. *Muslim Caliphs*

(From the death of the Prophet to the rise of the Abbasid Dynasty.)

"ORTHODOX" SUCCESSION

Abu Bakr	632–634
Umar	634–644

Uthman	644–656
Ali	656–661

UMAYYAD HOUSE

Mu'awiya I	661–680
Yazid I	680–683
Mu'awiya II	683–684
Marwan I	684–685
Abdalmalik	685–705
Walid I	705–715
Sulayman	715–717
Umar II	717–720
Yazid II	720–724
Hisham	724–743
Walid II	743–744
Yazid III	744
Ibrahim	744
Marwan II	744–750

(Succession after 750 to the Abbasid Dynasty)

Note: the basis for most of these lists is V. Grumel's *La Chronologie* ("Bibliothèque byzantine: Traité d'études byzantines," Vol. 1, Paris, 1958).

NOTES ON THE
ILLUSTRATIONS

I: Justinianic Medallion

The only known specimen of this magnificent gold medallion was discovered in the middle of the eighteenth century in the old Cappadocian city of Caesarea, and was preserved in the Cabinet des Medailles of the Bibliothèque Nationale in Paris until 1831, when it was stolen and destroyed. A cast of it had been made, however, and was preserved in the British Museum; it is from this cast that the electrotype shown in our photograph was made. A remarkable example of its kind, the original was struck in gold, of a weight equalling thirty-six Imperial *solidi*. On its obverse, Justinian is shown in a three-quarter-face bust, wearing a plumed helmet and full military armor, and carrying a spear. Around his head is the special Imperial halo, or *nimbus*. The inscription reads: D[ominus] N[oster] IVSTINII/ANVS P[er]P[etuus] AVG[ustus]; that is, "Our Lord Justinianus, Perpetual Augustus." For the mint mark CONOB, see the comments on the coins, Plate XI. On the reverse of this medallion, the Emperor is shown again, this time in full figure, wearing complete armor, mounted on horseback, spear in hand, and riding to the right, his horse led by a figure of Victory. The inscription here is: SALVS ET GL/ORIA ROMANORUM, or "The Welfare and Glory of the Romans." It is generally held that this medallion was issued in celebration of Belisarius' conquest of the Vandal kingdom. Thus, in the opinion of W. Wroth, *Catalogue of the Imperial Byzantine Coins in the British Museum*, 1 (London, 1908), 25: "The date of the medallion is therefore in all probability not later than A.D. 538, and may be as early as A.D. 534." Apparently this medallion was known or at least remembered for many centuries after its time: the later Byzantine historian Cedrenus, who wrote in the early twelfth century, describes an issue by Justinian in honor of Belisarius' victory in terms which fit our medallion. Cedrenus maintains, however, that, while the obverse pictures the Emperor, the reverse figure shown mounted is not Justinian but Belisarius himself; and Cedrenus further gives the reverse inscription, in Greek, as: *Belisários hi dhóxa tôn Rhōmaíon* ("Belisarius the Glory of the Romans"). Possibly, therefore, the word "salus" in the original Latin inscription might have been confused in later Greek tradition with the name Belisarius, in view of the medallion's association with the great general's victories. But from of old the Emperors were not accustomed to share the symbolic space of their official mint issues with any mere subject, and, though he had broken centuries of precedent by allowing Belisarius a triumph in his own right, the hyper-jealous Justinian would have been unlikely to go to such an extreme as to have his general represented with him on this commemorative issue. For some discussions of this medallion, its dating, its history, and its adventures in modern times, see E. C. F. Babelon's articles, "Histoire d'un médaillon disparu, Justinien et Bélisaire," in *Mémoires de la Société nationale des antiquitaires de France*, 57 (1896–98), 295–326, reprinted in the author's collection, *Mélanges numismatiques, IIIe séries* (Paris, 1898), 305–326, and his "Deux médaillons disparus de Domitien et de Justinien. Note additionnelle," *Revue numismatique*, IV:3 (1899), 1–8; also, J. M. C. Toynbee, *Roman Medallions* ("American Numismatic Society, Numismatic Studies," Vol. 5; New York, 1944), p. 183.

II: *Justinian's Cistern in Constantinople, Now Called Yere-Batan Serai*

This is one of two Byzantine cisterns surviving in modern Istanbul that apparently date from Justinian's period. It is generally agreed that this is the one whose construction is specifically described by Procopius in his treatise *On the Buildings*, Book I, chap. xi, secs. 12–14. The other of these two cisterns, now called by the Turks Bin Bir Derek, or the "Thousand and One Columns," seems to date from earlier in the Emperor's reign, or perhaps from the joint reign of Justin I and Justinian.

III: *Interior of Justinian's Church of Haghía Eiréné (St. Irene) in Constantinople*

Replacing an earlier edifice dedicated to Holy Peace, Justinian's building has undergone work of subsequent periods, but after the Turkish capture of the city in 1453 it did not share the fate of other Byzantine churches and become a mosque. Instead, it was used by the Turks as an armory, appropriate to its proximity to the Sultan's Seraglio and the Janissary headquarters in what used to be the old Imperial Palace area and its environs. In this century, however, the arms have been cleared out and the building is now a national monument attached to the Aya Sofya Museum complex.

In this photograph, looking down the nave to the apse, notice the curious set of tiered seats in the latter, apparently used for ecclesiastical gatherings.

IV: Apse Mosaic Panel Representing the Emperor Justinian with Attendants, Church of San Vitale, Ravenna;
V: Apse Mosaic Panel Representing the Empress Theodora with Attendants, Church of San Vitale, Ravenna

These two superb portrait panels are the best contemporary representations of the two rulers, and among the most famous of all Byzantine mosaics. They were executed when the octagonal Church of St. Vitalis was completed in the administrative capital of Italy not long after the first phase of the peninsula's reconquest by the Empire. In each panel, the Emperor or Empress is shown with his or her respective retinue, carrying an offering to the church of Ravenna. In Justinian's group, the Archbishop of Ravenna, Maximianus, is specifically identified; note also the soldier's shield bearing across its face the Christian Imperial symbol known as the *chrismon*, the first two initials of Christ's name in Greek, the letters *chi* and *rho*, superimposed on one another thus: ☧ .

VI: Mosaic Supposedly Representing Justinian (Originally Theodoric?), in Church of San Apollinare Nuovo, Ravenna

The "New" Church of St. Apollinaris, originally dedicated to St. Martin, was constructed under the Ostrogothic King Theodoric. After the Justinianic Reconquest, during the incumbency of Archbishop Agnellus (or Andreas) of Ravenna (A.D. 553–566), this church was transferred from Ostrogothic Arian usage to orthodox catholic service. During this period, our sources report, Agnellus had a pair of mosaics placed on the church's façade, one representing himself, the other the

Emperor Justinian. The present fragment (badly restored in 1863) is what survives of the latter of the two mosaics, transferred now to the interior of the building, at the end of the nave. That this mosaic was originally intended to represent Justinian has been questioned, however. In "Theodorich — nicht Justinian," in *Mitteilungen des Deutschen archäologischen Instituts, Römisch Abteilung*, 50 (1935), 339–347, F. von Lorentz argued that it was actually executed early in the sixth century, as a portrait of Theodoric himself, being then only adapted to the glorification of Justinian by Agnellus. This argument is now generally accepted as correct: see the article "Ultimi ritrovamenti ed ultimi indagini sui monumenti di Ravenna," in *Corsi d'arte ravennate e bizantina*, 1 (Ravenna, 1955), 29–33, by J. Bovini, who has also summarized the entire problem in his further article, "Note sul presunto ritratto musivo di Giustiniano in S. Apollinare Nuovo di Ravenna," in *Annales Universitatis Saraviensis*, 5 (Saarbrücken, 1956), 50–53. Consequently, this mosaic cannot be reckoned as a reliable portrait of the Emperor, but is of interest as an example of the uses of art works for political purposes in this age.

VII: *Exterior of Justinian's Church of Haghía Sophía (St. Sophia) in Constantinople;*
VIII: *Interior of Justinian's Church of Haghía Sophía (St. Sophia) in Constantinople*

Justinian's most famous building, the greatest landmark in Constantinople, and the third largest church edifice ever built, it is discussed frequently in this book, and is too well-known to require much comment here, save to note that the additions of the Turkish period — the four great minarets on the outside, and the large discs bearing Arabic inscriptions on the inside — have nothing to do with this supreme masterpiece of Byzantine architecture as originally built.

IX: *Mosaic Representing Justinian and Constantine with the Virgin and Child, in Haghía Sophía, Constantinople*

Dating from the end of the tenth century, this superb mosaic over the South Door of Justinian's Great Church demonstrates something of this Emperor's lingering fame in the Empire's later centuries (see the comments in the text, p. 264). Constantine, as founder of The City, offers a representation of it as his gift to its Protectress and

Her Son; Justinian, as builder of the majestic Temple of the Holy Wisdom, makes a representation of it his special offering to the Holy Pair.

X. Sketch of the Equestrian Statue Supposedly of Justinian

The great bronze statue which Justinian had placed atop a column in the Augoustaîon, near Haghía Sophía, in his own honor is described in detail by Procopius (*On the Buildings*, Book I, Chap. ii, secs. 5–12). According to Procopius, the Emperor was represented in this statue in the guise of the ancient hero Achilles: on the question of the symbolism thus involved, see the comments of G. Downey in his Appendix to the Loeb Classical Library edition of Procopius, 7 (London and Cambridge, Mass., 1940), 395–398; see also the same scholar's article, "Justinian as Achilles," *Transactions and Proceedings of the American Philological Association*, 71 (1940), 68–77. We have many descriptions of its survival and careful preservation through the centuries of the Empire thereafter, and we know that it remained in its original place at least until the capture of Constantinople by the Turks in 1453, at which time it may or may not have been pulled down. It continued to exist until the middle of the sixteenth century, when the Frenchman Pierre Gilles witnessed its destruction by the Turks, and recorded it in his book, *De topographia Constantinopoleos, et de illius antiquitatibus* (Leyden, 1562); see also the comments on this in the text, p. 265.

For some one hundred years now it has been assumed that the general aspect of this celebrated statue was preserved for us in a sepia-ink sketch made in the middle of the fifteenth century in some connection with the antiquarian work of the Italian Renaissance humanist, Cyriacus of Ancona. This sketch is on the back of one of the final pages (f. 144 *verso*) of a fifteenth-century manuscript long in the library of the Ottoman Sultans. It was first noticed by P. A. Dethier, in his capacity as librarian to Sultan Abdul Aziz (1861–1876). Dethier confidently concluded that the sketch represented no less than the famous equestrian statue of Justinian as it survived in the fifteenth century, and published his conclusions in several reports, the first of which appeared in 1864. Though the conclusions and the sketch have been frequently discussed in the century since then, the identification has been generally taken for granted, even though an actual photograph of the sketch — as against the inaccurate drawn copies of it circulated previously — was not made available until G. Rodenwalt published one, with some comments, in the *Archäologischer Anzeiger* of the *Jahrbuch der deutschen archäologischen Instituts*, 46 (1931), 331–334. Meanwhile, the manuscript containing this sketch had by this time changed location, for in 1877 Sultan Abdul Hamid II (1876–1909) presented it, together with some other manuscripts, as a gift to the Library of Budapest University. There it is to be found at present, as the *Codex latinus Budapestinensis Bibliothecae Universitatis*, No. 35 (*Codex italicus* 3).

Despite the long acceptance of the identification of the sketch's subject with the Justinianic statue, some problems have remained to puzzle and exercise scholars. One of these is the curious inscription on or around various parts of the horse: FON GLORIAE PERENNIS THEO/DOSI. This inscription has prompted various explanations, but it and a number of other questions have prompted the propounding of a bold thesis by Phillis Williams Lehmann in her richly annotated and documented article, "Theodosius or Justinian? A Renaissance Drawing of a Byzantine Rider," *The Art Bulletin* (*College Art Association of America*), 41 (1959), 39–57. Examining a wide range of evidence, and presenting much illuminating material, Mrs. Lehmann proposes that this sketch does not at all represent the Justinian statue, but is a drawing based on a hypothetical medallion of the Emperor Theodosius I (379–395) somehow obtained by or for Cyriacus of Ancona; thus, she suggests, the word FON in the drawing is a mistake for the mint mark CON (for Constantinople), while the rest of the inscription is what would have appeared around the edge of the medallion. Understandably, this thesis has provoked strong reactions, and is far from completely accepted. The most immediate rebuttal is contained in a long Letter to the Editor of the same journal (*ibid.*, 351–356) by Cyril Mango, who firmly rejects Mrs. Lehmann's arguments. He puts forward instead the theory, advanced by other scholars before him, that the sketch — still accepted as showing the Justinianic statue — proves, with the help of other corroborative evidence, that Justinian merely appropriated for his monument an already-existing equestrian statue instead of making a new one for himself; this earlier statue must have been one originally depicting either Theodosius I or Theodosius II, so that the inscription in the sketch must preserve an actual inscription which, in accordance with a contemporary practice not entirely unknown, was put on the statue itself when it was first made. Therefore, says Dr. Mango, the sketch's inscription may be read either as *Fon[s] gloriae perennis Theodosi[i?]*, or as *Gloriae fon[s] perennis Theodosi[us]*. Mrs. Lehmann replied immediately (*ibid.*, 356–358), rejecting Mango's arguments and reaffirming her own position. The question is therefore still open to further thought and speculation. For our purposes, the interested reader might note some points of parallelism between the figure in the sketch and the image on the reverse of the Justinianic medallion, especially the peacock-plumed helmet in both, but bearing in mind, of course, the continuity of conventions in Imperial iconography.

XI: A. *Justinianic Gold Coin of Constantinople (D.O. 3 h. 1)*
B. *Justinianic Gold Coin of Constantinople (D.O. 9 h 2)*
C. *Justinianic Silver Coin of Constantinople (D.O. 26. 2)*
D. *Justinianic Bronze Coin of Constantinople (D.O. 38 b. 1)*
E. *Justinianic Bronze Coin of Nicomedia (D.O. 113 b. 1)*
F. *Justinianic Bronze Coin of Antioch (D.O. 199 c.)*
G. *Justinianic Bronze Coin of Antioch (D.O. 203 b. 1)*

This series of seven specimens may serve to give some idea of Justinian's coinage, and of the Empire's money in general. All of these coins show the Emperor's portrait; in Justinian's case, we know that in his coinage his portrait was shown in profile, or sometimes in three-quarter face, until April of 538, after which he was always portrayed in full-face bust, or seated. Our specimens include examples of all of these. Consistently, over the Emperor's head is always the inscription: D[*ominus*] N[*oster*] IVSTINI/ANVS P[*er*]P[*etuus*] AVG[*ustus*], as in the medallion described above. In some types (as our D and E), the coin gives a dating of the issue from the year of the Emperor's accession, which Justinian eventually came to reckon from his appointment to co-rule with his uncle on April 1, 527 (here ANNO XIII, or 539–540). The coins often carry various other symbols of the Imperial power and faith, such as winged angels, succeeding pagan Victoria images, or crosses, orbs, and stars. The two gold coins, or *solidi* bear on their reverses the inscription: VICTORIA / AVGGG; while the reverse of our silver coin is marked: GLORIA / ROMANORVM [the latter word effaced in our sample]. In contrast with gold and silver types, the various types of the bronze *follis* would each carry on their reverse a sign of the coin's value: in all four cases here, the letter M representing the largest fractional denomination of 4 *nummia*. All coins of this period also bore mint marks, showing at which of the various Imperial mints throughout the Empire they had been struck. The first four of our coins are from the main mint in the capital, but the labeling of Constantinopolitan coins differed according to the metal category. Gold coins from Constantinople usually bore the legend, on their reverse, of CONOB, of which the first three letters represented the abbreviation of the city's name, and the last two apparently stood for the word *obryzum*, the late Latin term for "refined" or "purified" gold. Silver coins might bear a corruption of this, CONOS, but were more usually stamped COB, here the first letter only standing for Constantinople, and the OB again presumably representing *obryzum*, as applied to refined silver. Bronze coins from Constantinople merely bore the stamp CON, for the city alone. Our last three coins are examples of the products of two of the provincial mints: the first of them is stamped NIKO, for Nicomedia [*Nikomḗdeia* in Greek]; the other two are from Antioch, bearing the alternate stamps of ANTI [or, more normally, ANT], or THEVP [for *Theoúpolis*, the city's other name], which were both used for the issues of its mint. Our bronze coins also bear on their reverses, below the M denomination, the mark (all, in these cases, B) for the *officina* within the mint from which they came. For more information on Justinian's coinage and Imperial numismatics in general, the reader is directed to H. Goodacre's *A Handbook of the Coinage of the Byzantine Empire* (3 parts, London, 1928–31–33; reprinted, 1956), or to the more substantial compilation of W. Wroth, *Catalogue of the Imperial Byzantine Coins in the British Museum* (2 vols., London, 1908), extending the British Museum's series of catalogues of Roman Imperial coinage of the period before Justinian. It should be added, however, that a new landmark in Byzantine numismatic literature is soon to appear, a monumental catalogue of coins in the Dumbarton Oaks Collection; and it is to the numerical code of that catalogue that the numbers listed above refer.

SELECTED
BIBLIOGRAPHY

No attempt is made in this book to enumerate the vast modern literature dealing with the subject matter it covers. That task is undertaken rather in the bibliographical guide planned as a companion volume. The list which follows is designed to give the general reader a concise survey of some of the most important books available on the period of Justinian and on the broad history of the Later Roman and Byzantine Empires, for the convenience of those who might like to read or consult further. Works written in foreign languages as well as English are included. Most of the books cited have extensive bibliographies of their own, where more detailed citation of the literature may also be found.

In addition, though only a limited number of them are available in translation, a survey is also included of the major literary works which are our contemporary sources for the age of Justinian, giving the chief modern editions of their texts and any available translations. Fuller discussions of these sources, with extensive listings of scholarly writing on them may be found in the indispensable reference work of G. Moravcsik, *Byzantinoturcica* (2nd ed., 2 vols.; "Deutsche Akademie der Wissenschaften zu Berlin, Berliner byzantinistische Arbeiten," Vols. 10–11; Berlin, 1958), as well as in the older but still important handbook by K. Krumbacher, *Geschichte der byzantinischen Litteratur von Justinian bis zum Ende des oströmischen Reiches (527–1453)* (2nd ed.; "Handbuch der klassischen Altertumswissenschaften," No. 9; Munich, 1897; reprinted, 2 vols., New York, 1958); further useful comments may also be found in M. E. Colonna's *Gli storici bizantini dal IV al XV secolo*, Vol. 1: *Storici profani* (Naples, 1956). Note that in the list of sources, citations of the *"Bonn Corpus"* refer to the series of editions known as the *Corpus scriptorum historiae byzantinae* (50 vols., Bonn, 1828–97), and of "Migne's *Patrologia graeca*" to the series of reprints in J. P. Migne's *Patrologiae cursus completus, Series greco-latina* (161 vols., Paris, 1857–1903); both of these collections include old and relatively uncritical, but serviceable editions of the texts, together with old and not always reliable Latin translations.

I. Major Primary Sources
(In approximate order of chronology or importance)

Procopius. *History of the Wars*; *Anékdota* (*Secret History*); *On the Buildings*: critical Greek text ed. J. Haury, 3 vols. ("Teubner Series"), Leipzig, 1905–13; Haury's Greek text, with an English translation by H. B. Dewing (with G. Downey), 7 vols., London and New York: Loeb Classical Library, 1914–40; also ed. G. Dindorf, *Bonn Corpus*, Vols. 18–20, 1833–38; numerous other translations, especially of the *Secret History*, including one in paperback by R. Atwater, University of Michigan Press ("Ann Arbor" Series AA80), 1963. — As discussed in this book at some length, these are the writings of the most important contemporary literary historian, covering Justinian's era and its background down to the 550's, and are the starting point for all serious study of the period.

Agathias. *On the Reign of Justinian*: Greek text ed. L. Dindorf, in *Historici graeci minores*, Vol. 2, Leipzig, 1871; and ed. B. G. Niebuhr, *Bonn Corpus*, Vol. 1, 1828, and in Migne, *Patrologia graeca*, Vol. 88, 1864. — An incomplete continuation of Procopius, covering the years 552–558, much inferior in style to its predecessor.

Menander Protector. *History* (fragments): Greek text ed. L. Dindorf, in *Historici graeci minores*, Vol. 2, Leipzig, 1871; and ed. K. Müller, in *Fragmenta historicorum graecorum*, Vol. 4, Paris, 1851; and also ed. I. Bekker and B. G. Niebuhr in *Bonn Corpus*, Vol. 14, 1829, and in Migne, *Patrologia graeca*, Vol. 113, 1864. — Pieces of a continuation of Agathias, covering the period 558–582.

Peter the Patrician. *History* (fragments); *Descriptions of Ceremonies* (fragments): Greek texts ed. K. Müller, in *Fragmenta historicorum graecorum*, Vol. 4, Paris, 1851; and L. Dindorf, in *Historici graeci minores*, Vol. 1, Leipzig, 1870; also ed. B. G. Niebuhr, in *Bonn*

Corpus, Vol. 14, 1829, and in Migne, *Patrologia graeca*, Vol. 113, 1864. — Survivals of writings by a diplomat and *Magister officiorum* under Justinian; some coming down to us in the collection known as the *Excerpta de legationibus*, and others in the great treatise and anthology known as *De cerimoniis*, both compiled in the tenth century under the sponsorship and name of Emperor Constantine VII Porphyrogenitus.

John Lydus. *De magistratibus*: critical Greek text ed. R. Wuensch ("Teubner Series"), Leipzig, 1903; also ed. I. Bekker, *Bonn Corpus*, Vol. 31, 1837. — Valuable for historical as well as institutional and administrative information, from a contemporary of Justinian.

Cosmas Indicopleustes. *The Christian Topography*: critical Greek text ed. E. O. Winstedt, Cambridge, 1909; earlier edition in Migne, *Patrologia graeca*, Vol. 88, 1864; English translation by J. W. McCrindle, ("Hakluyt Society Publications," No. 98), London, 1897. — In spite of religious bias and geographical misconceptions, a work of much importance for the commercial and economic life of the Empire in the early sixth century, and for the general early Byzantine conceptions of the world.

John Malalas. *Chronographia*: Greek text ed. L. Dindorf, in *Bonn Corpus*, Vol. 15, 1831, and in Migne, *Patrologia graeca*, Vol. 97, 1865; English translation (but of Books VIII–XVIII only, and from an old version in Church Slavonic) by M. Spinka and G. Downey, Chicago, 1940. — A chronicle of events from legendary times to 563, perhaps as originally written extending to an earlier terminus: its text is in a shallow, monkish style which is itself of great literary interest; but, in spite of historical limitations and a preoccupation with the regional affairs of Egypt, it contains some important information.

John of Ephesus. *Ecclesiastical History* (Part III only): Syriac text, no complete critical edition; English translation by R. Payne Smith, Oxford, 1860; German translation by J. M. Schönfelder, Munich, 1862; and Latin translation by E. W. Brooks, Louvain, 1936. — An important Syriac source, covering originally the period from Julius Caesar to Maurice, of which only the most important section, Part III, survives, on the years 521–585; written from a Monophysite point of view, it gives valuable information as well as an insight into religious, sectarian, and local attitudes and events of the age.

Evagrius. *Ecclesiastical History*: critical Greek text ed. J. Bidez and L. Parmentier, London, 1898; reprinted: Amsterdam, 1964; earlier edition in Migne, *Patrologia graeca*, Vol. 86, pt. 2, 1865; English translation by E. Walford ("Bohn's Ecclesiastical Library"), London,

1854. — An addition to the sequence of earlier continuations of the original *Ecclesiastical History* by the great fourth-century Christian figure Eusebius of Caesarea; covering the period 431–593, this work gives attention to secular as well as religious matters, and contains much useful information, including some on the early Slavonic invasions.

John of Antioch. *Chronicle* (fragments): Greek text ed. K. Müller, in *Fragmenta historicorum graecorum*, Vol. 4, Paris, 1851; critical Greek texts of various passages ed. C. de Boor, in the collection *Excerpta de insidiis*, Berlin, 1905; and ed. T. Büttner-Wobst, in *Excerpta de virtutibus et vitiis*, Berlin, 1906. — A world chronicle by a Syrian author of disputed identity; originally encompassing the period from Creation to 610, this seems to have been a work of considerable quality and value, but it unfortunately survives only in fragments.

Anon. *Chronicon paschale* ("*Easter Chronicle*"): Greek text ed. L. Dindorf, in *Bonn Corpus*, Vols. 16–17, 1832, and in Migne, *Patrologia graeca*, Vol. 92, 1865. — A monkish compilation by an unknown author contemporary with Heraclius; covering a span from Creation to the year 629, it is mainly a list of events with occasional comments, but it contains some often unusual information on Justinian's period not to be found in other sources.

John of Nikiou. *Chronicle*: critical Ethiopic text, with French translation by H. Zotenberg as "Chronique de Jean, Évêque de Nikiou, Texte éthiopien publié et traduit," in *Notices et extraits des MSS. de la Bibliothèque Nationale*, 24, pt. 1 (1883), 125–605; and, previously, in the *Journal asiatique*, 7, No. 10 (1877), 451–517; No. 12 (1878), 245–347; No. 13 (1879), 291–386; English translation by R. H. Charles for the Text and Translation Society, London, 1916. — An important world chronicle written by an Egyptian churchman of the latter half of the seventh century, covering the period from Creation through the Arab conquest of Egypt; originally written in Greek, perhaps with some sections in Coptic, its text is lost, and it survives only in a mutilated Ethiopic version itself based upon a lost Arabic translation; its greatest value, despite some grave gaps, is its account of the period of Heraclius.

Theophanes Confessor. *Chronographia*: critical Greek text ed. C. de Boor, 2 vols. ("Teubner Series"), Leipzig, 1883–85; reprinted: Bardi Editore, 1963; ed. I. Classen and I. Bekker, in *Bonn Corpus*, Vols. 40–41, 1839–41, and in Migne, *Patrologia graeca*, Vol. 108, 1863. — A biased monk's chronicle for the years 284–814; important for its later sections, which often constitute virtually the only major source of information for parts of the seventh and eighth centuries; but its entries for the era of Justinian also include some helpful material.

II. Useful Modern Works
(Books both on the specific period of Justinian, and on the more general history of the Empire and the early Middle Ages)

Arragon, R. F. *The Transition from the Ancient to the Medieval World* ("Berkshire Studies in European History"), New York: H. Holt and Co., 1936; reprinted: Cornell University Press (paperback), 1939. — An old, but useful survey of the broad outlines.

Baynes, N. H., and H. St.L. B. Moss (eds.). *Byzantium: An Introduction to East Roman Civilization*, Oxford: Clarendon Press, 1948; reprinted: Oxford University Press (Paperback No. 16), 1961. — An outstanding topical survey of the Empire's history and life, with many valuable essays, contributed by a number of eminent scholars, on Byzantine history, government, institutions, culture, and achievement.

Bréhier, L. *Le Monde byzantin*, Vol. 1: *Vie et mort de Byzance*; Vol. 2: *Les institutions de l'Empire byzantin*; Vol. 3: *La civilisation byzantine* ("L'Évolution de l'humanité," Vol. 32, Pts. a–c), Paris, 1947, 1948, 1950, respectively. — An excellent tripartite survey by an outstanding scholar, the first volume comprising a particularly excellent narrative of the Empire's history.

Bury, J. B. *A History of the Later Roman Empire, from Arcadius to Irene (395 A.D. to 800 A.D.)*, 2 vols., London and New York: Macmillan & Company, Ltd., 1889; reprint in progress. — Though the bulk of this youthful tour de force by the great British historian is superseded by his own subsequent rewriting (the work cited next), its later chapters, on events after 565, are still of basic importance.

———. *A History of the Later Roman Empire from the Death of Theodosius I to the Death of Justinian (A.D. 395–565)*, 2 vols., London: Macmillan & Company, Ltd., 1923; reprinted: Dover Publications, 2 vols. (paperback, T–398/399), New York, 1958. — The author's second, fuller, and more authoritative treatment of material covered earlier in the foregoing work cited, and the one cited regularly in this book; the second volume is devoted entirely to the period from 518 to 565, and despite its age and a few shortcomings it remains the best comprehensive study of Justinian's reign currently available in English.

Cambridge Ancient History (various eds.), Vol. 12: *The Imperial Crisis and Recovery, A.D. 193–324*, Cambridge: The University Press, 1939.

Cambridge Medieval History (planned by J. B. Bury, with various eds.), 8 vols., Cambridge: The University Press, 1911–36; see especially Vol. 1: *The Christian Roman Empire and the Foundation of the Teutonic Kingdoms* (1911; rev. ed., 1924); and Vol. 2: *The Rise of the Saracens and the Foundation of the Western Empire* (1913; rev. ed., 1926). — This medieval history together with the ancient history cited above constitute a celebrated series of cooperative volumes, the individual chapters by various specialists and of variable quality, but often still very valuable. In the medieval series, the first volume covers the period from Constantine I's reign to the accession of Justinian, and the second volume from Justinian to 717 (note the individual citation below of Diehl's chapters in this volume); in the original series, the remaining history of the Empire and its neighboring peoples to the fifteenth century was covered in chapters of the fourth volume (1923), which is now to be superseded by a completely new two-volume equivalent, ed. J. M. Hussey, not yet published at this writing, but planned in the following division: Pt. 1, *Byzantium and its Neighbours*; Pt. 2, *Government, Church and Civilization.*

Dawson, C. *The Making of Europe. An Introduction to the History of European Unity*, London: Sheed and Ward, 1932; paperback reprint (Meridian Books, M–35), New York, 1956. — A very broad but stimulating popular survey of the early Middle Ages written from the point of view of Roman Catholic Christianity.

Diehl, C. *Byzance: Grandeur et Decadence*, Paris: E. Flammarion, 1919; trans. N. Walford, *Byzantium: Greatness and Decline*, with Bibliographical Note by P. Charanis, New Brunswick, N. J.: Rutgers University Press, 1957; also available as a paperback. — An attractive general sketch of Byzantine history and civilization for the layman; but this English version of the book is of considerable significance for the student and even the specialist by virtue of Professor Charanis' extensive bibliographical survey of the major secondary literature, arranged and discussed critically by topical categories.

———. *Figures byzantines, Premier séries*, Paris: A. Colin, 1906; 10th ed., 1925; and *Second séries*, Paris, 1908; 8th ed., 1927; trans. H. Bell as *Byzantine Portraits*, New York: Alfred A. Knopf, 1927; and a new selection of the essays entitled *Impératrices de Byzance*, Paris: M. Leclerc et Cie, 1959; also a new grouping drawn from these separate series, trans. H. Bell and T. de Kerpely as *Byzantine Empresses*, New York: Knopf, 1963. — A justly celebrated series of sketches of personalities and life through the full span of Byzantine history, including one of Theodora and others bearing on the periods covered in this book.

————. *Justinien et la civilisation byzantine au VIe siècle*, Paris: E. Leroux, 1901; reprinted: 2 vols., New York, 1959. — A lively and engagingly written study, still one of the best extended accounts of the Emperor to be had in French; particular emphasis is placed on the artistic activities of the age, and the book is appropriately very well illustrated.

————. "Justinian and the Imperial Restoration in the West," and "Justinian's Government in the East," Chapters I and II in the *Cambridge Medieval History*, Vol. 2, Cambridge, 1913; rev. ed., 1926, pp. 1–24 and 25–52, respectively. — In the cooperative work cited above: in effect, the author's summaries of his own foregoing major study, providing useful and well-balanced short sketches of the reign.

————. *Théodora, impératrice de Byzance*, Paris: H. Piazza, n.d., 3rd ed., 1904; reprinted, 1937. — A classic monograph, still virtually the best account of this perennially fascinating lady.

Diehl, C., and G. Marçais. *Le Monde oriental de 395 à 1081* ("Histoire générale, fondé par G. Glotz, Histoire du moyen âge," Vol. 3), Paris, 1936; 2nd ed., 1944. —A collaborative history of admirable substance and usefulness.

Downey, G. *Constantinople in the Age of Justinian* ("Centers of Civilization," Vol. 3), Norman, Okla.: University of Oklahoma Press, 1960. — A vivid and stimulating picture of the Empire and the capital in this period, and a useful introduction to the history both of the city and of this Emperor for the general reader.

Every, G. *The Byzantine Patriarchate, 451–1204*, London: Society for Promoting Christian Knowledge, 1947; 2nd ed. rev., 1962. — A perceptive survey of the Empire's ecclesiastical history until the Fourth Crusade.

Foord, E. *The Byzantine Empire. The Rearguard of European Civilization*, London: A. and C. Black, 1911. — Though old, a lively popular sketch of the Empire's history.

Harrison, F. *Byzantine History in the Early Middle Ages* (*Rede Lecture*), London and New York: Macmillan and Co., 1900; reprinted in the author's collection, *Among My Books: Centenaries, Reviews, Memoirs*, London, 1912, pp. 180–231. — Despite its age, and its somewhat derivative nature, an interesting attempt to characterize Byzantine civilization and to suggest its impact on the Latin Medieval West.

Holmes, W. G. *The Age of Justinian and Theodora*, 2 vols., London: G. Bell and Sons, 1905–7; 2nd ed., 1912. — One of the more extended accounts of the period, but rather limited in depth or penetration.

Hussey, J. M. *The Byzantine World* ("Hutchinson's University Library" Series), London, 1957; reprinted: Harper paperback (Torchbook TB–1057), New York, 1962. — One of the best compact introductions, stressing the historical development, with supplementary sections on Byzantine institutions and civilization.

Hutton, W. H. *Constantinople: The Story of the Old Capital of the Empire* ("Medieval Towns" Series), London: J. M. Dent and Co., 1900; 3rd ed., 1907. — A dated but engaging short history of the great city through the Roman, Byzantine, and Ottoman Turkish imperial periods.

Jones, A. H. M. *The Later Roman Empire, 284–602: A Social, Economic and Administrative Survey*, 4 vols., Oxford, 1964; and 2 vols., Norman, Okla.: University of Oklahoma Press, 1964. — Combining a somewhat ill-balanced historical narrative with a series of analytical chapters on a comprehensive range of topics, this new work is an indispensable mine of information on the Empire's transitional period.

Kulakovsky, J. A. *History of Byzantium* [in Russian], Vol. 1: *395–518*; Vol. 2: *518–602*; Vol. 3: *602–717*, Kiev, 1910 (2nd ed., 1913), 1912, 1915, respectively. — One of the leading products of the illustrious tradition of Byzantine studies in pre-Revolution Russia, it is, despite shortcomings, a work of great importance in the study of the early phases of Byzantine history.

LaMonte, J. L. *The World of the Middle Ages. A Reorientation of Medieval History*, New York: Appleton-Century-Crofts, 1949. — Though designed as a college textbook, it may serve as reliable narrative and a substantial reference work; it is especially of significance for its broader, all-Mediterranean perspective, thus giving a much more equitable and balanced picture of the medieval East in relation to the medieval West than the traditional, myopic preoccupation with the exclusively Latin world of northwestern Europe that is maintained by most histories and texts on the Middle Ages.

Lemerle, P. *Histoire de Byzance*, Paris: Presses universitaires de France, 1943; 2nd. ed., 1948; trans. A. Matthew as *A History of Byzantium*, New York: Walker & Co., 1964, also available in paperback (W–18), — A good short history, by an eminent scholar.

Lot, F. *La fin du monde antique et le début du moyen âge* ("L'Évolution de l'humanité," Vol. 31), Paris: Rennaisance du livre, 1927; trans. P. and M. Leon as *The End of the Ancient World and the Beginnings of the Middle Ages*, New York and London, 1931; reprinted: Harper paperback (Torchbook TB–1044), New York, 1961. – A classic evaluation of the period of the third through the eighth centuries, and one of the best books of its kind, though its focus is mainly on the West with only limited material on Eastern developments in this period; the paperback reprint is of particular value for the new introduction and bibliographical annotations provided for it by G. Downey.

Moss, H. St.L. B. *The Birth of the Middle Ages, 395–814*, Oxford: The Clarendon Press, 1935; reprinted: Oxford University Press (paperback, No. 60), 1963. – A very worthwhile survey, tracing both Eastern and Western development in the period covered.

Oman, C. W. C. *The Byzantine Empire* ("The Story of the Nations," Vol. 33), New York and London: G. P. Putnam's Sons, 1892; 3rd ed., 1897. – Like the work of Foord cited above, an old but still very readable survey of the Empire's history for the general public, written by the eminent historian of medieval warfare.

Ostrogorsky, G. *Geschichte des byzantinischen Staates* ("Handbuch der Altertumswissenschaft," No. XII, Pt. I, Vol. 2), Munich: C. H. Beck, 1940; 3rd ed. rev., 1963; trans. J. M. Hussey, from the 2nd ed. (1950) as *History of the Byzantine State*, Oxford: B. H. Blackwell, 1956, and New Brunswick, N.J.: Rutgers University Press, 1957. – The outstanding history of the Empire in German, and, in any language, by far the best one-volume history; the emphasis is placed upon political, institutional, social, and economic development, with invaluable citation and discussion of both sources and modern literature, though its coverage of the earlier periods, including that of Justinian, tends to be rather cursory.

Rubin, B. *Das Zeitalter Iustinians*, Vols. 1 –, Berlin: Walter de Gruyter Co., 1960 –. – A multi-volume work still in progress, this somewhat formidable but exhaustive specimen of Germanic scholarship will, when completed, be the most thorough and authoritative detailed study of the Emperor and his age for some time to come; when this book went to press, only the first volume had appeared.

Runciman, S. *Byzantine Civilisation*, New York and London: Longman, Green, and Co., 1933; paperback reprint (Meridian Books, M–23), New York, 1957. – Long a popular and attractive survey, by an author who is both a sound scholar and an accomplished writer, this

is not as intensive or profound a work as some of the foregoing outlines of Byzantine history, society, and culture, but it is a stylish and
enjoyable introduction.

Stein, E. *Geschichte des spätrömischen Reiches*, Vol. I: *Vom römischen
zum byzantinischen Staat (284–476)*, Vienna: L. W. Seidel & Sohn,
1928; rev. French ed. by J.-R. Palanque as *Histoire du Bas-Empire*,
Vol. 1: *De l'état romain à l'état byzantin (284–476)* (printed in 2
vols.), Paris, Brussels, and Amsterdam: Desclée de Brouwer, 1959;
Vol. 2: *De la disparition de l'empire d'Occident à la mort de Justinien
(476–565)*, posthumous rev. ed., by J.-R. Palanque, Paris, Brussels,
and Amsterdam, 1949, – A major work written by one of the great
German scholars of late Roman and early Byzantine history, the
second part of which never appeared in his original text, and the first
is now superseded by Palanque's revision; the second part is the best,
and certainly the most up-to-date, single-volume scholarly coverage
of Justinian's age in any language at present, and is fundamental for
the serious student of this period.

Sullivan, R. E. *Heirs of the Roman Empire* ("Development of Western
Civilization"), Ithaca, N.Y.: Cornell University Press (paperback),
1960. – A handy outline on the period of the barbarian kingdoms, including the phase of Justinian's Reconquest program.

Ure, P. N. *Justinian and his Age*, Harmondsworth, Eng., and Baltimore:
Penguin Books, Ltd. (Pelican paperback, A–217), 1951. – Perhaps
the best compact and small-scale book on Justinian in English, written by a noted English classicist; though it presupposes some advance knowledge of ancient history and culture, and of the historical
setting of Justinian's period, it offers the cultivated general reader
some stimulating and provocative insights into this Emperor's age
and society.

Vasiliev, A. A. *History of the Byzantine Empire, 324–1453*, Madison,
Wis.: University of Wisconsin Press, 1952; paperback reprint, 2
vols., 1958. – The final result of a long sequence of versions and editions through several languages, written by one of the most distinguished Byzantinists of this century; though its organization is con-
fusing for the novice, and it is on the whole far less effective as a
general history than that by Ostrogorsky cited above, it still contains
much of value, in discussion of modern literature and interpretations,
and especially for its sections on cultural history, an area not included
in Ostrogorsky's book.

———. *Justin the First: An Introduction to the Epoch of Justinian
the Great* ("Dumbarton Oaks Studies," No. 1), Cambridge, Mass.,

1950. — The most important and, indeed, the only comprehensive study on the early phase of the Justinianic period by itself.

Wallace-Hadrill, J. M. *The Barbarian West: The Early Middle Ages, A.D. 400–1000* ("Hutchinson's University Library" Series), London, 1952; reprinted: Harper paperback (Torchbook TB–1061), New York, 1962. — A useful and well-balanced outline, tracing the emergence of a new European order in the Latin West out of the barbarian epoch, both before and after the Justinianic Reconquest.

INDEX

Theodora, Empress (9th century), 260

Theodore (brother of Heraclius), 244

Theodore Askidas, 107–108, 110, 273

Theodore of Mopsuestia, 108, 273

Theodoret of Cyrrhus, 108, 273

Theodoric, the Amal: in the Balkans, 42–43, 127; King in Italy, 43, 102, 104, 131, 141, 146–149, 269, 270; apparent portrait of, 288–289

Theodoric Strabo, 40–41, 42

Theodosius I, "the Great," Emperor: religious policies of, 18, 20, 95; reign of, 21; German policies, 25–26, 96; and St. Ambrose of Milan, 96; mentioned, 80, 115, 224, 252, 291

Theodosius II, Emperor: reign of, 30–31, 38, 39; Higher School founded by, 30, 100; Law Code of, 30, 167–168; religious policies of, 49, 50; mentioned, 115, 291

Theodosius III, Emperor, 257

Theodosius, Patriarch of Alexandria, 106–107, 271, 272, 273

Theopaschite doctrine, 103–104, 271

Theophilus, legal scholar, 168, 170

Theophilus, Patriarch of Alexandria, 48

Theotókos, 45, 48

Theoúpolis (Antioch), 293

Thermopylae, 195, 199

Thessalonica, 96, 196, 224, 231, 254, 274

Thessaly, 199

Theudebald, 165

Theudebert I, 156, 157, 163, 165

Thrace, 40, 42, 56, 61, 174, 178, 195, 196, 198, 199, 220, 224, 230, 255, 274

Three Chapters controversy, 108–111, 188, 273, 274

Thucydides, 76

Tiberius II, Emperor: under Justin II, 203–212, 215, 218; reign of, 218–221, 223

Tiberius III (Apsimar), 256, 257

Tomus, 49, 51

Totila (Baduila), 159, 160–164, 272, 273, 274

Toulouse, 28, 131

Tours, Battle of, 259

Toynbee, Arnold, 209

Trade, Imperial, 83, 92, 216–217. *See also* Silk trade

Trajan, Emperor, 113, 114

Tribonian, 72, 85, 90, 168, 170, 270, 271

Tricamaron, Battle of, 142, 143, 271

Triságion, 60

Trocundes, 41–42

Turks, 197, 216–217, 263, 264, 288, 289, 290

Tuscany, 215

Twelve Tables, 166

Týpos, 252

Ulfilas, 24, 45

Ulpian, 169, 265

Umayyad Dynasty, 248, 257, 258; table of rulers of, 285

Unogundur (Onogur) Huns, 56, 198, 249

Ure, P. N., quoted, 176–177*n*

Utigur Huns, 198, 199, 274, 275

Vahram VI, Choben, 222

Valens, Emperor, 21, 24–25

Valentinian I, Emperor, 21, 24

Valentinian II, Emperor, 21

Valentinian III, Emperor, 29, 32–33, 140

Valerian, Emperor, 114

Vandals: migrations of, 23, 28, 29, 33; kingdom of, 29, 33, 36, 37, 41, 131, 135, 139–143, 144, 151, 248, 269, 270; Justinian's war with, 77, 119, 136, 141–143, 150, 158, 271, 286; table of rulers of, 282

Vasiliev, A. A., quoted, 67*n*

Venice, 76*n*, 181

Verdi, Giuseppe, 76*n*

Vergil, quoted, 6–7

Verina, Empress (wife of Leo I), 40, 41–42, 212

Vesuvius, Mt., 164–165

Victorinus, 264*n*

Vigilantia (mother of Justinian), 269

Vigilantia (sister of Justinian), 187, 203

Vigilius, Pope, 105, 106, 107, 109–111, 154, 188, 272, 273, 274, 275

Visigoths: migrations of, 24–25, 27–28; kingdom of, 28, 32, 33, 37, 131, 135, 258; Justinian's war with, 136, 138–139, 274

Vitalian, 60–61, 63, 64, 66, 84, 101, 155, 195, 269

Völkerwanderung, 23–24 *et seq*, 194

Wittigis, 119, 153, 154–158, 162, 272

Wulfila. *See* Ulfilas

Xenophon, 77

Xerxes, 112, 234

Yarmuk River, Battle on the, 244

Yazdigerd III, 243

Yemen, 127–128, 217, 242, 269, 270

Yere-Batan Serai, 287

Zabergan, 198–199

Zeno, Emperor: reign of, 37, 41–43, 116, 140; rise to power of, 39, 40–41; religious policy, 53–54, 101

Zenobia, 123

Zoroastrianism, 114, 115, 121, 217, 232–233, 235